Introduction to Claims

Introduction to Claims

Pamela J. Brooks, CPCU, AAM, AIM
Assistant Director of Curriculum
AICPCU/IIA

Donna J. Popow, JD, CPCU, AIC
Director of Curriculum
AICPCU/IIA

Doris L. Hoopes, CPCU, AIC, ARe

Third Edition • Third Printing

American Institute for Chartered Property Casualty
Underwriters/Insurance Institute of America
720 Providence Road, Suite 100
Malvern, Pennsylvania 19355-3433

Foreword

The American Institute for Chartered Property Casualty Underwriters and the Insurance Institute of America (the Institutes) are independent, not-for-profit organizations committed to expanding the knowledge of professionals in risk management, insurance, financial services, and related fields through education and research.

In accordance with our belief that professionalism is grounded in education, experience, and ethical behavior, the Institutes provide a wide range of educational programs designed to meet the needs of individuals working in risk management and property-casualty insurance The American Institute offers the Chartered Property Casualty Underwriter (CPCU®) professional designation, designed to provide a broad understanding of the property-casualty insurance industry. CPCU students may select either a commercial or a personal risk management and insurance focus, depending on their professional needs.

The Insurance Institute of America (IIA) offers designations and certificate programs in a variety of disciplines, including the following:

- Claims
- Commercial underwriting
- Fidelity and surety bonding
- General insurance
- Insurance accounting and finance
- Insurance information technology
- Insurance production and agency management
- Insurance regulation and compliance
- Management
- Marine insurance
- Personal insurance
- Premium auditing
- Quality insurance services
- Reinsurance
- Risk management
- Surplus lines

You may choose to take a single course to fill a knowledge gap, complete a program leading to a designation, or take multiple courses and programs throughout your career. No matter which approach you choose, you will gain practical knowledge and skills that will contribute to your professional growth and enhance your education and qualifications in the expanding insurance market. In addition, many CPCU and IIA courses qualify for credits toward certain associate, bachelor's, and master's degrees at several prestigious colleges and universities, and all CPCU and IIA courses carry college credit recommendations from the American Council on Education.

The American Institute for CPCU was founded in 1942 through a collaborative effort between industry professionals and academics, led by faculty members at The Wharton School of the University of Pennsylvania. In 1953, the American Institute for CPCU merged with the Insurance Institute of America, which was founded in 1909 and which remains the oldest continuously functioning national organization offering educational programs for the property-casualty insurance business.

The Insurance Research Council (IRC), founded in 1977, helps the Institutes fulfill the research aspect of their mission. A division of the Institutes, the IRC is supported by industry members. This not-for-profit research organization examines public policy issues of interest to property-casualty insurers, insurance customers, and the general public. IRC research reports are distributed widely to insurance-related organizations, public policy authorities, and the media.

The Institutes strive to provide current, relevant educational programs in formats and delivery methods that meet the needs of insurance professionals and the organizations that employ them. Institute textbooks are an essential component of the education we provide. Each book is designed to clearly and concisely provide the practical knowledge and skills you need to enhance your job performance and career. The content is developed by the Institutes in collaboration with risk management and insurance professionals and members of the academic community. We welcome comments from our students and course leaders; your feedback helps us continue to improve the quality of our study materials.

Peter L. Miller, CPCU
President and CEO
American Institute for CPCU
Insurance Institute of America

Preface

Insurance claims offer professionals fascinating career opportunities in a fast-paced, ever-changing, legally responsive work environment. This text gives students an introduction to that environment and the skills and qualities that will help them succeed in claim work.

This third edition of *Introduction to Claims* incorporates material presented in the second edition, plus added material to assist new claim personnel in developing a strong general insurance and claim background.

This revision begins with an introduction to insurance concepts, terminology, and policy structure. It describes the claim function, including the roles of claim personnel and the skills and qualities that assist them. The text examines the various types of laws, court systems, and forms of dispute resolution, good faith claim-handling practices, and regulatory compliance issues. The text introduces and examines a systematic approach to handling claims and examines the investigation of auto physical damage, property, bodily injury, workers' compensation, and fraud claims. The final chapters review insurance policy coverages and endorsements that apply to first-party auto, first-party property, liability, and workers' compensation losses, respectively, and each chapter examines claim considerations that apply to those losses. Sections describing insurance products that require claim specialization and catastrophe claim-handling are included where appropriate.

Because insurers often use customized insurance forms, this revision approaches policy coverages more generally rather than referencing specific coverage forms; however, most exhibits are based on Insurance Services Office (ISO) forms. Students should examine their employer's coverage forms to properly apply the course material to their work.

The Institutes appreciate the knowledge and contributions of the following individuals who wrote material for the previous edition of the text or other Institute materials used as resources:

Michael J. Betz, AIM

Sara J. Harty

Alison Kittrell

Carol B. Szender, CPCU

Eric A. Wiening, CPCU, ARM, AU

For more information about the Institutes' programs, please call our Customer Support Department at (800) 644-2101, e-mail us at customersupport@cpcuiia.org, or visit our Web site at www.aicpcu.org.

Pamela J. Brooks

Donna J. Popow

Doris L. Hoopes

Contents

Chapter 1

Direct Your Learning

Insurance Basics

After learning the content of this chapter and completing the corresponding course guide assignment, you should be able to:

■ Describe the benefits, costs, and underlying principles of insurance.

■ Describe the parties to, the roles the parties play, and who else might benefit from insurance policies.

■ Explain how the following parties help to provide insurance products and services:

- Producers
- Underwriters
- Loss control specialists
- Actuaries
- Claim representatives
- Special investigation unit (SIU) personnel
- Lawyers

■ Explain how premium dollars are used.

■ Explain how an insurer's financial condition is evaluated.

■ Explain how the claim representative interacts with the following parties:

- Insured/claimant
- Producer
- Underwriter
- Loss control specialist
- Actuary
- Special investigation unit (SIU) personnel
- Lawyer

■ Describe the parts of an insurance policy, including the following categories of insurance policy provisions:

- Declarations
- Definitions
- Insuring agreements
- Exclusions
- Conditions
- Miscellaneous provisions

■ Describe insurance policy endorsements and their use.

■ Define or describe each of the Key Words and Phrases for this chapter.

Develop Your Perspective

What are the main topics covered in the chapter?

This chapter introduces the concept of insurance: the purposes, benefits, and costs of insurance; the parties to the insurance policy and other parties associated with the policy; and the parts of an insurance policy. The chapter also explains how insurance is sold, how policies are processed, how premium dollars are used, and how and why an insurer's financial condition is evaluated.

Identify the role of your employer in the insurance business.

- Is your employer a producer, an underwriting or a claim department, or another type of insurance unit or organization?

- What role does your department or employer play in the claim process?

Why is it important to learn about these topics?

The operation of insurance, the parties to an insurance policy, the parties who help provide insurance products and services, and the interaction among the parties establish the purpose and the environment for claim work. To analyze insurance policies and determine coverage for claims, claim representatives must understand the provisions of insurance policies and endorsements. For any given loss, the claim representative must be able to read and interpret the policy. To properly determine coverage for a claim, the claim representative must understand that some policy provisions cancel or extend other policy provisions; therefore, all policy provisions must be analyzed to determine whether coverage exists for the loss.

Review a personal policy and a commercial policy that your organization uses.

- Where are the definitions located in each policy?

- What are some provisions that cancel or modify other provisions?

How can you use what you will learn?

Analyze an insurance claim.

- For any given claimant in the claim file, is the claim a first-party or a third-party claim?

- Which interactions between the claim representative and others can you identify from the claim file?

Chapter 1

Insurance Basics

Individuals and organizations use insurance as one technique to protect their financial interests. Insurance helps to restore people and organizations to their pre-loss financial positions by paying losses that are covered under the insurance policy.

Without insurance, few people could afford to bear the financial losses associated with their activities and property, with the exception of small, infrequent losses. For example, most homeowners would be financially strained if they had to pay for the cost to repair or replace their homes in the event of serious damage or destruction. Most at-fault automobile drivers would find it difficult to pay for injuries that others sustain or for damage to others' property for which they are responsible. In addition, organizations could lose income if their property were damaged or destroyed and they could not readily repair the property and replace any lost income.

This chapter presents basic insurance concepts that provide a foundation for claim personnel to understand insurance and the insurance business. To investigate and settle claims, claim representatives must be knowledgeable about the operation of insurance, the parties to the insurance policy, the parties who provide insurance products and services, and how and why an insurer's financial condition is evaluated, among other important concepts. Claim representatives must also understand and be able to interpret the various types of insurance policies (also called insurance contracts) and the provisions that make up those policies.

WHAT IS INSURANCE?

This section describes concepts that are basic to insurance and explains how individuals and organizations use insurance to protect their financial interests. Individuals and organizations encounter **loss exposures**, which are conditions, situations, or property that present the possibility of a loss. The possibility that an auto owner faces of suffering an auto accident, or the possibility that a business owner's warehouse might be damaged by a storm or that the business's inventory might be stolen are examples of loss exposures. Typically, they use insurance as one technique to manage those loss exposures. **Insurance** is a system for transferring the potential financial consequences of loss from people and organizations (insureds) to insurance

Loss exposure
A condition, situation, or property that presents the possibility of a loss.

Insurance
A system for transferring risk from people and organizations to insurers, which reimburse those people and organizations for covered losses.

Insured
A person or an organization whose property, life, or legal liability is covered by an insurance policy.

Insurer
A company that sells insurance policies to protect insureds against financial hardship caused by financial losses.

Claim
A demand by a person or an organization seeking to recover from an insurer for a loss that an insurance policy might cover.

companies (insurers), which reimburse those people and organizations for covered losses. The **insured** is the person or organization that agrees to the insurance policy terms (to provide protection for property, life, or legal liability) by signing an application (contract) and paying the appropriate fee, called an insurance premium. According to the policy terms, in return, the **insurer**, a company that sells insurance policies, agrees to protect insureds against financial hardship caused by financial losses by paying those losses covered by the policy. Such losses may result from bodily injury, property damage, loss of income, or damage to reputation.

Insureds or others present **claims** to the insurer after they suffer a loss that they believe is covered by the policy. Insurers then use premiums that they receive from all of their insureds to investigate the claim and reimburse those insureds or others who suffer covered losses.

The insurance transaction (buying and selling insurance) might seem like an unequal exchange. For example, for a small percentage of a home's value, homeowners can purchase insurance that will reimburse them for the full value of the home if it is destroyed. But insurers collect a premium for that coverage based on their projection of the number of insured homes that will be destroyed or damaged. In any given year, because relatively few insureds suffer a loss as compared to the total number of insureds, insurers usually collect enough premiums to pay those losses that do occur. Therefore, the insurance policy can benefit both the insured and the insurer—by providing protection to the insured and revenue to the insurer.

Benefits of Insurance

In addition to paying insureds' covered losses (under the policy terms), insurance provides other direct and indirect benefits. Among those benefits are the following:

- *Reduction of uncertainty.* Because insurance provides financial compensation when covered losses occur, it greatly reduces the financial uncertainty created by many loss exposures. For example, a family's major financial concerns probably center around the possibility of an income earner's death or serious illness or the destruction of their home. If the family transfers the uncertainty about the financial consequences of such losses to an insurer, the family reduces these financial concerns.

Loss control
A risk management technique that attempts to decrease the frequency or severity of losses.

- *Loss reduction and prevention.* Insurers often recommend loss control practices for individuals and organizations. **Loss control** involves taking measures to prevent some losses from occurring or to reduce the financial consequences of losses that do occur. Individuals, families, and organizations can use measures such as burglar alarms, smoke alarms, and deadbolt locks to prevent or reduce losses. Loss control generally reduces the amount of money insurers must pay in claims. As a result, loss control helps to improve the financial results of insurers and to reduce insurance costs to consumers. Therefore, society also benefits from activities that prevent and reduce losses.

- *Efficient use of resources.* People and organizations that face an uncertain future often set aside funds to pay for the financial consequences of potential future losses. Insurance makes it unnecessary to set aside a large amount of money to pay for insurable losses. Money that would otherwise be set aside to pay for possible losses can be used to improve a family's quality of life or to contribute to the growth of a business. In exchange for a relatively small premium, families and businesses can free up funds that they would otherwise need to reserve to pay for unforeseen future losses. For example, suppose George owns a small craft shop that is his sole source of income. If the shop were destroyed by fire, George would be deprived, at least temporarily, of his livelihood. Additionally, if a customer tripped over an electrical wire in the shop and broke her leg, George might be held responsible for paying the customer's medical bills and other costs. George could set aside enough money to pay for rebuilding the shop or for customers' injuries, or he could purchase property and liability insurance. The insurance premium would be much lower than the cost to repair the building or pay for customers' injuries, so purchasing insurance would allow George to use his remaining money more efficiently—to expand his business, for example.

- *Support for credit.* Before lending money for a major purchase such as a house, a bank or another lender requires assurance that the money will be repaid. If the borrower should fail to repay the loan, the lender can repossess the house. However, if the house were destroyed by fire, repossession would not be a viable alternative because the property the lender would repossess would likely be worth less than the lender's insurable interest. Additionally, the borrower would have less incentive and fewer resources to make future loan payments. For these reasons, lenders require that parties seeking loans purchase insurance on the property they buy with the loan proceeds, and they require that the insured indicate the lender's interest in that property on the insurance policy. If the property were destroyed by a covered cause of loss, insurance would pay for the destroyed home on the insured's behalf. Therefore, insurance facilitates lending by increasing lenders' certainty that the borrower will be able to repay the loan.

- *Satisfaction of legal requirements.* Insurance is often used or required to satisfy legal requirements. In many states, for example, automobile owners must prove they have auto liability insurance before they can register their autos. All states have laws that require employers to pay for the job-related injuries or illnesses of their employees, and employers generally purchase workers' compensation insurance to meet this financial obligation.

- *Satisfaction of business requirements.* Certain business relationships require proof of insurance. For example, building contractors are usually required to provide evidence of liability insurance before a construction contract will be granted. In fact, almost anyone who provides a service to the public, from an architect to a tree trimmer, might need to prove that he or she has liability insurance before being awarded a contract for services.

- *Source of investment funds.* One of the greatest benefits of insurance is that it provides funds for investment. When insurers collect premiums, they do not usually need funds immediately to pay losses and expenses. Insurers use some of these funds to make loans to businesses. Such loans provide investment money for projects involving new construction, research, and technology. Investment funds promote economic growth and job creation. Insurers also invest in social projects, such as cultural events, education, and economic development projects. Investments bring additional funding to insurers in the form of interest. This additional income helps to keep insurance premiums reasonable.

- *Reduction of social burdens.* Accident victims who are not compensated for their injuries and families who lose all their belongings in a fire can become serious burdens to society. Insurance helps reduce these and similar burdens by providing compensation for lost wages and medical expenses, and by paying for the repair or replacement of damaged or destroyed property.

Through a simplified example, Exhibit 1-1 illustrates the benefits of insurance to a group of plumbers and their community. The illustration demonstrates that insureds and society benefit from insurance well beyond the payment of claims.

EXHIBIT 1-1

Benefits of Insurance

In a community, twenty-five plumbers each invest $50,000 in tools and a truck. Statistics show that each year, the tools and truck of one plumber in this community will be stolen. The following example illustrates some of the benefits that insurance would provide to these plumbers and their community.

Reduction of uncertainty for insureds	Insurance ensures that the plumbers can continue to earn a living even if a loss occurs.
Loss reduction and prevention for insureds	Insurers would encourage loss control by offering premium discounts for specific loss control practices that the plumbers use that have proved effective.
Efficient use of resources for insureds	The expected loss each year for the group of plumbers is $50,000. This amount is divided among all twenty-five plumbers. Each plumber would pay $2,000 each year in insurance premium to support the one unfortunate plumber whose truck and tools are stolen. Doing this frees up cash for all the plumbers to use for other business needs. Without insurance, each should set aside $50,000 for the possibility of a loss.*
Support for credit for lenders	Banks are more likely to lend money to the plumbers because they have insurance protection. A plumber who qualifies for credit can obtain loans for tools and a truck and begin work.
Satisfaction of legal requirements for insureds	Insured plumbers would meet state or local requirements to insure their business property.
Satisfaction of business requirements for insureds	Insured plumbers would meet insurance requirements of businesses that contract for plumbing services.
Source of investment funds for organizations	Plumbers and other businesses can benefit from business loans offered by insurers using funds they collect in premiums but do not yet need to pay claims.
Reduction of social burdens for society	Any of the insured plumbers can continue doing business following a loss (such as the theft of tools and truck).

*This example has been simplified to show the insurance benefits. Insurance must also reflect administrative costs that are not considered in this example.

Costs of Insurance

In exchange for the benefits insurance provides to insureds, other parties, and society, insurance imposes costs on insureds, insurers, and society. The following are some direct and indirect costs of insurance:

- *Premiums paid by insureds.* Premiums are an obvious cost of insurance for insureds and can vary widely among insurers for many reasons. Premiums vary in different parts of the country because they must cover loss exposures that vary. For example, medical expenses, construction material and labor costs, and the cost of vehicle parts and repairs are higher in some areas than in others, which affects claim costs. Some areas are subject to greater chances of storm damage, such as from hurricanes on the coasts and tornados in the Midwest, and property insurance premiums must be higher in those areas to offset the greater exposures.

- *Operating costs of insurers.* Like any business, an insurer has operating costs resulting from running the business day to day. These costs often include salaries, agent commissions, advertising costs, building expenses, equipment costs, taxes, licensing fees, and many others. In addition, most insurers are in business to make a profit. A reasonable amount of profit (after operating costs) must be calculated in the premiums that insureds pay.

- *Opportunity costs of insureds.* An indirect cost of insurance is opportunity costs. **Opportunity costs** are those costs associated with using resources for one purpose instead of another. They represent income not earned because an opportunity to earn income was not pursued. Dollars that insureds spend on premiums cannot be used for other purposes that could be more productive for the economy. For example, the money the insured used to pay premiums could instead have been invested to start a small business or used to help finance the down payment on a house.

- *Increased losses.* A **moral hazard** is a condition that increases the likelihood that a person will intentionally cause or exaggerate a loss. Moral hazards exist because insurance can provide an economic incentive for insureds to have losses. For example, excessive debt might induce an insured to intentionally cause a loss or exaggerate a loss that has occurred to gain insurance claim money. Deliberate losses include arson, staged auto accidents, or other intentional losses. Exaggerated claims are a common result of moral hazard. For example, in a liability claim arising from a fall in a store, the claimant (the third party who reports an injury) might sustain a back or neck injury that results in an alleged disability that is difficult to disprove and that could be exaggerated. Moral hazards are an indirect cost of insurance because they cause more frequent or more severe losses than would have occurred in the absence of insurance.

  Another hazard that can increase losses is a morale hazard. Morale hazard occurs not when losses are caused deliberately but when an insured is careless or indifferent to potential loss because insurance exists to cover it. For example, an insured might leave an expensive piece of jewelry or

Opportunity costs
The costs associated with using resources for one purpose instead of another. They represent income not earned because an opportunity to earn income was not pursued.

Moral hazard
A condition that increases the likelihood that a person will intentionally cause or exaggerate a loss.

a laptop computer in an unlocked, unattended car. The insured takes no precautions to protect the item because he or she knows insurance will pay the cost to replace it if the item is stolen.

- *Increased lawsuits.* Liability insurers sometimes pay large sums of money to protect people who could be held responsible for injury to other people or for damage to others' property. Some people incorrectly view liability insurance as a pool of money available to pay the claims of any person or organization that suffers injury or whose property is damaged, regardless of fault. Therefore, the existence of insurance might encourage these people to sue an insured to recover for their bodily injury or property damage.

Underlying Principles of Insurance

An explanation of the underlying principles of insurance is necessary to help claim personnel understand insurance concepts and their roles and responsibilities in handling claims. Insurance is based on the **principle of indemnity**, which states that no insured should be in a better financial position *after* a loss than *before* it. For example, assume that Jill purchases insurance for her five-year-old car and that her car is later destroyed in an auto accident. The principle of indemnity states that Jill should be paid (indemnified) for the value of the five-year-old car. Under this principle, Jill would not be entitled to the value of a new car because that would put her in a better position than she was in before the loss occurred, because her car was not new. The principle of indemnity is important because it discourages people from causing losses when they would benefit from them. (In this case, being paid for the value of a new car rather than an older car would create an incentive to cause a loss.) The principle of indemnity supports the coverage of losses that are accidental or over which the individual or organization has limited control.

Insurance enables people and organizations to share the financial consequences of their losses. Insureds pay relatively small insurance premiums compared to the value of their property or the value of their assets exposed to the possibility of loss. In return, insurers pay for the covered losses that occur. Insurers can project the number of losses that will occur in a given time period based on a principle called the law of large numbers. The **law of large numbers** is a mathematical principle stating that, as the number of similar but independent exposure units increases, the relative accuracy of predictions about future outcomes (losses) based on these exposure units also increases.

The law of large numbers enables insurers to offer large dollar amounts of insurance coverage to insureds in return for a relatively small premium. For example, assume that Bountiful Insurance Company sells homeowners insurance to homeowners all over the United States. Bountiful insures thousands of homes and, over several years, the percentage of its insured homes that are destroyed or damaged remains fairly consistent. This consistency allows Bountiful to project, with reasonable accuracy, the amount of money it will need to pay claims for insured losses in any given year and set aside appropriate funds to pay them.

Principle of indemnity
The principle that insurance policies should provide a benefit no greater than the loss suffered by an insured.

Law of large numbers
A mathematical principle stating that, as the number of similar but independent exposure units increases, the relative accuracy of predictions about future outcomes (losses) based on these exposure units also increases.

The law of large numbers requires that the units (called exposure units) of property insured (such as homes) be independent. This means that the exposure units must be geographically separated and diverse so that one event does not affect all of the insured exposure units. An insurer that has exposure units spread throughout a broad geographic area can take advantage of the law of large numbers. For example, an earthquake that damages homes in California will probably not damage homes in Tennessee, and a tornado that damages homes in Kansas will probably not damage homes in New Jersey. In the Bountiful example, the individual homes that Bountiful insures are located throughout the country. By insuring exposure units all over the country, Bountiful can charge each of its homeowners insureds a reasonable premium, with the confidence that no single event will cause losses for a large percentage of its insureds.

The law of large numbers similarly affects liability insurance. Liability insurance protects insureds from the possibility of a claim for injury or damage suffered by another party who alleges the insured's legal responsibility.

Insurance is also based on the requirement for an insurable interest, which is required for purchasing insurance. To have an **insurable interest** in property, an individual or organization must stand to suffer a financial loss related to that property. This principle prevents parties from profiting from insurance because of another's loss that does not financially affect them. For example, if Jason were able to purchase insurance for a home that he does not own and the home was subsequently damaged, he would suffer no financial loss. Similarly, because Jason does not own the home, he would have no incentive to repair or replace it, so he could profit from the loss payment. An insured party that has nothing to lose (no insurable interest) could behave recklessly and could cause losses or intentionally damage property to make a claim. A greater number of losses results in higher premiums for all insureds, and losses not tied to insurable interest contradict public welfare.

Insurable interest
An exposure that a party has to financial loss.

The requirement for insurable interest reinforces the principle of indemnity, which specifies that insurance policies pay claims only to the extent of the insured's insurable interest. For example, if an insured owns 50 percent of a building and the building is destroyed, that insured can collect only 50 percent of the building's value, even though the building was totally destroyed.

In summary, insurance is a system for transferring the potential financial consequences of loss from insureds to insurers. Insurance provides numerous benefits to insureds, other parties, and society, but not without costs. In the next section, an examination of the parties to the insurance contract builds on this insurance foundation.

WHO ARE THE PARTIES TO AN INSURANCE POLICY?

An insurance policy is a legal contract. Identifying the parties to an insurance policy is essential to understanding the coverage provided under the policy because each party has different roles and responsibilities or obligations. This section describes the two parties to an insurance policy—the insured and the insurer—and explains third-party beneficiaries.

Insured

The insured is the first party because insurance protects the insured. Insurance for losses that the insured incurs pertaining to its own property or person is called first-party insurance. Property-casualty insurers sell insurance to two broad groups of customers: (1) individuals and families and (2) for-profit and not-for-profit organizations.

Personal insurance
Insurance that covers the financial consequences of losses to individuals and families caused by death, illness, injury, disability, and unemployment.

Individuals and families purchase **personal insurance** to insure their non-business exposures. Typical personal property and liability insurance policies cover such exposures as an auto, a home, a motorcycle, or a boat. Life insurance and health insurance are other types of personal insurance that cover nonbusiness exposures.

Commercial insurance
Insurance that covers for-profit businesses or not-for-profit organizations against the adverse financial effects of property and liability losses.

Generally, the property-casualty insurance needs of organizations are more complex than those of individuals and families. For-profit and not-for-profit organizations purchase **commercial insurance** to insure their business exposures. Business exposures are those that affect a business operation—for example, damage to business property from weather or vandalism and liability for injuries to customers and clients. Typical commercial coverages include building and business personal property insurance, workers' compensation insurance, commercial general liability insurance, business auto insurance, and crime insurance.

First-party claim
A demand by an insured person or organization seeking to recover from its insurer for a loss that its insurance policy might cover.

Because the insured is the party protected by an insurance policy, the insured is usually named in the policy. However, property and liability policies can also cover parties other than named insureds. For example, under a home-owners policy, coverage is provided for family members who reside in the home of a couple who are named insureds. When any insured suffers a loss, he or she files a first-party claim with the insurer. A **first-party claim** is a demand by an insured person or organization seeking to recover from its insurer for a loss that its insurance policy might cover.

Third-party claim
A demand by a claimant (plaintiff) against an insured based on the legal duties the insured owes to claimants (plaintiffs); seeks to recover from the insured's insurer for a loss that the insured's policy might cover.

Persons and entities that are not parties to the policy can also benefit from property and liability policies . These parties, who suffer bodily injuries or property damage because of the insured's actions, are third-party beneficiaries of the insurance policy, but they are not insureds. Individuals purchase personal liability insurance and organizations purchase commercial liability insurance to protect themselves from the claims of third parties. Third-party beneficiaries make insurance claims (**third-party claims**) against insureds and their insurers, so their relationship to the policy is important even though they are not parties to the policy.

Insurers

The second party to the insurance policy is the insurer. Insurers accept the exposures of insureds when they write and sell insurance policies, collect premiums, and pay covered losses. In the U.S., private insurers offer private insurance, and state and federal governments provide government insurance programs.

Private Insurers

Private insurers are owned by individuals or organizations other than the government. They are formed to meet the needs of insureds and to make a profit or share the costs of insurance with other insureds. Private insurers can be differentiated by their legal form of ownership, which also indicates the purpose of the insurer, as follows:

- Stock insurers are corporations owned by stockholders. The stockholders became owners by purchasing shares of stock to earn profit from the business.

- Mutual insurers are corporations owned by their policyholders. If a mutual insurer makes a profit, it might pay dividends (money from its earnings) to its policyholders. Conversely, if losses exceed premiums, policyholders might be assessed, although assessments are uncommon.

- Reciprocal insurance exchanges are unincorporated associations owned by their members that provide insurance services to their subscribers (members).

- Insurance exchanges are marketplaces (similar to a stock exchange) owned by the members of a syndicate (a pool of insurers formed to jointly insure potentially high loss exposures). Members in an insurance exchange choose the types and amounts of insurance for which they assume liability and underwrite the coverages.

- Captive insurers are subsidiaries of and owned by their parent companies. Captives are formed expressly to write all or part of the insurance for the parent company or companies.

Private insurers are divided into two broad categories: property-casualty insurers (sometimes called property-liability insurers) and life and health insurers.

Private insurers vary in size, structure, the products they sell, and the territories they serve. Although thousands of insurers are based in the U.S., they do not sell every type of insurance that consumers need or want because some loss exposures are not readily insurable. Government insurance programs have evolved to meet many of those needs; private insurers rarely cover exposures that should be covered by government insurance programs.

Government Insurance Programs

The U.S. federal government, as well as state and local governments, offers insurance programs. In certain cases, governments provide insurance protection that private insurers are unwilling to provide against the financial consequences of specific loss exposures. For example, people who own homes along rivers are exposed to loss by flood. Typically, homeowners who want to buy flood insurance are those who are most likely to suffer a flood loss, creating a situation known as adverse selection. **Adverse selection** occurs when only those people or organizations with a high probability of experiencing loss are interested in purchasing insurance. Governments often provide insurance programs to protect individuals and organizations who cannot obtain insurance from private insurers because of adverse selection.

Adverse selection
A situation that occurs when only those people or organizations with a high probability of experiencing loss are interested in purchasing insurance.

Based on the law of large numbers, insurers must have a large number of independent exposure units (such as insured properties). When adverse selection occurs, both the number of exposure units and their independence are reduced. In the preceding example, the pool of insureds is small because relatively few homes are prone to loss by flood. Independence is reduced because many of those homes could be destroyed by the same flood. Therefore, private insurers are reluctant to write flood insurance. To remedy this problem and make flood insurance available to individuals and organizations that need it, the federal government created the National Flood Insurance Program. This program federally subsidizes the cost of flood insurance policies, which can be sold by any licensed insurance producer.

Other government insurance programs include the following:

- The Social Security program is a federal program that provides retirement benefits and health insurance (through Medicare) for elderly persons, survivorship benefits for the dependents of deceased workers, and disability benefits for totally disabled workers.

- Medicaid insurance is a state and federal program offering health insurance to people with low or no income, regardless of their ages.

- Unemployment insurance plans, offered by each state and financed by the federal government, ensure that all eligible workers have some unemployment insurance protection.

- Workers' compensation insurance is offered by some state governments to pay expenses and wages for workers who become injured or ill on the job.

- Crop insurance, offered through the Federal Crop Insurance Program, insures the losses of crop farmers.

In summary, the two parties to the insurance policy are the insured—the first party—who purchases the policy and its benefits, and the insurer—the second party—who provides the policy benefits. Third-party beneficiaries also receive policy benefits. Insureds purchase property and liability insurance to protect themselves from the claims of third-party beneficiaries, so their relationship to the policy is important. The next section builds on the foundation laid by the preceding sections by examining the parties who help to provide insurance products and services.

WHO HELPS TO PROVIDE INSURANCE PRODUCTS AND SERVICES?

Many parties have roles in providing insurance products and services to insureds. Payment of claims is one of those services; therefore, this section introduces the roles of certain claim personnel, along with the roles of the parties who provide insurance policies. These parties, all of whom are described in the next few sections, include the following:

- Producers
- Underwriters
- Loss control specialists
- Actuaries
- Claim representatives
- Special investigation unit (SIU) personnel
- Lawyers

Producers

One party who has a role in providing insurance products and services is the producer. Many insurance policies are sold through a **producer**, either an agent or a broker who works with or for one or more insurers to sell insurance products. Agents and brokers differ in that agents represent insurers to sell insurance products, but brokers represent insurance consumers (buyers) in locating insurance products that meet consumers' needs.

Producer
Any person or organization who sells insurance products for an insurer or insurers.

Producers often market and sell insurance to consumers within the following marketing systems:

- Independent agency and brokerage marketing system
- Exclusive agency marketing system
- Direct writing marketing system

Other marketing systems exist as well, but the following section describes these three most commonly used systems.

Independent Agency and Brokerage Marketing System

In the independent agency and brokerage marketing system, an independent agent contracts with several unrelated insurers to represent them by selling and servicing their insurance policies to consumers. **Independent agents** are independent contractors and are not employees of any insurer. They select insurers with which they have developed a business relationship; sell those insurers' products to consumers; and provide policy services, such as analyzing the consumer's insurance needs, explaining and recommending various coverages, completing the insurance application, and collecting loss information and submitting any claims to the insurer.

Independent agent
An independent contractor who sells insurance under the independent agency marketing system, usually on behalf of more than one insurer.

A broker is similar to an agent in that he or she also sells insurance products to consumers and provides policy services, but the broker represents insurance consumers. A broker locates insurance policies from all insurers that best meet the consumer's individual needs and provides the same policy services that independent agents provide.

Insurers pay independent agents and brokers a commission, typically a percentage of the premium, for each policy sold. Commission rates might vary for new and renewal business and by type of policy.

Independent agents and brokers have some control over whether a policy is renewed. They can allow their client's policies to renew, or they might propose that the client purchase a different insurer's policy. This control is called "owning expirations." If an independent agent does not renew its contract with a particular insurer, the independent agent can place the policies written by that insurer with another insurer. Brokers, on the other hand, have no contract with any insurer and are always free to place business with other insurers.

An independent agent's organization is called an independent agency. An agency can consist of one person working alone, or it can include several agents working with customer service representatives and other specialists. A broker's organization is called a brokerage and can also vary in size. A brokerage can consist of one broker or many brokers who work with customer service representatives and other specialists.

Exclusive Agency Marketing System

Exclusive agent
An independent contractor who has a contract to sell insurance exclusively for one insurer (or a group of related insurers) under the exclusive agency marketing system.

In the exclusive agency marketing system, an **exclusive agent** has a contract to sell insurance only for a particular insurer or a group of related insurers, possibly under common ownership. Like independent agents, exclusive agents are independent contractors and are not employees of an insurer. But in contrast to independent agents, most exclusive agents have contracts that prohibit them from selling insurance for any other insurer. Exclusive agents are usually paid commissions, and the commission percentage is often higher for new business than for renewal business. Unlike with independent agents, the insurer owns the expirations. Therefore, if an exclusive agent does not renew its agency contract with the insurer, the insurer retains control of the policies written by the exclusive agent.

Direct Writing Marketing System

Direct writing agent
An insurer's employee who markets policies directly rather than through independent agents or brokers.

In the direct writing marketing system, a **direct writing agent** acts like an exclusive agent in that it sells insurance for only one insurer or group of insurers. However, in contrast to an exclusive agent, a direct writing agent is employed by the insurer. A direct writing agent might receive a salary, a commission, or a combination of the two. The term "direct writing" also refers to an insurer that sells insurance directly to insurance buyers through its employees. This type of marketing system does not involve producers.

As described, producers can use several types of marketing systems to sell insurance products and provide insurance services. Being able to distinguish among these systems can help claim representatives understand the insurer's relationship with the producer, who often gathers and submits claim information.

Underwriters

Another party who has a role in providing insurance products and services is the underwriter. When a potential insured completes an application for insurance, the producer sends that application to the underwriting department. **Underwriting** is the process of deciding which insurance applicants to accept, which to reject, and for which to provide modified coverage. Insurers need to have favorable underwriting results for profitable growth and survival. Therefore, the underwriting department's primary purpose is to select and maintain a growing, profitable book of business (all of the policies written) for the insurer. Underwriting activities include (1) selecting insureds and their exposures, (2) pricing coverage, (3) determining policy terms and conditions, and (4) monitoring the exposures and loss experience on the policies written.

Underwriting
The process of selecting insureds, pricing coverage, determining insurance policy terms and conditions, and then monitoring the underwriting decisions made.

The first underwriting activity is selection. Underwriters select insureds based on underwriting guidelines that include criteria such as the loss exposures presented by the applicant, the applicant's likelihood of paying the insurance premium, and the insurer's policy concentration in the applicant's location (for example, if an insurer insures a number of properties along a particular coast and a hurricane strikes that coast and destroys those properties, the insurer's loss payments could cause the insurer to become insolvent).

Underwriters rely on their producers to recommend applicants with loss exposures that meet their underwriting guidelines and whose financial reports and credit ratings help ensure their ability to pay their premiums and reveal any incentives the applicant might have to commit fraud (such as a failing business or excessive debt). Insurers are selective about the property and applicants (often collectively called loss exposures) they accept for two reasons. The first reason is to avoid the consequences of adverse selection. Insurers accept a limited number of loss exposures with above-average loss potential, unless they can charge adequate premiums to pay for anticipated losses. The second reason insurers are selective is that they are limited in the volume of business they can handle. This limitation stems from financial capability limitations (capacity) and operational limitations (such as staffing). Underwriters must be selective in accepting applications so that insurers use their capacity to write only business on which they can anticipate earning a reasonable profit. Underwriters examine many aspects of loss exposures to determine whether they would be profitable to insure.

The second underwriting activity is pricing coverage. Underwriters' pricing goal is to charge a premium that reflects the loss exposure. An insured's premium should be determined so that the total premium collected from a large group of insureds is adequate to pay the group's claims and the expenses associated with providing the insurance, while also allowing the insurer to make a reasonable profit.

Selection and pricing are intertwined with the third underwriting activity, determining policy terms and conditions. Rather than reject an unacceptable insurance application, underwriters can accept an application subject to modifications. For example, the underwriter can offer to accept the application if the applicant agrees to increase or reduce the amount of coverage, change the exposure by installing fire alarms or sprinkler systems, or pay a higher premium.

The fourth underwriting activity is monitoring the exposures and loss experience. Underwriters must monitor insureds' exposures and loss experience to determine whether any significant changes have occurred. Changing exposures and related conditions could affect an insured's loss experience and require the underwriter to raise the insured's premium. For example, as the insured ages, he or she might be more prone to auto accidents because of slower reflexes, so the insurer might raise the premium based on the number of accidents or might not renew the policy if the insured's health prevents him or her from driving safely.

Loss Control Specialists

Another party who helps to provide insurance products and services is a loss control specialist. Loss control specialists perform inspections called loss control surveys (usually for organizations that apply for commercial insurance or that have just been accepted), and they summarize the results in loss control reports for underwriters. These reports describe the operations and loss exposures of the applicant's or insured's business. They also recommend safety programs and other methods to control losses. Loss control reports describe an applicant's or insured's insurance-related strengths and weaknesses and recommend improvements. Through their recommendations, loss control specialists try to reduce loss frequency and severity.

The contents of a loss control report depend on the type of insurance involved. For example, in a business auto insurance loss control report, vehicle maintenance is important. Well-maintained vehicles usually cause fewer accidents than do poorly maintained vehicles; therefore, the loss control specialist will evaluate the applicant's or insured's maintenance procedures and report the results of that evaluation to the underwriter. The loss control specialist might recommend improvements in vehicle maintenance procedures, such as hiring a full-time mechanic or changing the maintenance schedule. In a workers' compensation insurance loss control report, the loss control specialist might suggest protective eye equipment, include information on the use of such equipment, and comment on the frequency of workers' breaks from physically demanding jobs.

Actuaries

Another party who has a role in providing insurance products and services is the actuary. An **actuary** develops and uses systems for calculating insurance premiums. Actuaries use complex mathematical methods and statistics to analyze loss data and other information and project losses as accurately as possible based on the law of large numbers. The results of their analyses are used to determine premiums. The actuary's goal is to develop competitive and equitable insurance rates. Actuaries usually have an educational background in mathematics or statistics and other specialized training.

Actuary
A person who uses complex mathematical methods and statistics to analyze loss data and other information and to develop systems for determining insurance premiums.

Claim Representatives

Another party who has a role in providing insurance products and services is a claim representative. Losses occur, despite the best underwriting efforts. The primary purpose of the claim department is to fulfill the promise that the insurer makes in the insurance policy by paying the covered claims of insureds and others fairly, efficiently, and promptly, according to the policy provisions. A **claim representative** is an insurer's employee who investigates, evaluates, and settles claims. Agents and brokers also have employees who handle claims.

Claim representative
The person responsible for investigating, evaluating, and settling claims.

Special Investigation Unit (SIU) Personnel

Special investigation unit (SIU) personnel also have a role in providing insurance products and services. Many state insurance laws require insurers to establish **special investigation units (SIUs)**, claim department units with the expertise to investigate suspicious claims and other possible fraud. Insurers in many other states have established SIUs voluntarily. SIU personnel perform many of the same tasks as claim representatives, but their focus is to investigate claims that appear to be fraudulent. SIU personnel investigate all types of claims that other claim staff refer to them. They also investigate organized rings of claimants who submit fraudulent claims and the medical providers, lawyers, and body shops that help these claimants make their claims appear to be legitimate. When SIU personnel are confident that they have detected fraud, they deny the claims and alert the proper authorities to prosecute the wrongdoers. In addition to fulfilling their investigative duties, SIU personnel conduct training for claim personnel to remind them of fraud indicators and of the types of cases that should be referred to SIU personnel.

Special investigation unit (SIU)
A claim department unit with the expertise to investigate suspicious claims and other possible fraud.

Lawyers

Lawyers also have a role in providing insurance products and services. When a claimant or a lawyer representing the claimant files a lawsuit naming the insured as the defendant, the insurer hires a lawyer to represent that insured. For example, liability insurance coverages typically include promises that the insurer will defend the insured in lawsuits that relate to the coverages provided by the insurance policy. Claimants might also hire lawyers to represent them in claims against insureds and insurers.

HOW IS INSURANCE SOLD, AND HOW ARE POLICIES PROCESSED?—AN ILLUSTRATION

This section illustrates how insurance can be sold through a case study, starting with a hypothetical applicant's insurance needs and ending with the issuance of the insurance policy.

John Thomas, who owns a small accounting firm, wanted to purchase insurance protection for all of his loss exposures, including his home, his automobiles, his snowmobile, any additional personal liability loss exposures, and his business loss exposures. John's friend recommended Millwright Insurance Agency, so John met with its agent, Vivian Slade. Vivian spoke with John about his personal and business loss exposures and recommended that he purchase the following:

- A homeowners policy for his home

- A personal automobile policy for his two personal vehicles

- A recreational vehicle policy for his snowmobile

- A personal umbrella liability policy to cover any additional personal liability loss exposures not covered by the three preceding policies and to provide higher liability limits than those provided by those three policies

- A commercial package policy that covers all of John's business property, his business vehicle, and his business liability, and that provides workers' compensation coverage for any of John's employees who are injured on the job

Vivian explained the basic coverage provided by each of these policies, and John agreed with Vivian's recommendations.

Millwright Insurance Agency is an independent agency that represents KYL Insurance Company, among other insurers. KYL offers insurance coverages that meet all of John's insurance needs. Vivian completed all of the appropriate application forms, secured John's check for the premiums she estimated for all of the policies, and sent the forms and check to KYL. The following day, Vivian took photos of John's home and business facility and sent them to KYL.

KYL received the application and the check, and staff entered the information into the underwriting system for distribution to the appropriate underwriters. They also processed the check for deposit. When Vivian's photos arrived, staff sent them to the appropriate underwriters.

Jennifer, a personal insurance underwriter, reviewed all of the personal applications and ordered a motor vehicle report (MVR) and a personal credit report on John. Later, Jennifer reviewed those reports along with all of the other documents. From the photos, John's home appeared to be well-maintained and in good repair. Based on the collected information, Jennifer approved the policy issuance and sent the application forms to Don, a data entry clerk. Don completed the entry work needed to issue the policy, printed the policy forms and endorsements, and assembled the policies to be mailed to Millwright.

Howard, a commercial insurance underwriter, reviewed all of John's commercial applications and ordered MVRs on all reported drivers of John's business vehicle. Howard also ordered a business credit report and a financial report from a reputable financial reporting agency. Later, Howard reviewed all of the documents. He contacted Jill, KYL's loss control specialist, and asked her to inspect John's business premises and complete a loss control report.

Jill inspected John's business site and interviewed office personnel to verify information in the insurance applications. Jill compiled a report of her findings, including two loss control recommendations, and sent it to Howard. Based on all of the collected documents, Howard approved John's application for a commercial package policy, with the added provision that John comply with the recommendations from Jill's loss control report. Howard sent the applications to Don for data entry. Don completed the data entry, printed the policy forms, and assembled the forms into a commercial package policy folder to be mailed to Millwright.

Vivian reviewed KYL's policy forms for accuracy and sent them to John. In her cover letter, Vivian explained that John should contact her if any of his personal or business loss exposures change; for example, if he were to replace one of his automobiles or change the nature of his business. Finally, John received the policies in the mail, confident that his loss exposures were covered.

This case study illustrates insurance concepts presented in previous sections of the chapter. It shows how a producer might sell insurance policies that meet a consumer's needs and how an insurer might underwrite and issue those policies. The case study also illustrates some ways in which a producer provides insurance services to consumers. Different producers and insurers follow different procedures and might request other reports as part of underwriting, but this case study offers insight into common procedures. The next section examines how insurers use premium dollars collected from the sale of insurance.

HOW ARE PREMIUM DOLLARS USED?

Insurers receive income from two major sources. The first is the sale of insurance, which generates underwriting income. Underwriting income (gain or loss) is the amount remaining after underwriting losses and expenses are subtracted from premiums. The second source is the investment of funds, which generates investment income. Investment income (gain or loss) is the amount remaining after investment expenses are subtracted from the gross amount earned on investments during the period. While some insurers receive other income from the sale of specialized services or other incidental activities, most of the income an insurer receives is either underwriting income or investment income.

As mentioned, underwriting income is the amount of income (gain or loss) after losses and expenses are subtracted from premiums that are earned. Premiums are the money an insurer receives from its policyholders in return for the insurance coverage provided. In effect, premiums are the revenue from the insurer's underwriting operations. The losses paid by the insurer's policies plus the expenses associated with controlling and adjusting those losses are the primary underwriting expenses.

When calculating underwriting income for the year (or any other period), an insurer must determine the portion of its total policy premiums generated during the period (written premiums) that it earned (earned premiums) and the portion it did not yet earn (unearned premiums). For example, assume that an insurer writes only one policy during the year: a one-year policy effective October 1 with an annual premium of $120. The written premium for the year is $120—that is, premium for the entire policy period. On December 31, the earned premium would be $30, because only three months of protection have been provided ($^3/_{12} \times \$120 = \$30$). The remaining $90 of premium would be considered unearned premium. Insurers use written premiums as a source of cash, to pay expenses and claims, and for investment purposes. However, insurers consider only *earned* premiums as income for financial reporting purposes.

Because insurers collect premiums from their insureds and do not use them to pay claims and other expenses immediately, they have money available for investing to generate investment income. Insurers invest money from written premiums that they have set aside for claim reserves (money set aside to pay specific claims), money collected in unearned premiums, and money that they have already earned from investments. Insurers invest in stocks, bonds, Treasury bills, and other securities. Their goal is to earn the highest possible return from prudent investments that meet regulatory requirements, while making sure that funds are always available to meet their expense and claim obligations.

When insurers pay large claims, they withdraw some of their invested claim reserve funds. To be able to pay claims from invested funds as needed, insurers must invest their reserve funds in short-term (more liquid) securities that earn a lower rate of return than long-term securities.

Insurers routinely spend slightly more for claims and other expenses than they collect in premiums. Therefore, managing investments wisely provides them with enough income to balance their revenues and expenses, to continue their operations, and, ideally, to make a profit.

According to the Insurance Information Institute, in the U.S., the cost of property-casualty underwriting operations in 2002 was $1.07 for every premium dollar collected. Underwriting operations are associated with the following expenses:[1]

- Sales and administrative costs, including costs to acquire new business (such as advertising, commissions, and promotions for producers) and operating costs (such as salaries, employee benefits, and building maintenance)
- Dividends to policyholders or stockholders
- State taxes and license fees
- Claims and the expenses incurred in handling them

In 2002, U.S. insurers used the entire premium dollar collected to pay for operating expenses, plus they spent an additional $0.07 for every premium dollar collected. That $0.07 was obtained from investment earnings or additional operating income. Any profit was attributable to investment income. Exhibit 1-2 depicts the 2002 allocation of property-casualty insurance premium dollars.

EXHIBIT 1-2

Where the Premium Dollar Goes, Property/Casualty Insurance, All Types, 2002

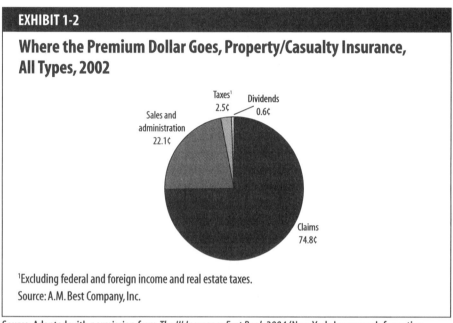

[1]Excluding federal and foreign income and real estate taxes.
Source: A.M. Best Company, Inc.

Source: Adapted with permission from *The III Insurance Fact Book 2004* (New York: Insurance Information Institute, 2004), p. 14.

To summarize, insurers receive income from two major sources: insurance sales and investment income. Insurers collect premiums from insurance sales that can be categorized into earned and unearned written premiums. By far the largest percentage of the premium dollar is used to pay claims. The next largest percentage is used for sales and administration, with small percentages used for taxes and dividends. Premiums that are not yet needed to pay claims are used to invest, along with other operating income, to earn investment income. An insurer's income is considered in determining the insurer's overall financial condition. The next section examines how an insurer's financial condition is evaluated.

HOW IS AN INSURER'S FINANCIAL CONDITION EVALUATED?

An insurer's premium and investment income help determine its overall financial condition. State insurance regulators evaluate an insurer's financial condition based on how the insurer's operating expenses compare to the premiums that it collects. Regulators want to ensure that insurers maintain enough profit to pay their current claims and to remain viable to pay future claims. For example, if an insurer spent $0.95 of each premium dollar on operating expenses and claims in one year, then that insurer would have an underwriting profit of $0.05 per dollar for that year. The insurer could invest 5 percent of its total written premium ($0.05 of each dollar = 5%) for future growth. In contrast, if the insurer spent $1.05 for each dollar collected in premiums on operating expenses and claims in that same year, then that insurer would be operating at an underwriting loss. Investment income results would determine whether the insurer was operating at an *overall* loss.

The combined ratio measures an insurer's profitability. It uses a formula to compare losses and expenses incurred and premiums earned during a fiscal year. A combined ratio of more than 1.00 means that the insurer's operations were not profitable. For example, a combined ratio of 1.04 means that the insurer spent $1.04 for each premium dollar it earned. A combined ratio of less than 1.00 means that the insurer was profitable. For example, a combined ratio of 0.95 means that the insurer spent only $0.95 of each premium dollar it earned. State regulators and investors examine an insurer's combined ratio over a period of years to determine whether that insurer is likely to remain financially solvent.

Insurance business fluctuates over time. Fortunately, insurers can have a combined ratio of more than 1.00 for several years and still remain solvent—if they have made prudent investments. Insurers' investment income helps them survive the less profitable years.

In summary, state insurance regulators evaluate insurers by comparing their operating expenses to their premiums collected. Regulators use insurers' combined ratios to determine their profitability. Because insurance business fluctuates over time, insurers invest available funds to earn income that enables them to remain solvent through years in which they suffer underwriting losses. While this and previous sections examined general insurance concepts, the next section focuses on claim representatives and their interactions with other parties who are associated with insurance.

WHOM DOES THE CLAIM REPRESENTATIVE INTERACT WITH?

Claim representatives interact with numerous parties, both inside and outside insurers' offices. In many ways, the claim representative is the insurer from others' perspectives; therefore, positive interactions with these parties can influence an insurer's success. The next section describes interactions among the following parties:

- Claim representative and insured/claimant
- Claim representative and producer
- Claim representative and underwriter

- Claim representative and loss control specialist
- Claim representative and actuary
- Claim representative and special investigation unit (SIU) personnel
- Claim representative and lawyer

Claim Representative and Insured/Claimant

Two of the primary parties with whom claim representatives interact are insureds and claimants. Because claim representatives represent the insurer when they handle claims, insureds and claimants often recognize the claim representative as the insurer. Therefore, the claim representative's skill at communicating directly with insureds and other claimants affects their satisfaction with the insurer. For purposes of this discussion, the term "claimant" is used to describe both insureds (who are first-party claimants) and third-party claimants. A claimant could be an individual or a representative of an organization.

Claim representatives' first contact with a claimant occurs after the claimant has sustained a loss. Most claimants suffer some type of emotional reaction to a loss. Depending on the extent and type of loss, that claimant might experience a range of emotions, such as anger or rage, depression, frustration, or hopelessness. Claim representatives must empathize with claimants to interact effectively with them. Claim representatives must be prepared to explain the policy's claim provisions to the claimant as those provisions apply to the claimant's property damage or injury. A well-prepared, professional claim representative who empathizes with the claimant will gain the claimant's confidence and increase the likelihood of reaching a mutually agreeable settlement.

If the claim representative is concerned that coverage will not apply to the damage or injury, he or she must be prepared to explain those concerns to the claimant and preserve the insurer's right to deny a claim that is not covered (details about preserving this right appear in a subsequent chapter). Even in a case in which a claim is denied, a claim representative who carefully explains the issues and empathizes with the claimant might be able to avoid costly litigation.

Claim Representative and Producer

Claimants often contact their producer, instead of the claim office, to report claims on insurance policies. The producer then represents the insurer in explaining the insurer's claim process to the claimant and in establishing positive interactions with the claimant.

The producer can serve as an excellent resource for the claim representative. The producer might have information about the claim that is not part of the loss notice (the initial report of a claim). Also, because producers' offices are usually located near their insureds, the producers might know about community events that affect losses. A producer might know, for example, the local, unofficial information on the cause of a fire loss or whether the claimant had experienced financial difficulties before the loss. Having such information could lead a claim representative to consider the possibility of a fraudulent claim. Because claimants often report losses to their producer first, the producer might be able to provide more details. Producers are usually more helpful to claim representatives who are friendly, composed, and professional.

Claim Representative and Underwriter

The insurance business operates effectively if underwriters accept loss exposures that are likely to experience only the types and amounts of losses anticipated in the insurance rates. If underwriters accept loss exposures that experience more losses than anticipated, the rates charged by the insurer will be inadequate and the insurer could become financially insolvent. Claim personnel help underwriters in this regard by ensuring that claims are paid fairly and according to the policy. Proper, consistent, and efficient claim handling enables underwriters to evaluate, select, and appropriately price loss exposures based on consistent claim costs.

When claim representatives inspect accident scenes in homes or at work sites as part of the claim investigation, they sometimes notice loss exposure characteristics, either negative or positive, that were not readily apparent in the insurance application. When claim representatives report such findings to the underwriter, the underwriter might adjust the premium or take other actions to accommodate the difference in the exposure from the application information. For example, based on information from the claim representative, the underwriter might cancel coverage or renew it only if the insured implements corrective measures. Alternatively, the underwriter might grant a premium credit based on a claim representative's report of an above-average loss exposure.

Claim representatives' interaction with underwriters is not limited to providing loss information. Although claim personnel are typically the final authority on coverage interpretation, underwriters can provide insight into the intentions of the two parties to the insurance policy using the insurance application and producer's notes, which might affect coverage interpretation. When claim representatives explain their interpretations of coverage to underwriters, the underwriters can reassess coverage forms and endorsements and make any needed changes to clarify the coverages.

Claim Representative and Loss Control Specialist

As mentioned earlier, loss control specialists conduct on-site inspections and write loss control reports that give underwriters an assessment of each loss exposure. Loss information provided by claim representatives can supplement those reports or trigger another loss control inspection. Loss control specialists can provide useful information to claim representatives because they have knowledge of the insured site before any loss occurs. For example, if a property is damaged by fire, the loss control specialist who inspected the property might provide valuable information about the property's pre-loss condition. This information helps the claim representative determine the value of the loss or any factors that might have contributed to the extent of damage.

Claim Representative and Actuary

Using mathematical methods and statistics, actuaries analyze loss data to project the number of losses that will be reported and the dollar amount of claims that insurers will pay. Then, they use those projections to set rates for insurance coverages. The raw data that actuaries use to perform their analyses and from which they draw their conclusions are generated by claim transactions. Those transactions include payments that claim representatives have made and reserves set aside for future payments. When claim representatives or other claim personnel accurately record claim payments and set realistic reserves in insurers' claim processing systems, the raw data that actuaries use to develop rates will be accurate, and rates will reflect the insurer's loss experience.

Claim Representative and Special Investigation Unit (SIU) Personnel

Special investigation unit (SIU) personnel are effective in detecting insurance fraud only if claim representatives refer claims to them that indicate possible fraud. SIU personnel should help train claim representatives on fraud indicators and should periodically remind or update claim representatives about new fraud schemes that have been discovered. Because SIU personnel are specifically trained to investigate and handle fraud cases, claim representatives should refer any suspicious claims to them as soon as fraud is suspected. Claim representatives should also provide SIU personnel with all information that might assist in a fraud investigation. Cooperation between claim representatives and SIU personnel helps insurers avoid paying fraudulent claims and having to inflate insureds' premiums to cover invalid claims.

Claim Representative and Lawyer

Claim representatives often work with lawyers. Some lawyers represent the insurer and advise claim representatives about specific losses and legal issues. These lawyers might also serve as insurers' counsel in litigation. Claim representatives should assist these lawyers as needed by sharing claim details and assembling information that supports the insurer's legal position.

Claim representatives also interact with lawyers who represent claimants. In such cases, claim representatives who are composed and professional and who have strong negotiating skills can help avoid litigation. Even if litigation ensues, claim representatives should continue to interact in a cordial, professional manner with claimants' lawyers.

WHAT ARE THE PARTS OF AN INSURANCE POLICY?

Insurance personnel must understand the parts of an insurance policy to properly handle insurance claims. Before analyzing the coverage provided in an insurance policy to determine whether a claim is covered, claim representatives should make sure that they have all of the relevant forms, with the effective dates shown, that are cited in the policy. Property-casualty insurance policy provisions describe the coverage that is provided, the types of losses that will not be covered, and the responsibilities of the parties to the insurance policy. These policy provisions create a structure for examining the policy. They can be categorized as follows:

1. Declarations
2. Definitions
3. Insuring agreements
4. Exclusions
5. Conditions
6. Miscellaneous provisions

Some policy provisions appear in sections of the policy that match the provision's category, such as definitions that are located in the Definitions section of the policy. Other policy provisions are interspersed throughout the policy; for example, a definition might be found in the Exclusions section of the policy. Consequently, claim representatives must examine the entire policy to determine whether coverage is provided for a loss.

Declarations

One category of provisions in a property-casualty policy is the declarations. Declarations contain (declare) information about the insured from the insurance application. They also describe the insurer's statement of the coverage it provides under the policy, along with other information that is unique to the policy.

The declarations or information page is typically the first page(s) of an insurance policy or is included in a coverage section. Declarations often contain the information listed in the box on the next page.

Sometimes policy forms or endorsements also contain information that qualifies as declarations, often in the form of a schedule. For example, a schedule of contractor's equipment describes each piece of equipment, the coverage amount for each piece, and the premium for the schedule.

Standard Declarations Information

- Policy number
- Policy inception and expiration dates
- Insurer's name
- Producer's name
- Insured's name
- Named insured's mailing address
- Physical address and description of the covered property or operations
- Numbers and edition dates of all attached forms and endorsements
- Dollar amount of applicable policy limit
- Dollar amounts of applicable deductibles
- Names of persons or organizations whose additional interests are covered (such as mortgag-ees, loss payees, or additional insureds)

Definitions

·A second category of provisions in a property-casualty policy is the defini-tions. Generally, terms used throughout the policy or form are defined in the Definitions section. As mentioned, definitions could be included anywhere in the policy, or they could be presented in a specific Definitions section. Policies typically use boldface type or quotation marks to distinguish words and phrases in the policy descriptions that are defined elsewhere in the policy.

The way in which words will be used could be described in the definitions or in a policy introduction. For example, many policies explain that the term "we" indicates the insurer and that "you" indicates the named insured. Policies might also describe the meaning of the pronouns "us," "our," and "your" as used in the policy.

Undefined words included in policy forms are interpreted by insurers and the courts according to the following rules of contract interpretation:

- Everyday words are given their ordinary meaning.
- Technical words are given their technical meaning.
- Words with an established legal meaning are given their legal meaning.
- Words that have local, cultural, and trade-usage meanings are considered, if applicable.

Insuring Agreements

A third category of provisions in a property-casualty policy is insuring agree-ments. An insuring agreement is any insurance policy statement indicating that the insurer will make a loss payment or provide a service under described circumstances. The insuring agreement often follows the declarations and sometimes follows the definitions.

If a policy provides more than one coverage, it can have more than one insuring agreement. For example, the Personal Auto Policy typically provides liability, medical payments, uninsured motorists, and physical damage coverages. Each coverage part has its own insuring agreement. An insuring agreement usually introduces a policy coverage, but it can also introduce other policy sections such as coverage extensions, additional coverages, and supplementary payments.

An insuring agreement that introduces a coverage section broadly states what the insurer agrees to do under the policy, subject to clarification in other parts of the policy such as the policy definitions. Insuring agreements usually contain one or more defined terms that are crucial to understanding the coverage provided.

As mentioned, insuring agreements can also apply to extended, additional, or supplementary coverages. A coverage extension generally extends a portion of basic policy coverage to apply to a type of property or loss that would not otherwise be covered. Additional coverage (such as debris removal) adds a type of coverage not otherwise provided. Supplementary payments coverage clarifies the extent of coverage for certain liability insurance expenses, such as the insured's loss of earnings because of attendance at a hearing. Other policy provisions grant or restore coverage otherwise excluded. Therefore, these provisions serve as insuring agreements and might appear within a definition, as an exception to an exclusion, or elsewhere in the policy.

Exclusions

A fourth category of provisions in a property-casualty policy is exclusions. Exclusions are policy provisions that state what the insurer does *not intend* to cover. The primary function of exclusions is to clarify the coverages granted by the insurer. Specifying what the insurer *does not* intend to cover is a legally enforceable way of clarifying property or situations that the insurer *does* intend to cover.

Exclusions can serve one or more purposes, as described in the following box.

Purposes of Exclusions

Exclusions can perform the following functions:

- Eliminate coverage for uninsurable loss exposures—Some loss exposures (such as intentional acts) are not insurable. Exclusions allow insurers to eliminate coverage for those exposures.

- Assist in managing moral and morale hazards—Exclusions help insurers minimize loss exposures that are affected by moral and morale hazards, as described previously.

- Reduce likelihood of coverage duplications—In some cases, two different types of insurance policies may provide coverage for the same loss. For example, a car is parked in the garage when the house and garage are destroyed by fire; the car is destroyed as well. The insured's homeowners policy excludes the car, but her auto policy covers it. Exclusions ensure that policies work together to provide complementary, but not duplicate, coverages.

- Eliminate coverages that the typical insured does not need—Exclusions sometimes allow insurers to exclude coverage for loss exposures that typical insureds do not face. These exclusions eliminate the chance that all insureds would have to share the costs of covering substantial loss exposures of relatively few insureds, such as physical destruction of a motorboat—many insureds do not own a motorboat. Watercraft policies or endorsements can provide coverage for this exclusive loss exposure.

- Eliminate coverages requiring special treatment—These coverages might require rating, underwriting, loss control, or other treatment that is different from that normally applied to the policy. One example is workers' compensation coverage.

- Assist in keeping premiums reasonable—Exclusions allow insurers to decline loss exposures that would drive up overall insurance costs. By declining such loss exposures, insurers can offer premiums that most insureds will consider reasonable for their exposures.

Conditions

A fifth category of provisions in a property-casualty policy is conditions. A policy condition is any provision that qualifies an otherwise enforceable promise of the insurer or a duty of the insured. Some policy conditions are included in a "Conditions" section of the policy, while others are found in the forms, endorsements, or other documents that together form the entire insurance policy.

In a policy's insuring agreement, the insurer promises to pay covered losses, furnish a defense, and provide other services to the insured *only* if the insured has fulfilled its contractual duties as specified in the policy conditions. Examples of such conditions include the insured's obligations to pay premiums, report losses promptly, provide appropriate documentation for losses, cooperate with the insurer, and refrain from jeopardizing an insurer's rights to recover from responsible third parties (subrogate). If the insured fails to perform these duties, the insurer may be released from its policy obligations.

Miscellaneous Provisions

A sixth category of provisions in a property-casualty policy is miscellaneous provisions. These provisions do not strictly qualify as declarations, definitions, insuring agreements, exclusions, or conditions, but they affect coverage. They do not, however, have the force of conditions; if the insured does not follow procedures specified in miscellaneous provisions, the insurer typically must still fulfill its contractual promises.

An example of a miscellaneous provision is descriptions of standards the insurer uses when determining the value of a loss, such as basing the value of an auto on the National Automobile Dealers Association (NADA) Blue Book. Or, miscellaneous provisions might be unique to a particular type of insurer, such as a mutual insurer, in which policyholders have voting rights. In this case, one miscellaneous provision might describe the policyholders' right to elect the board of directors.

WHAT ARE INSURANCE POLICY ENDORSEMENTS?

In addition to examining insurance policy provisions, claim representatives must study the property and liability provisions contained in endorsements. An endorsement is a provision that adds to, deletes, replaces, or otherwise modifies another provision in an insurance policy. Other terms that describe endorsements are "policy change," "addition," and "amendment." Some endorsements have only a descriptive title, such as "loss payable clause." Endorsements form a part of an insurance policy when they are listed in the declarations and are physically attached to the policy. Endorsements can also be added to a policy after the policy has been issued, but the endorsements must be listed in a policy amendment (change) form.

Endorsements can be preprinted, computer-printed, or typewritten, or simply a handwritten line, sentence, paragraph, or set of paragraphs on a separate sheet of paper attached to other policy documents. To be enforceable, endorsements must be dated and initialed by an authorized representative of the insurer, such as the chief executive officer or president.

Endorsements are often intended to modify a basic policy form. The provisions in an endorsement usually differ from the provisions in the basic policy to which it is attached. To properly interpret an insurance policy with an endorsement, insurance personnel must apply the following two rules:

1. An endorsement takes precedence over any conflicting terms in the policy to which it is attached.
2. A handwritten endorsement supersedes a computer-printed or typewritten one.

These rules are based on the premise that an endorsement added to a policy, particularly if it is handwritten, tends to reflect the intent of the parties more accurately than do other, preprinted policy terms.

SUMMARY

Individuals and organizations use insurance as one technique to manage their loss exposures. Insurance is a system for transferring risk from insureds to insurers. The insured agrees to the policy terms by signing an application and paying the premium. The insurer agrees to pay for losses covered by the policy. Insureds or others present claims after they have suffered a loss that they believe is covered by the policy.

The benefits of insurance include reduction of uncertainty, loss reduction and prevention, efficient use of resources, support for credit, satisfaction of legal requirements, satisfaction of business requirements, source of investment funds, and reduction of social burdens. In exchange for the benefits provided by insurance, insurance has many costs, such as premiums, operating costs of insurers, opportunity costs of insureds, increased losses, and increased lawsuits.

Insurance is based on the principle of indemnity, the law of large numbers, and the insurable interest requirement. The principle of indemnity and the insurable interest requirement affect the amount that an insured can recover through loss payments, while the law of large numbers helps determine the amount of coverage insurers can provide.

The parties to an insurance policy are the insured and the insurer (through private and government insurance). Third parties who suffer injury or property damage because of the insured's actions are beneficiaries of the insurance policy, even though they are not insureds. Parties who help to provide insurance products and services include producers, underwriters, loss control specialists, actuaries, claim representatives, special investigation unit (SIU) personnel, and lawyers.

Insurance can be marketed and sold through various marketing systems, including the independent agency and brokerage marketing system, the exclusive agency marketing system, and the direct writing marketing system, all of which involve producers. Producers send completed applications to underwriters, who examine them and collect other documents to decide which insurance applicants to accept and which to reject. The primary purpose of underwriting is to select and maintain a growing, profitable book of business. Underwriting activities include selecting insureds and their exposures, pricing coverage, determining policy terms and conditions, and monitoring the exposures and loss experience on the policies written.

Loss control specialists perform loss control surveys and submit loss control reports to underwriters, in which they evaluate the applicant's or insured's operations and recommend improvements. Actuaries use complex mathematical methods and statistics to analyze loss data and other information so that insurance premiums can be determined. A claim representative is an insurer employee who investigates, evaluates, and settles claims. Claim representatives fulfill the insurer's promise to pay the insured's claims efficiently and promptly, according to the policy provisions. SIU personnel specialize in investigating claims that appear to be fraudulent and conduct training for claim personnel on fraud indicators and cases that should be referred to the SIU. Insurers sometimes hire lawyers to defend insureds in legal proceedings. Claimants sometimes hire lawyers to represent them in claims against insureds and insurers.

In many cases, insurance is sold through a producer, who helps customers identify their insurance needs and submits the applications. Underwriters for an insurer collect additional information and decide whether to accept the loss exposures presented in the applications. If they accept a loss exposure, the insurer issues an insurance policy to that insured. The collected premiums are processed and deposited in the bank.

Insurers receive income from the sale of insurance (underwriting income) and investment of funds (investment income). When calculating underwriting income, an insurer determines written premiums, earned premiums, and unearned premiums. These premiums are used to cover the expenses of an insurance operation and invested to pay future claims. State insurance regulators evaluate an insurer's financial condition based on the insurer's combined ratio. Because insurance business fluctuates over time, insurers invest funds to earn income that enables them to remain solvent in years when they have underwriting losses. When insurers pay large claims, they usually must withdraw some of their invested claim reserve funds.

Because claim representatives are often viewed as the insurer by claimants and others, a claim representative's positive interaction with parties inside and outside the insurer's office can influence the insurer's success. Through interaction with insureds/claimants, producers, underwriters, loss control specialists, actuaries, SIU personnel, and lawyers, claim representatives develop crucial relationships. A claim representative who is friendly, composed, and knowledgeable can develop effective relationships with these parties and others.

Insurance personnel must understand the parts of an insurance policy to properly handle claims. Property and liability insurance policies contain policy provisions that can be categorized as declarations, definitions, insuring agreements, exclusions, conditions, and miscellaneous provisions. Endorsements add to, delete, replace, or otherwise modify other provisions in the policy.

The basic insurance concepts presented in this chapter provide a foundation for insurance personnel to understand insurance and the insurance business. This foundation is crucial to understanding insurance claims and to handling them efficiently and promptly in the best interests of the insurer and the insured. The next chapter introduces the claim function, including the claim-handling process, the roles of claim personnel, and the skills and qualities that claim personnel should possess.

CHAPTER NOTE

1.   Adapted from Insurance Information Institute, *The III Insurance Fact Book 2004* (New York: Insurance Information Institute, 2004), p. 14.

Chapter 2

Direct Your Learning

The Claim Function

After learning the content of this chapter and completing the corresponding course guide assignment, you should be able to:

- Identify the activities in the claim-handling process.

- Describe the roles of the following claim personnel and others who help handle claims:
  - Managers
  - Supervisors
  - Claim representatives
  - Customer service representatives
  - Other support staff
  - Special investigation unit (SIU) personnel
  - In-house counsel
  - Third-party administrators

- Describe the technical skills that claim representatives should possess and why they should possess them.

- Describe the work skills that claim representatives should possess and why they should possess them.

- Describe the following interpersonal skills that claim representatives should possess and why they should possess them:
  - Managing customer expectations
  - Communicating effectively
  - Projecting empathy and establishing rapport
  - Resolving conflicts
  - Providing exceptional customer service

- Describe the following qualities that claim representatives should possess and why they should possess them:
  - Ethical behavior
  - Other desirable qualities, including creativity and innovation, the desire to learn, inquisitiveness, and adaptability.

- Define or describe each of the Key Words and Phrases for this chapter.

Develop Your Perspective

What are the main topics covered in the chapter?

This chapter provides an overview of the claim-handling process. It also describes the roles of claim personnel and others who help handle claims and the essential skills and qualities that claim representatives should possess, including technical skills, work skills, interpersonal skills, and desirable qualities.

Interview a claim representative whom you know well.

- What skills or qualities does this claim representative find helpful in performing his or her work?
- With which other departments does this claim representative interact during the course of the day?

Why is it important to learn about these topics?

Claim personnel must be familiar with the activities in the claim-handling process in order to handle claims properly and thoroughly. They must also understand the roles of the various claim department personnel with whom they interact during the claim-handling process. New claim personnel can strive to develop the skills and qualities that they need to possess to be successful in their jobs, and experienced claim personnel can strive to improve those skills and qualities.

Review an insurer's claim-handling procedures and a claim file.

- What claim-handling activities can you identify by reviewing notes in the claim file?
- What claim personnel were involved or consulted during the claim process?

How can you use what you will learn?

Assess your skills and qualities as they compare to those that successful claim personnel possess.

- What skills and qualities do you have that make you well-suited for claim department work?
- What skills and qualities should you work to develop?
- What resources are available to you to help you develop the skills and qualities you need?

Chapter 2
The Claim Function

The previous chapter described insurance, the parties to an insurance policy, the parties who provide insurance products and services, the operation of insurance, the parties whom claim representatives interact with, and the provisions of insurance policies. This chapter expands on that information by providing an overview of the claim-handling process, the roles of claim department personnel, and the skills and qualities required for a claim representative to handle claims successfully.

When an insurer processes claims, it delivers on the promise in the insurance policy. Insureds buy insurance so that their covered claims will be paid and so that they will be returned to their financial position before the loss. The insurer is obligated to properly handle all claims submitted and to pay for covered losses. The following general overview of the claim process lays a foundation for more-detailed descriptions of the multi-faceted claim-handling process that are presented in subsequent chapters.

OVERVIEW OF THE CLAIM-HANDLING PROCESS

Different types of claims, such as first-party auto physical damage, first-party property, liability, and workers' compensation claims, require different treatment from the claim representative to be properly investigated and paid. Despite these differences, claim representatives can perform the same basic activities to handle any type of claim. These claim-handling activities appear in the box below and are briefly introduced in the sections that follow.

Claim-Handling Activities

- Acknowledging and assigning the claim
- Identifying the policy
- Contacting the insured or the insured's representative
- Investigating and documenting the claim
- Determining the cause of loss and the loss amount
- Concluding the claim

These activities are not sequential; they can begin and end at any point in the process, and they can overlap. Depending on the severity and complexity of the loss, claim handling can be a quick process, completed within hours or days of receiving a claim report, or it can extend over many months. These activities provide a guideline for handling all types of claims, regardless of the severity or complexity of the loss.

When a loss occurs, the insured reports the loss either to the producer, who reports it to the insurer, or directly to the insurer's claim department. Either way, the claim is presented to the insurer for claim handling.

Acknowledging and assigning the claim involves the insurer acknowledging the claim with the insured or the insured's representative and assigning it to a claim representative. This claim representative might be a member of the claim department staff, such as a telephone or field claim representative, or might be a claim representative for an independent adjusting firm (a business that contracts with insurers to handle claims).

Identifying the policy requires the claim representative to check the insurance policy to determine whether coverage applies to the loss. In addition, the claim representative establishes loss reserves, which are estimated amounts necessary to pay the claim, based on the applicable policy limits. These reserves might be for property damage, bodily injury, or other damages. **Property damage** is physical injury to, destruction of, or loss of use of tangible property. **Bodily injury** is physical injury to a person, including sickness, disease, and death. In some cases, reserves are established as "record-only," which indicates that a claim was presented but that coverage is not provided for the loss. A record-only claim is often indicated by a very small reserve amount.

Contacting the insured or the insured's representative occurs soon after the claim has been assigned and the claim representative has established reserves (although some claims are concluded immediately without establishing reserves). This activity involves the claim representative reviewing the loss notice and the policy to verify whether coverage exists, and then contacting the insured. Often, the claim representative schedules a time to meet with the insured or a party representing the insured at the loss location as part of this activity.

Investigating and documenting the claim are ongoing activities that involve the claim representative investigating the loss and documenting the claim to create a complete claim file and to avoid duplicate work. Claim representatives commonly complete many investigations, such as insured/witness investigations, claimant investigations, accident scene investigations, and others. They might also consult numerous experts as part of these investigations. Claim representatives also investigate subrogation possibilities in conjunction with their other investigations. Subrogation is the recovery of payment amounts from responsible third parties.

Claim representatives document claims based on the type of loss. For example, a medical liability claim might include, in addition to the file status notes,

Property damage
Physical injury to, destruction of, or loss of use of tangible property.

Bodily injury
Physical injury to a person, including sickness, disease, and death.

recorded statements of witnesses, medical bills, a physician's diagnosis, and a diagram of the accident scene. In contrast, a broken windshield claim might include only an estimate for the glass replacement with the claim representative's file status notes. Many insurers have claim-handling guidelines that outline the possible ways to document each type of claim. Documenting a claim can involve the following activities:

- Gathering records
- Photographing or taking visual recordings of a loss scene
- Drawing floor plans and diagrams of damaged areas or accident scenes
- Reviewing financial records to help determine the scope of loss
- Examining damaged or missing inventory

Determining the cause of loss and the loss amount occurs when the claim representative uses the results of the investigations and documentation as a basis for an opinion about the loss. The claim representative determines whether the loss resulted from a covered cause of loss and, if so, what amount of the loss is covered.

Concluding the claim takes place after the claim representative investigates the claim and determines the cause of loss and the loss amount. This activity involves the claim representative preparing a loss statement and settling the claim. Claim representatives settle claims through negotiation or alternative means and complete closing reports. As part of this activity, claim representatives also issue appropriate payments or deny claims that are not covered by the policy.

Claim representatives need a basic understanding of these claim-handling activities to understand the roles of claim personnel and the importance of the skills and behaviors required of claim personnel. The next section examines these various roles.

ROLES OF CLAIM PERSONNEL

Both insurers and independent adjusting firms employ claim personnel. The structure of insurers' and adjusting firms' claim departments varies, along with the job titles these organizations use to describe claim department personnel. However, claim personnel perform basically the same duties, despite differences in department structures, job titles, and whether they are employed by insurers or adjusting firms. Claim personnel fulfill the promise that insurers make in insurance policies. This section describes the duties of the following claim personnel and others who help handle claims:

1. Managers
2. Supervisors
3. Claim representatives
4. Customer service representatives

5. Other support staff
6. Special investigation unit (SIU) personnel
7. In-house counsel
8. Third-party administrators

Managers

The first common position in a claim department is manager. Usually, insurers appoint a claim vice president as a key member of the insurer's management team. Insurers typically appoint one or more assistant vice presidents, who report directly to the claim vice president. Assistant vice presidents have responsibility for specific types of insurance, such as workers' compensation or auto insurance. Insurers might appoint one or more claim managers to report to each of the assistant vice presidents.

Some claim departments are divided into sub-departments, each with its own manager—for example, for property losses, liability losses, workers' compensation losses, subrogation, fraud investigation, appraisal, and legal work. Each manager holds some or all of the following responsibilities:

- Setting goals
- Budgeting
- Staffing
- Developing staff
- Monitoring workload
- Monitoring losses and expenses
- Establishing claim procedures and ensuring compliance

Managers set goals for their departments and motivate their staff to reach those goals. Typical goals include reducing the response time for contacting insureds and claimants, concluding claims that are ready for settlement, managing the cost of each claim, and recovering subrogation amounts. Each year, managers revise departmental goals to improve on the previous year's performance.

Managers estimate future needs and develop a budget based on the costs required to meet those needs. Managers often involve supervisors or other key staff in these activities.

Managers forecast changing workloads or other circumstances that might require staff changes, such as acquiring or losing accounts, employee retirements, or replacing employees who have performance problems. If additional or replacement staff will be needed, managers seek hiring authority from upper management, prepare written job descriptions and profiles of ideal candidates, and assist in interviewing and selecting candidates.

Managers encourage employees to develop professional skills. For example, managers might circulate news articles to claim staff on landmark court decisions or current claim issues, or they might urge their staff to pursue insurance education. Training is also part of staff development. Some insurers hire training directors to develop training programs, to coordinate departmental training, and to staff training facilities. Other insurers form small training units within the claim department or rely on outside sources for training. Some insurers send claim representatives to independent training schools to learn claim-handling skills, such as estimating auto or property losses.

Managers monitor claim representatives' workloads to ensure that each claim representative is responsible for a manageable number of claim files. A **claim file** is a paper or an electronic file that contains information for a loss. Factors that help determine whether the number of claim files is appropriate include the type of claim; the claim representative's experience, expertise, and time-management skills; and the insurer's procedures for documentation, reporting, and on-site inspections. Managers should assign appropriate types and numbers of claim files to claim representatives to maximize productivity and to reduce the stress that is inherent in claim handling. Additionally, managers should ensure that claim representatives have all of the resources required to work efficiently.

Claim file
A paper or an electronic file that contains information for a loss.

Managers monitor losses and expenses to identify training needs, loss trends, and any claim-handling practices that need to be improved. The results of monitoring expenses might indicate the need for additional staff or a different approach to handling difficult claims.

Finally, managers establish claim procedures to ensure that claims are handled promptly and efficiently. Managers often develop procedures for auditing claim files and other processes that help ensure compliance with claim-handling procedures.

Supervisors

The second common position in a claim department is supervisor. Supervisors report to managers. Managers might divide departments into units by type of coverage, such as auto or property, or by geographic location, such as by state or designated territories. Then they assign a supervisor to direct each unit's daily activities. Supervisors should have technical claim-handling knowledge, good interpersonal skills, and the ability to motivate others. Supervisors' responsibilities are more narrowly defined than managers' responsibilities. A claim supervisor's typical responsibilities include unit budgeting, monitoring claim-file quality, answering customer inquiries and resolving problems, conducting performance appraisals, and training and motivating employees.

Supervisors, like managers, have budget responsibilities. However, supervisors develop budgets only for their units. These unit budgets then become part of the manager's departmental budget. Supervisors must support managers' and the insurer's goals to manage expenses and keep costs within the established budget.

Supervisors periodically monitor claim files to ensure consistent and accurate claim handling (some insurers assign this task to quality control staff).

They might review each file, files that meet specific criteria (such as those with reserves that exceed a certain amount), or a random sample of files.

Supervisors encourage claim representatives to develop strategies for resolving problems independently; however, supervisors help solve problems as needed. They advise claim representatives and discuss problems identified through file reviews.

Like managers, supervisors are responsible for training and must support managers' training goals for the department. Supervisors should use their technical expertise to train claim representatives; for example, they can hold informal training meetings to update staff on medical and legal developments that affect claims or on other claim issues. Claim supervisors can also act as role models by pursuing continuing professional education themselves.

Supervisors regularly assess the technical and behavioral performance of their staff. They typically conduct performance appraisals once per year, but they might conduct them more frequently if company policy dictates it, such as for new employees.

Supervisors can strive to motivate claim representatives to achieve better performance by listening carefully and by publicly recognizing staff for exceptional job performance. Successful supervisors exhibit good interpersonal skills, self-control, and motivational skills in their interactions with claim representatives and upper management.

Claim Representatives

The third common position in a claim department is claim representative. Insurers employ various kinds of claim representatives, including telephone claim representatives, field claim representatives, and specialized claim representatives. Additionally, insurers sometimes give claim-handling authority to agents. The next sections focus on these different types of claim representatives.

Telephone Claim Representatives

Telephone claim representative, or inside claim representative
An insurer's employee who handles claims that can be settled, usually by telephone or letter, from inside the insurer's office.

Managers assign claims to **telephone claim representatives**, or **inside claim representatives**, who handle claims from the insurer's office. Telephone claim representatives investigate claims and evaluate damages based on telephone interviews and correspondence and sometimes ask field claim representatives to help with the investigation. Telephone claim representatives can handle small, uncomplicated claims or larger, more complex claims, as determined by claim department procedures and the types of policies the insurer writes (for example, personal auto lends itself well to telephone claim handling). These claim representatives sometimes handle bodily injury claims, review damage estimates, and settle certain fire losses by telephone. Some insurers, because of the types of insurance they provide, use telephone claim representatives to handle nearly every claim.

Field Claim Representatives

Claim representatives who work both inside and outside the insurer's office are called **field claim representatives**, or **outside claim representatives**. They generally handle claims that require visiting the scene of a loss; interviewing witnesses; investigating damage; and meeting with insureds, claimants, lawyers, and others involved in the claim. Field claim representatives inspect damaged property and work closely with damage appraisers, and they often prepare damage estimates.

Specialized Claim Representatives

Some claim representatives specialize in handling certain types of claims or certain aspects of claims. Catastrophe claim specialists are trained to handle disasters (such as floods, hurricanes, tornadoes, and earthquakes) and liability losses involving multiple claimants. Catastrophe claim specialists might travel to the site of a catastrophe and remain there until all claims have been settled.

Claim representatives might also specialize in one or more of the following areas:

- Auto physical damage
- Building physical damage
- Heavy equipment damage
- Maritime property damage
- Automobile liability
- Workers' compensation
- Homeowners liability
- General liability
- Environmental liability

For example, a field claim representative might specialize in auto physical damage appraisals and be called a damage appraiser. If an insured's auto is damaged but can still be driven, the insured can take it to a drive-in claim center. The damage appraiser can estimate the cost to repair the vehicle by using computer software or by checking a crash manual. A **crash manual** (also called an **estimating guide**) is a book that describes procedures for estimating the cost to repair damage to vehicles and that lists auto part prices and typical labor times to repair or replace the part. Most manuals are now available electronically. Frequently, the damage appraiser can issue a check for the appropriate amount to the insured immediately after completing the damage appraisal. This approach enables the insured to choose where to have the car repaired. Alternatively, the insured might present a repair facility's estimate to the damage appraiser and, if the appraiser believes that the estimate is appropriate, the appraiser will issue the insured a check for the appraisal amount.

Other field claim representatives might specialize in heavy equipment or pollution environmental liability claims. In some cases, specialized claim

Field claim representative, or **outside claim representative**
An insurer's employee who handles claims that are best handled in person; much of the field claim representative's time is spent visiting the scene of a loss; interviewing witnesses; investigating damage; and meeting with insureds, claimants, lawyers, and other persons involved in the claim.

Crash manual, or **estimating guide**
A book that describes procedures for estimating the cost to repair damage to vehicles and that lists auto part prices and typical labor times to repair or replace the part.

representatives can use their expertise to take steps to reduce the damage amount. For example, a specialist might know whom to contact to quickly contain a pollutant spill and reduce the resulting damage.

Some claim representatives deal only with certain aspects of claims. They include the following:

- Material damage appraisers
- Medical consultants
- Rehabilitation nurses

Total loss

A loss that exists when the cost to repair a damaged vehicle (or other property) equals or exceeds the value of the vehicle.

Constructive total loss

A loss that exists when a damaged vehicle (or other property) cannot be repaired for less than its actual cash value minus the anticipated salvage value.

Salvage

Damaged property that is turned over to the insurer after the insurer pays the claimant or insured the total value of the property. Often, it can be sold to recover part of the claim payment.

Material damage appraisers inspect damage to autos and other types of property to determine whether the property is repairable, a total loss, or a constructive total loss. A **total loss** is a loss that exists when the cost to repair a damaged vehicle (or other property) equals or exceeds the value of the vehicle. A **constructive total loss** is a loss that exists when a damaged vehicle (or other property) cannot be repaired for less than its actual cash value (the cost to repair it or replace it with property of like kind and quality) minus the anticipated salvage value (the amount that the insurer might obtain by selling the damaged property). Generally, the appraiser helps determine only damages and not coverage and liability. If the property can be repaired, he or she prepares an estimate of the repair costs. The appraiser then negotiates the repair price with the insured's selected repair facility, contractor, body shop, or other organization. If the property is damaged beyond repair, the appraiser helps the claim representative determine the value of the property and helps locate a buyer for any salvage. **Salvage** is damaged property that is turned over to the insurer after the insurer pays the claimant or insured the total value of the property. Often, it can be sold to recover part of the claim payment.

Medical consultants and rehabilitation nurses are resources that help insurers assess the medical requirements in injury claims. Medical consultants arrange independent medical examinations (IMEs) for injured insureds and claimants and request second opinions from physicians for treatments or surgical procedures. In some jurisdictions, these exams are called defense medical exams (DMEs)—claim representatives must use the proper terminology for the particular jurisdiction to avoid state fines or penalties. Medical consultants also review medical reports and audit bills from physicians and other medical providers to determine whether the treatment being provided follows the physician's treatment instructions. Rehabilitation nurses help claim representatives assess whether rehabilitation is possible for the claimant and, if so, to what extent.

Agents

Draft authority

The authority expressly given to an agent by an insurer allowing the agent to settle and pay certain types of claims up to a specified limit.

Insureds are likely to call their agent first when a loss occurs. Most insurers who market insurance through independent agents give selected agents **draft authority**, which allows the agent to settle and pay claims up to a certain amount, such as $2,500. Those agents can issue drafts (checks) directly to insureds for covered claims and thereby reduce the time necessary to pay insureds. In this capacity, agents perform a role similar to that of a telephone claim representative, but only for small claims.

Agents appreciate the opportunity to help when insureds need the coverage that they purchased through the agent. Agents can also use this contact as an opportunity to remind their clients of the value of their services. If the agent does not have draft authority, he or she can report the loss to the insurer immediately, give the insured the telephone number of the insurer's claim office, and explain how the insured can expect the claim to be handled.

Customer Service Representatives

The fourth common position in a claim department is customer service representative. When an insured reports a loss directly to its insurer, a customer service representative (CSR) generally records the loss information for the insurer. The CSR is often the insured's first contact with the insurer. CSRs answer telephone inquiries from insureds and claimants and perform routine processing and clerical tasks. Some CSRs have limited authority to handle claims for small amounts and that require little investigation, such as windshield damage claims.

Other Support Staff

The fifth common position in a claim department is support staff. Many insurers have support staff, instead of CSRs, who perform routine claim-related tasks that enable other claim department personnel to work more efficiently. Support staff might complete technical and clerical tasks such as data entry, although many claim representatives also perform those tasks.

Data entry clerks enter information about each claim into the insurer's claim information system. Accurate data entry is crucial to the success of claim departments and insurers. The information often includes claim codes to identify the type of reserves and payments. If the wrong code is entered (for example, glass breakage instead of collision), payments for that claim will be allocated to the wrong type of coverage. Insurers use claim payment data to develop some rates, and they report this data to advisory organizations, such as Insurance Services Office (ISO). Advisory organizations use the reported data to develop loss costs that many insurers use to develop rates. Incorrectly coded claim payments result in inaccurate rates, regardless of who is developing the rates. Incorrect loss reserve amounts can cause serious problems. For these reasons, accurate data entry is essential.

In addition to performing data entry, support staff might also handle the following tasks:

- Locating and retrieving files, matching incoming mail with the appropriate claim files, and other filing duties
- Sorting, date-stamping, and delivering mail
- Transcribing memos, letters, statements, and reports from rough drafts or from audiocassette tapes
- Answering telephones, directing incoming calls, and greeting visitors

---

Insurance Services Office (ISO)

Insurance Services Office, Inc. (ISO), is a national insurance advisory organization that develops policy forms, manual rules, and loss costs for its member insurers. ISO files these forms, rules, and loss costs with insurance regulators in the various states, and it provides actuarial and statistical services. Policy forms are printed forms that members can use to make up insurance policies. Manual rules instruct insurers in providing insurance policies to customers; for example, ISO provides rules for insurance eligibility, limits of insurance, and insurance premium calculation. Loss costs form the basis for insurance rates and are described in a subsequent chapter.

ISO forms are often referred to as standard forms. Some insurers develop their own forms in order to offer unique products, but standard forms serve as a benchmark for insurance personnel in analyzing comparable nonstandard forms. Most of the forms described in this text are ISO forms.

- Entering settlements and payments in computer systems
- Processing agents' payments

Additionally, support staff might handle routine claims. For example, support staff might handle auto towing claims, for which they verify that towing coverage applied to the auto that was towed and then issue the claim payment. Support staff might verify that other than collision coverage is provided and issue claim payments for auto glass repair or replacement.

Special Investigation Unit (SIU) Personnel

The sixth common position in a claim department is special investigation unit (SIU) personnel. Fraud costs insurers billions of dollars annually, and the amount escalates every year. To combat this problem, many state insurance regulators require insurers to establish SIUs, and insurers in other states often establish SIUs voluntarily to detect and investigate fraudulent claims.

SIUs investigate property claims, auto accident and theft claims, workers' compensation claims, and bodily injury liability claims. They also investigate organized rings of professional claimants (claimants who conspire and create false or exaggerated insurance claims to collect insurance payments), including the medical providers, lawyers, and body shops that help professional claimants make fraudulent claims look legitimate. When SIUs are confident that they have detected fraud, they deny the claim and alert the proper authorities, who try to prosecute the wrongdoers. Successful prosecution requires expert collection and preservation of evidence, so SIUs often employ former police officers or other law enforcement authorities with expertise in gathering evidence and investigating crime. SIU investigations can also prove that claims are legitimate and should be paid.

SIU personnel perform many of the same tasks as other claim personnel, such as maintaining claim files and communicating with insureds, claimants, and witnesses. However, claims assigned to SIUs require extensive investigation and knowledge of the standards for preserving physical evidence that are used by law enforcement officers investigating criminal cases. SIU personnel usually conduct personal investigations of insureds or claimants who attempt fraud.

Claim personnel selected for SIU work are highly skilled. They typically have many years of experience in investigating and negotiating claims. SIU personnel usually become experts in particular areas, such as origin and cause analysis or financial records analysis.

SIUs provide lists of fraud indicators for their claim departments. If a claim representative recognizes a fraud indicator while handling a claim, he or she should refer the file to the SIU. SIU personnel determine which claims referred to them are candidates for intensive investigation. An unusual com-bination of circumstances or a single compelling circumstance may indicate fraud to a veteran SIU member.

SIU personnel research information using broad databases and online services. For example, SIU personnel might search for a claimant's place of employ-ment and court records, such as civil or criminal investigation records and records of divorce or bankruptcy proceedings.

Many states have passed antifraud laws requiring insurers to share their inves-tigations of suspicious claims with law enforcement authorities. SIU personnel also cooperate with authorities because a claimant's criminal conviction for fraud supports a claim denial. However, SIU personnel conduct their own fraud investigations and do not depend on law enforcement authorities to investigate fraudulent claims. Those authorities rarely have the staff or budget to investigate every possible crime.

In addition to performing their investigative duties, SIU personnel conduct seminars and meetings for claim department staff to remind them of the SIU's role and of fraud indicators. Because SIUs receive claims by referral from other claim personnel, all claim personnel are crucial to the successful identi-fication and investigation of fraud.

In-House Counsel

The seventh common position in a claim department is in-house coun-sel. Insurers employ lawyers called in-house counsel or staff counsel. These lawyers defend insureds in court proceedings, but they are employees of the insurer; therefore, in-house counsel are especially vulnerable to conflict of interests charges. They cannot simultaneously represent the insured and advise the insurer as to possible coverage issues because doing so violates their duty to represent the best interests of their client. A denial of coverage is rarely in the best interests of the insured.

Whether using in-house counsel or independent lawyers to defend insureds, claim representatives must realistically assess the insurer's chance of achieving a verdict favorable to the insured. Because defense costs can be substantial, an incorrect assessment could be costly to the insurer.

Third-Party Administrators

Third-party administrator (TPA)
A firm that contracts to provide administrative services to other businesses; often hired to handle claims by organizations that have self-insurance plans.

Third-party administrators (TPAs) are firms that contract with other organizations to provide administrative services, including claim handling. Claim departments might encounter TPAs who are hired to handle claims for organizations that self-insure their losses up to a certain limit but purchase insurance for their loss exposures above that limit. Self-insured organizations are firms that use their own funds to cover some or all of their loss exposures.

TPAs hire claim representatives to handle claims in much the same manner as claim representatives who work for insurers and independent adjusting firms. TPA claim representatives handle claims for the self-insured organization such as liability claims and/or workers' compensation claims. The claim-handling activities that these claim representatives perform may differ from those of claim representatives who work for insurers, depending on the terms of the TPA contract. TPA claim representatives may have many of the same job duties and responsibilities as insurers' claim representatives, or their activities may be limited to investigation and reporting.

When a self-insured organization hires a TPA, it generally purchases claim recordkeeping and statistical analysis services, along with claim-handling services. Large independent adjusting firms sometimes function as TPAs for self-insured organizations in addition to providing claim-handling services for insurers. Some property-casualty insurers have established subsidiary companies that serve as third-party administrators.

This section and the previous section outlined a claim representative's job duties and role in the claim department, as well as the roles of other claim department personnel. The following section describes the skills and qualities that claim representatives should possess to be successful in their jobs.

ESSENTIAL SKILLS AND QUALITIES

Successful claim representatives come from a wide range of backgrounds, and each representative possesses unique skills and qualities. Nevertheless, all effective claim representatives have certain skills and qualities that enable them to do their jobs well, as follows:

1. Technical skills
2. Work skills
3. Interpersonal skills

Although this section focuses on these skills and qualities as they apply to the work of claim representatives, most of these skills and qualities are equally appropriate for other claim department personnel.

Technical Skills

One set of essential skills for claim representatives is technical skills and technical knowledge. Claim representatives should possess the following technical skills:

- Investigative skills
- Evaluation skills
- Negotiation skills

To properly complete claim investigations, claim representatives require certain investigative skills. During their investigations, claim representatives collect information, sometimes from reluctant sources such as the party responsible for the damages who avoids self-incrimination. Investigative skills that claim representatives have or acquire through experience include the ability to recognize important details and resources and to extract needed information. Claim representatives must verify the information that they collect for accuracy and credibility. They can verify accuracy by examining statements from insureds and witnesses, or through other resources. For example, if an insured covered by automobile insurance says that it was pouring rain when an accident occurred, the claim representative can verify weather information by checking local news accounts or meteorologists' records. The claim representative can verify a claimant's statements by interviewing witnesses. Claim representatives can compare the information they collect with information available from other sources as well. For example, the claim representative could compare the insured's statement and the police report. When new information contradicts existing information, the claim representative should reexamine all of the information obtained and investigate further to resolve the conflict or determine which information is most credible.

Successful claim representatives also possess evaluation skills. Claim representatives generally improve their evaluation skills through experience and education. Claim representatives evaluate property damage, bodily injuries, liability, and the quality of evidence. In doing these evaluations, they must be able to interpret insurance coverages in light of the facts. They consult numerous sources of information, such as valuation guides, previous similar claims, and supervisors. After evaluating a claim, the claim representative should be comfortable with the established range of settlement values and should know the maximum amount that the insurer would be willing to pay on a claim. Claim representatives who properly evaluate losses are then prepared for negotiating a settlement.

Successful claim representatives possess negotiation skills as well. Claim representatives resolve differences with other parties to the claim through negotiation. Negotiation is the process of exchanging information to resolve differences and reach an agreement. Negotiation is most apparent during the claim settlement process, but claim representatives negotiate with almost every person they encounter during their work.

The claim representative should prepare specific strategies and arguments for negotiating a claim. The strategies and arguments should be based on a thorough investigation of the facts of that claim. Claim representatives who are successful at negotiating claims have strong knowledge of coverage, liability, and damages.

Because negotiation is a form of communication, strong communication skills are essential to successful negotiations. Effective negotiators communicate their position clearly and strive to understand the other party's position.

In addition to having the technical skills of investigation, evaluation, and negotiation, successful claim representatives possess technical knowledge to handle claims. Claim representatives can gain this knowledge through experience, training and education, and working with other claim professionals.

Claim representatives need technical knowledge applicable to the types of claims they handle. Property claim representatives learn about building construction to compare building damage estimates to the actual damage. Liability claim representatives and workers' compensation claim representatives learn about legal systems, medical terminology, and the human skeletal and muscular systems. Claim representatives who handle auto damage claims must have specialized knowledge about parts of a car, auto repair, and body shops.

Work Skills

A second set of essential skills for claim representatives is work skills, including the following:

- Positive work ethic
- Organizational skills
- Time management skills
- Decision-making skills
- Stress management skills
- Computer skills
- Math skills

Having a positive work ethic is essential to being a successful claim representative. The following factors contribute to a claim representative's work ethic:

- *Ability to work well with others.* Claim representatives work with numerous other people. The ability to work well with others requires seeing issues from other, possibly different perspectives and respecting others' opinions.
- *Persistence.* Good claim representatives follow through and finish what they start.
- *Positive attitude.* Difficult claimants, aggressive lawyers, and heavy caseloads can be discouraging to claim representatives. Claim representatives who realize the valuable role they play can usually keep a positive attitude despite these challenges.
- *Punctuality.* Claim representatives encounter many crucial deadlines. Arriving on time for an appointment or completing a report on time, for example, shows that a claim representative can meet deadlines.

- *Self-confidence.* Claim representatives develop confidence from knowing that they can handle the emotional, intellectual, and physical demands (such as climbing on roofs) of their profession. Self-confident claim representatives are less likely to suffer from stress. However, successful claim representatives also know when to seek help with a claim and know not to be overly confident about their knowledge and abilities.

- *Self-discipline.* Claim representatives must work independently and manage their own work. They must identify what needs to be done and when, and ensure that they perform the work expected of them. They cannot rely on supervisors or managers to direct every task or rely on anyone else to perform the necessary work on their claim files.

Being organized is crucial to effective claim handling. Claim representatives decide when to make appointments, when to report on claims, and when to perform other tasks associated with their jobs. Claim representatives must organize their work and perform the most important tasks first. They must organize their claim files so that they and others can locate information quickly.

Both field and telephone claim representatives need organizational skills to manage their time. Field claim representatives spend much of their time outside the office conducting investigations. Field claim representatives might organize several appointments and meetings each day at various locations. They should coordinate trips and use waiting time to review files. If an appointment must be canceled, the field claim representative should schedule another appointment to fill that time. Although telephone claim representatives rarely work outside the office, they must also organize their daily routines. Claim representatives can use a diary or a calendar to organize their work so that they do not overlook any tasks that are essential to handling claims effectively.

Successful claim representatives also need to have time management skills. Claim representatives must deal with constant interruptions to their work and must manage multiple tasks simultaneously. For example, while working on one claim file, a claim representative might be interrupted by a phone call about another claim. When the call is completed, other department staff might ask questions about a third claim. Claim representatives must manage their time well, especially regarding telephone time, paperwork, and work duties performed outside the office. Claim representatives should prioritize their return calls to give immediate attention to those calls that require it. Claim representatives should schedule time each day for returning calls and should make calls at times when those receiving the calls are likely to be available. Similarly, when managing paperwork, claim representatives should prioritize their mail to handle the most important matters first, and they should aim to handle each piece of mail only once.

Successful claim representatives also possess decision-making skills. Claim representatives must be decisive. They should identify problems with claims and resolve them by developing solutions and choosing and implementing the best solution. Claim representatives should also seek input or guidance from supervisors when needed.

Successful claim representatives need to have stress management skills. Claim handling can be stressful, and effective claim representatives learn how to manage stress by recognizing its sources and understanding its effects.

Claim representatives experience stress because of the volume and complexity of claims; the difficulty of dealing with claimants, insureds, and witnesses; and the competing demands placed on them. Claim representatives' caseloads can expand suddenly if a disaster increases the number of claims assigned or if a coworker resigns, retires, or becomes ill and a manager transfers that coworker's claims to a claim representative who already has a full caseload. Complex claims are stressful by their nature, such as total fire losses to homes, death claims, and fraud investigations. Such claims involve a great deal of work, tend to remain open for a long time, and can involve lawsuits. Claim representatives sometimes encounter difficult people, which causes additional stress, and they experience many competing demands. For example, although they should investigate claims thoroughly, they must also settle them at an appropriate time. Claim representatives might also feel torn between the competing demands of the claimant and the insurer.

Stress can adversely affect a claim representative's well-being and the quality of work performed. Avoiding difficult situations and decisions produces more anxiety, guilt, and denial and results in greater stress. Claim representatives can never eliminate all of the stress from their jobs, but they can manage it. They can control how fast they work at settling claims, and effective time management can help them reduce stress. Other claim representatives might have tips for controlling stress or provide an example of how to manage it. When they feel overwhelmed, claim representatives should consult supervisors and managers to communicate the problem and jointly seek solutions.

Having computer skills is essential to being a successful claim representative. The insurance business relies heavily on computers. Computer software efficiently processes records and transactions and speeds communications within and outside insurers' offices. For example, claim representatives access coverage and loss information through computerized policy and claim processing systems. Claim payments are handled through or recorded in claim processing systems. Property and auto estimating can be completed with the help of estimating software. Using software that automates repetitive, routine, and tedious tasks helps claim representatives focus on investigating, evaluating, and negotiating claims. Claim representatives who possess good knowledge of the operation and use of personal computers and common production software can improve the quality and quantity of their work and create a competitive advantage over those who do not.

Finally, successful claim representatives need to possess math skills. Claim representatives need math skills for many claim-handling tasks, such as the following:

- Setting reserves
- Assessing the value of damage to real and personal property
- Assessing the value of bodily injury claims
- Calculating claim payments

Claim representatives measure distances, calculate areas and percentages, subtract deductibles, and determine totals. Although calculators and computers can perform many of these functions, claim representatives still need good math skills to properly perform their duties.

Interpersonal Skills

A third set of essential skills for claim representatives is interpersonal skills. Effective claim representatives have good interpersonal skills that enable them to deal with the many people they encounter while handling claims. The following interpersonal skills are important to claim representatives' success:

- Managing customer expectations
- Communicating effectively
- Projecting empathy and establishing rapport
- Resolving conflicts
- Providing exceptional customer service

Managing Customer Expectations

One interpersonal skill that is important to claim representatives' success is managing customer expectations. Claim representatives work closely with insureds and claimants (who are collectively called claimants in this section). After a loss occurs, claimants often feel uncertain about how a claim will be handled and whether they should retain legal counsel to achieve a fair claim settlement. They are often bombarded with mixed messages from friends and advertisements on how best to approach their claims. These influences could cause claimants to set unrealistic expectations for their claim settlement. Claim representatives can reduce the effect of these influences by contacting the claimant as soon as possible to fully explain the claim-handling process and its goals and to answer any questions from the claimant. If claimants ask whether they should retain legal counsel, claim representatives should not advise them either way, but instead should explain how the claim-handling process would be affected by that decision.

Throughout the claim-handling process, claim representatives should speak realistically with claimants about the costs of repairs, replacement of damaged property, and the medical expenses that are eligible for reimbursement, such as medical treatments for covered injuries and transportation expenses associated with those treatments. Claim representatives should frankly explain that any claim payments depend on coverage and policy conditions and limitations.

Communicating Effectively

Another interpersonal skill that is important to claim representatives' success is communicating effectively. Claim representatives convey information to insureds, claimants, supervisors, underwriters, lawyers, and others, and they must communicate that information using language that each of these groups can understand. Claim representatives routinely deal with distracted, distressed, and suspicious people, and they must know how to communicate to gain the cooperation of those people so that they can settle claims.

Claim representatives employ written, oral, and nonverbal communication. Much of a claim representative's communication is done in writing. Claim representatives can avoid causing the insurer serious business and legal problems by writing clear, concise, and legally accurate memos, letters, and reports. For example, a claimant who receives a confusing letter from a claim representative might hire a lawyer to intercede on the claimant's behalf and, if an insured, might be likely to switch insurers. A claim representative's written communications reflect on the professionalism of the insurer and the claim representative. Some claim representatives dictate routine documents; however, most use form letters that can be adapted to specific claims or prepare their own correspondence using word processing software.

Except when referring to policy provisions, to write clear, concise, legally accurate materials, claim representatives should follow these guidelines:

- Use simple, familiar words.
- Write in short sentences.
- Read the completed document aloud to find errors that might otherwise be missed.
- Avoid using abbreviations and technical claim language in external communications.

Faxes and e-mail have significantly increased the speed with which written messages can be sent and received. However, those messages affect others in the same manner regardless of how they are delivered. Claim representatives must follow the same standards for all written communications regardless of the delivery method. And claim representatives must communicate using appropriate methods; for example, although it is acceptable to discuss claim denial with a claimant or an insured over the phone, claim representatives must follow up with a claim denial letter to properly document the claim.

Claim representatives communicate with others in person and by telephone. In addition to considering word choice and tone, claim representatives should consider the nonverbal aspects of their oral communications. People send and receive nonverbal cues and messages when they communicate orally. Claim representatives should be aware that eye contact, facial expressions, gestures, and personal appearance influence the oral messages they send and receive.

Because claim personnel conduct much of their business by telephone, they must know how to communicate effectively by phone. For example, they

must be courteous and maintain a professional demeanor even with claimants who are angry or upset. Claim representatives should show consideration
for the other party by not interrupting when he or she is speaking. Active
listening techniques, such as saying "I see" or "Go on," reassure the other
party that the claim representative is listening closely. Providing feedback by
paraphrasing the other person's comments helps to ensure that the meaning
of those comments is clear to everyone involved. Finally, people form mental
pictures of the person at the other end of the telephone. Claim representatives can project a warm, friendly, and sincere tone to positively influence
that mental image.

Projecting Empathy and Establishing Rapport

Another interpersonal skill that is important to claim representatives' success
is projecting empathy and establishing rapport. Claim representatives must be
able to empathize with insureds and claimants who have recently experienced
trauma. Successful claim representatives strive to establish rapport with the
many people they contact while handling claims.

Resolving Conflicts

Another interpersonal skill that is important to claim representatives'
success is resolving conflicts. In claim work, conflict often arises because
of differing expectations about the claim process and disagreements over
the amount of the loss and who is responsible for the loss. Effective claim
representatives learn to employ methods for conflict resolution. Four of
those methods are as follows:[1]

1. *Avoidance.* When claim representatives avoid conflict, they prevent it
    from arising. For example, to avoid conflict, they might quickly and clearly
    explain the claim process to the claimant and prevent misunderstandings.
2. *Accommodation.* When claim representatives accommodate others, they
    let the desires of the other side prevail. For example, they might agree to a
    request to meet an insured at an unusual time or place to reduce conflict.
3. *Compromise.* When claim representatives compromise, they give up
    something in return for something else. For example, a claim representa-
    tive might agree to settle a claim at a value that is mid-way between the
    claimant's demand and the claim representative's proposal.
4. *Collaboration.* When claim representatives collaborate, they work with
    others to achieve their goals. For example, they might work closely with
    a claimant to evaluate the extent of the claimant's injuries and establish a
    claim value that is agreeable to both the insurer and the claimant.

Providing Exceptional Customer Service

Another interpersonal skill that is important to claim representatives' success
is providing exceptional customer service. Successful claim representatives
know that others with whom they interact are the insurer's customers or

potential customers. Those customers have many demands and expectations for claim representatives. Insurance customers deserve high-quality service in exchange for their insurance premiums. They expect claim representatives to settle their claims quickly and fairly and to treat them with courtesy, respect, and understanding. They like to know that the insurer appreciates their business. Consequently, claim representatives must constantly consider their customers' needs and provide the customer service that meets those needs.

Qualities

In addition to having the essential skill sets described earlier, successful claim representatives possess certain personal qualities. Claim representatives must hold themselves to high standards of ethical, professional conduct. In addition, claim representatives' behavior should reflect other personal qualities. The following sections describe the ethical behavior and the other desirable personal qualities exhibited by successful claim representatives.

Ethical Behavior

Ethics refers to a person's beliefs about how that person should behave in general and in a given situation. Ethics are derived from moral values; however, moral decisions can be differentiated from ethical decisions. Moral decisions involve deciding between right and wrong and obeying the law. Ethical decisions involve choosing between two right or legally acceptable decisions. Ethical decisions can involve honesty versus loyalty, long-term versus short-term benefits, justice versus mercy, and community versus individual.

Situation-based approach
An approach to ethical decision making that is based on the best possible outcome, given the circumstances.

Rule-based approach
An approach to ethical decision making that is based on rules that apply regardless of the effect.

People-based approach
An approach to ethical decision making that is based on how the decision maker would want to be treated in the same situation.

Claim representatives face conflicting demands and needs, such as those of insureds or claimants and those of the company's stockholders. To assess the different demands and needs, claim representatives can use three approaches to ethical decision making: situation-based, rule-based, or people-based. These approaches are commonly used in the field of ethics and can help claim representatives resolve difficult ethical decisions. Using a **situation-based approach**, the claim representative decides what the best possible outcome would be, given the circumstances. Taking a **rule-based approach**, the claim representative follows the rules that apply to the situation, regardless of the effect. With a **people-based approach**, the claim representative considers how he or she would want to be treated in the same situation. No single approach is best for every situation, even within a given profession. Also, these approaches have their weaknesses: the decision maker must decide what set of rules to follow and must consider when and under what circumstances the rules were made and whether those rules still apply. For example, in the absence of claim-handling guidelines, a claim representative might decide between guidelines that a former employer used or that he or she learned through educational resources. The claim case in Exhibit 2-1 illustrates an ethical decision based on each of the three approaches.

EXHIBIT 2-1

Illustration of Approaches to Ethical Decision Making

Following a series of hurricanes in an area, an insurer's claim department staff was faced with an ethical dilemma. Should they pay the insureds who lost their homes $5,000 to help them pay for temporary housing and living expenses before thoroughly investigating their claims, or should they withhold payments until the claims have been investigated thoroughly and coverage has been confirmed? When the department staff discussed what to do, they considered the decision from three approaches, as follows:

- *Situation-based approach*: They should write the checks. The small amount of funds that may be paid fraudulently would be dwarfed by the legitimate needs of insureds with valid claims. Besides, in the long run, the goodwill that the insurer would reap from providing immediate relief would more than compensate for any financial loss related to fraud.

- *Rule-based approach*: They could ask their producers from that area to vouch for their insureds before writing the checks; they could ask producers or insureds for enough information on the amount of coverage, home location, and years insured to generate reasonable credibility, or they could arrange to pay nearby hotels and restaurants directly for temporary housing and meals.

- *People-based approach*: They should write the checks. The staff would consider how they would want to be treated. If they were awaiting payment after losing everything they owned, receiving a check is exactly what they would want.

Claim representatives have an ethical and a legal obligation to keep certain information confidential. They have access to a great deal of personal information about insureds and claimants, much of which is private and some of which could harm others if it were to become public. A partial list of such confidential information includes the following:

- Details about arson and fraud investigations (because not every investigation results in the conclusion that the insured or the claimant has committed arson or fraud)

- Medical records

- Underwriting data (such as an insured's employment history or limits of liability)

- Case reserve amounts

- Information from the National Insurance Crime Bureau or other such services about previous claims

Claim representatives must also avoid conflicts of interest. They should make decisions based on the best interests of their customers and the insurer. Anytime claim representatives allow their personal interests to interfere with their customers' or employers' interests, **conflicts of interest** arise.

Conflict of interest
A situation that occurs when a decision maker's personal interests interfere to the extent that he or she makes decisions that adversely affect customers or employers.

Claim representatives, supervisors, managers, and other professionals who refer clients to vendors or assign files to adjusting firms for claim handling are actively lobbied by people seeking referrals. These people might try to influence claim representatives with incentives such as dinners at fine restaurants, the use of boats or other equipment, access to condominiums at popular vacation spots, and even payments of cash. Because claim representatives stand between the client and vendor, they are positioned for potential conflicts. Claim representatives should check their companies' policies in this regard.

People prefer to do business with persons and organizations that they like and are comfortable with. Salespeople for vendors make a deliberate effort toward establishing camaraderie with those they want to influence. Claim representatives should recommend and select outside services based strictly on the merits of the vendor and the needs of the insured/claimant in the given situation. Any other factors, such as friendship or common activities, that influence a claim representative create a conflict of interest.

Claim representatives can cultivate relationships with vendors, but they should remain alert to vendors' goals to sell products or services. Claim representatives must consider whether these relationships are based on friendship or sales efforts. Answering the following questions can help claim representatives evaluate their relationships with vendors:

- Does the vendor offer special services, favors, or gifts solely because of the claim representative's position?

- Do the vendor and claim representative share common interests? Do they occasionally disagree on issues, or do they always seem to agree? If they seem to share common interests and always seem to agree, then the vendor could be patronizing the claim representative.

- When the claim representative and the vendor go places together, such as to dinner or a sports activity, are expenses shared, or does the vendor always pay the bill?

- Could the claim representative return a bill for services to the vendor if it were above the standard charge? Would the insurer give that bill preferential treatment compared with other vendors' bills? Could business with that vendor still be conducted in a professional manner?

Preventing conflicts of interest requires claim representatives to strive to behave with honesty and integrity at all times. Claim representatives who are approached by vendors with offers for inappropriate gratuities must document the vendor's offer and their own response.

Managers of claim representatives may be able to offer guidelines for reducing conflicts of interest, such as the following:

- Have a strong commitment to ethical practices in all areas of claim handling.

- Have a strong and an enforceable written policy that is not open to interpretation and that is signed by every employee at least annually.

- Encourage claim representatives to consult with their supervisors and managers on ethical problems, as long as these supervisors and managers did not contribute to the problems.
- Conduct an independent reinspection of physical damage and a file review at random intervals.
- Dismiss unethical employees and defend those decisions in court.

Other Desirable Qualities

Claim representatives, in addition to behaving ethically, should exhibit other desirable qualities. These qualities include creativity and innovation, the desire to learn, inquisitiveness, and adaptability.

Successful claim representatives are creative and innovative in their work. Much of the work that claim representatives do (such as setting reserves, evaluating losses, conducting investigations, and negotiating settlements) involves judgment and discretion, so claim representatives must be creative to develop unique solutions to unique problems. For example, assume that a claim representative has located an eyewitness to an auto accident, but the witness does not speak English and has recently arrived in the United States from Thailand. The claim representative expects that this witness's statement will be valuable in proving that the insured was not liable for the accident, but the language barrier is a challenge. As a solution, the claim representative might find a family member or neighbor to act as an interpreter. Local colleges and universities that teach Thai as part of their foreign language program could be good resources for interpreters. The claim representative could call a local Thai restaurant to identify people fluent in both English and Thai who would be willing to act as interpreters. Or, the claim representative could use phone interpretation services, such as those provided by AT&T Language Line services. These are examples of the creative problem-solving that is an asset in claim work.

Claim representatives must also possess a desire to learn. For example, claim representatives who handle auto physical damage claims must keep current on automotive technology and repair methods. Claim representatives who handle bodily injury claims must keep abreast of new medical treatments and alternative treatments. Changes in a state's laws might have implications for all claim department personnel. Claim representatives who continually update their knowledge are valuable employees.

Similarly, claim representatives should be inquisitive. For example, while a claim representative is taking a witness's statement, the witness's remarks could open a new path of inquiry. Following that path could lead to additional information.

Finally, claim representatives need to demonstrate adaptability. Priorities change, and claim representatives need to adapt their work to the new priorities. Emergencies might require claim representatives to change their focus. If a claim department is staffed for multiple shifts, claim personnel might share work spaces. If two or more employees share work space and supplies, they must adapt their work habits to a routine that will enable all employees to work harmoniously.

Claim representatives should strive to develop the combination of skills and personal qualities that will help them handle claims effectively. They can use education and training services, along with personal and work experience, to help develop these skills and qualities.

SUMMARY

When an insurer handles claims, it delivers on the promise that is provided in the insurance policy. The activities in the claim-handling process guide claim representatives in handling all types of claims, regardless of the severity or complexity of the loss. These activities include acknowledging a claim and assigning it, identifying the policy, contacting the insured or the insured's representative, investigating and documenting the claim, determining the cause of loss and the loss amount, and concluding the claim.

Claim departments employ personnel as managers, supervisors, claim representatives, customer service representatives, other support staff, special investigation unit (SIU) personnel, and in-house counsel. They also work with third-party administrators that employ claim representatives.

Managers' responsibilities include setting goals, budgeting, staffing, developing staff, monitoring workload, monitoring losses and expenses, and establishing claim procedures and ensuring compliance.

Supervisors should have technical claim-handling knowledge, good interpersonal skills, and the ability to motivate others. Supervisors' responsibilities typically include unit budgeting, monitoring claim-file quality, answering inquiries, resolving problems, conducting performance appraisals, and training and motivating employees.

Claim representatives can be telephone claim representatives, field claim representatives, or specialized claim representatives, and insurers sometimes give claim-handling authority to agents. Claim representatives' duties include handling claims using the claim-handling process as it applies to various types of losses.

Customer service representatives (CSRs) generally record loss information for the insurer, answer telephone inquiries, and perform other routine processing and clerical tasks. Other support staff perform routine claim-related tasks, including data entry and filing.

Special investigation unit (SIU) personnel investigate suspicious claims and organized rings of professional claimants. They also teach other claim department staff about fraud indicators.

In-house counsel are lawyers whom insurers employ to defend insureds in court proceedings.

Third-party administrators (TPAs) are independent firms that contract with other organizations to provide administrative services, including claim handling. Many self-insured organizations contract with TPAs.

To be successful, claim representatives need technical skills (investigative, evaluation, and negotiation skills) along with technical knowledge. They also need work skills, including a positive work ethic, organizational skills, time management skills, decision-making skills, stress management skills, computer skills, and math skills. Finally, claim representatives need interpersonal skills to be able to work effectively with the many people they encounter while handling claims.

Claim representatives must hold themselves to high standards of ethical behavior. Ethical decision making involves choosing between two right or legally acceptable decisions. Three approaches to ethical decision making can help claim representatives make the best choice. They include the situation-based approach, the rule-based approach, and the people-based approach. Claim representatives are obligated to behave ethically regarding maintaining confidentiality and avoiding conflicts of interest. In addition to behaving ethically, claim representatives should exhibit other desirable personal qualities, including creativity and innovation, the desire to learn, inquisitiveness, and adaptability.

The first two chapters of this text describe general insurance concepts and the function of claims in insurance, including claim department personnel and operations. The next chapter examines the legal environment of claims, including legal and regulatory requirements, good faith claim-handling practices, and regulatory compliance.

CHAPTER NOTE

1.   Adapted from Kathryn M. Bartol and David C. Martin, *Management*, 1st CPCU ed. (New York: McGraw-Hill, Inc., 1994), p. 492.

Chapter 3

Direct Your Learning

Factors Affecting the Claim Environment

After learning the content of this chapter and completing the corresponding course guide assignment, you should be able to:

■ Describe the following types of laws, court systems, and forms of dispute resolution:
- Criminal, civil, common, statutory, and administrative law
- State and federal court systems
- Negotiation, arbitration/mediation, and lawsuit

■ Describe state and federal laws that influence claim-handling practices.

■ Explain how claim-practice regulations focus on complaints and unfair claim settlement practices.

■ Describe the areas on which good faith claim-handling practices should focus.

■ Explain how the following measures are used to ensure regulatory compliance:
- Claim guidelines, policies, and procedures
- Controls
- Supervisor and manager reviews
- Claim audits

■ Explain how each of the following benefits of regulatory compliance helps insurers and/or the public:
- Recording accurate information
- Fulfilling reporting requirements
- Detecting and preventing fraud
- Ensuring adequate reserves
- Preserving insurer solvency
- Encouraging good faith and fair claim handling

■ Define or describe each of the Key Words and Phrases for this chapter.

Develop Your Perspective

What are the main topics covered in the chapter?

This chapter builds on the discussion of the claim function in the preceding chapter by describing the claim environment. Factors that affect the claim environment include legal requirements, regulatory requirements, good faith claim-handling practices, and compliance measures.

Review an insurer's claim guidelines and procedures.

- What laws influence the various guidelines and procedures?
- What good faith claim-handling practices do you find in the guidelines and procedures?

Why is it important to learn about these topics?

Good faith claim handling should be a goal of all claim departments. To handle claims properly, claim representatives must understand the types of laws that apply to insurance and claims, the workings of the court system, forms of dispute resolution, and state and federal laws that influence claim-handling practices. Claim representatives should also understand how regulators handle complaints and regulate unfair claim settlement practices and know proper compliance measures and the benefits of regulatory compliance.

Review a closed claim for any type of loss.

- What types of laws apply to the claim?
- If a dispute ensued on the claim, what form(s) of dispute resolution were used?
- What state and federal laws applied to the claim?

How can you use what you will learn?

Assess good faith claim-handling practices and compliance measures that apply to your organization or another organization you know well.

- Does the state in which you handle claims have an unfair claim practices act?
- Does the state have licensing laws? If so, what are they?
- What controls does the employer use to ensure compliance with those laws?

Chapter 3

Factors Affecting the Claim Environment

The first chapter described insurance basics and the parties with whom claim representatives interact. The second chapter built on the first by introducing the claim-handling process that claim representatives follow and by describing the roles, skills, and qualities of claim personnel. This chapter examines the legal requirements associated with insurance claim handling and the regulatory requirements that insurers and claim departments must meet. Additionally, it describes claim-handling practices that help insurers and their claim representatives meet these regulatory requirements and handle claims fairly.

LEGAL REQUIREMENTS

Because insurance policies are legal contracts, claim representatives must observe numerous legal requirements when handling claims. Consequently, claim personnel must understand various types of laws and how they apply in insurance. Although most claims are resolved without litigation (lawsuits), claim representatives should understand the litigation process because some claims will inevitably be concluded through litigation. They should investigate and document each claim file in anticipation of such a conclusion.

Claim representatives resolve claim disputes, such as for the amount of damages, as prescribed by law. Legal procedures and claim-handling practices are affected by numerous state and federal laws. This section examines the legal environment in which claims are handled by describing the various types of laws, the court systems, forms of dispute resolution, and laws that influence claim-handling practices.

Types of Laws

Different types of laws establish legal requirements for insurance. This section discusses criminal law versus civil law, common law versus statutory law, and administrative law.

Criminal Law Versus Civil Law

Criminal law is a body of law that applies to wrongful acts that society deems so harmful to the public welfare that government takes responsibility for

Criminal law
The body of law that applies to wrongful acts that society deems so harmful to the public welfare that government takes responsibility for prosecuting and punishing the wrongdoers.

prosecuting and punishing the wrongdoers. Criminal law protects the interests of the public rather than the interests of individuals. Criminal law is always statutory law. When a crime is committed, the government, rather than the injured party, decides whether to pursue legal action against the responsible party. Criminal law governs many actions, such as murder, rape, assault, theft, arson, and fraud. Criminal law governs how suspects are investigated; charged; tried; and, when found guilty, punished. Crimes are punishable by fines; imprisonment; or, in some states, death. Losses that the wrongdoer incurs, such as fines, are not usually insurable.

Civil law

The body of law that deals with the rights and responsibilities of citizens with respect to one another; applies to legal matters not governed by criminal law.

Civil law is a body of law that deals with the rights and responsibilities of citizens with respect to one another; it applies to legal matters not governed by criminal law. Civil law includes common and administrative law and some statutory law. Civil law governs liability for civil wrongs, such as negligent acts, or breach of contract. It also addresses matters such as divorce, bankruptcy, or property zoning. When civil wrongs occur, injured parties decide whether to pursue their right of redress against the wrongdoer(s). Civil lawsuits are brought by individuals and are designed to remedy a wrong through monetary awards and fines. Punishment in civil cases never includes imprisonment when the party accused of wrongdoing is found liable. Penalties include awards of money; performance of certain acts, such as paying child support; or prohibition of certain acts, such as allowing a dog to run loose.

Under some circumstances, a person might violate criminal and civil law at the same time and might be subject to prosecution by both the government and the injured party. For example, a person responsible for a fatal car accident might face a liability lawsuit seeking compensation brought by the victim's family and criminal charges of vehicular homicide brought by the government. Exhibit 3-1 distinguishes between criminal and civil law. Criminal wrongs are not covered by insurance, but costs and penalties resulting from a civil action could be covered under insurance.

EXHIBIT 3-1

Comparison of Criminal Law and Civil Law

Criminal Law	Civil Law
Protects the public	Protects the rights of individuals
A legal action brought by the government	A legal action brought by injured individuals
Based on statutory law	Based on common, administrative, and statutory law
Designed to punish the wrongdoer	Designed to compensate the victim
Punishments such as fines or imprisonment	Punishments such as monetary awards and fines

Common Law Versus Statutory Law

Common law, or **case law**, is a body of law that consists of principles and rules established over time by courts on a case-by-case basis. Most United States common law is rooted in the common law of early colonists, which was based on common sense and English court judgments.

Common law varies by state because the courts in each state interpret and develop that state's common law over time. Under common law, courts use the rulings of other courts to help guide their decisions in similar cases. However, as society and values change over time, some common laws may no longer seem applicable, so common law evolves along with society. Because common law evolves at different paces in different areas of the country, common law rulings can vary significantly among states.

One example of common law is most contract law.[1] **Contract law** is the branch of civil law that governs contracts and settles contract disputes. (A **contract** is a legally enforceable agreement between two or more parties.) Civil law also protects contract rights and enables contract enforcement. Contract law promotes commerce by making contracts more reliable. People and organizations are more willing to enter into contracts with others when they know that the contracts are enforceable. If one party does not honor a contract, the other party to the contract can ask the court to compel that party to perform the contract, or the court can assess damages.

Because insurance is a contract between the insurer and insured, it is subject to contract law. How insurance policy language is interpreted is governed by the principles of contract law. An insurance policy is considered a **contract of adhesion**, which is a contract in which one party (the insured, in insurance) must adhere to the agreement as written by the other party (the insurer). Therefore, because the policy is usually written by the insurer with no input from the policyholder, courts generally interpret any ambiguities in the policy language in the insured's favor. Courts often interpret policy language in coverage disputes. Therefore, claim representatives should be aware of the common law that relates to insurance policy interpretation in the states where they handle claims.

Legislatures at the local, state, and federal levels of government have the power to enact formal laws, or statutes, which form the basis of **statutory law**. State statutes are passed by state legislatures, and federal statutes are passed by the U.S. Congress and signed into law by the President. If the government believes that a common-law court decision is unwise or contrary to public interests, the legislature could create a statute modifying the effect of the court decision. Although common law evolves from court decisions, a relationship exists between common law and statutory law. Sometimes a statute is enacted to amend a common law. When the meaning of a statute is unclear, the courts must interpret it, and the result is the development of common (case) law. Some civil law is governed by statutory law; in contrast, all criminal law is statutory.

Common law, or **case law**
The body of law that consists of principles and rules established over time by courts on a case-by-case basis.

Contract law
The branch of civil law that governs contracts and settles contract disputes.

Contract
A legally enforceable agreement between two or more parties.

Contract of adhesion
A contract in which one party (the insured, in insurance) must adhere to the agreement as written by the other party (the insurer).

Statutory law
The body of law that consists of the formal laws, or statutes, enacted by federal, state, or local legislative bodies.

All states have statutes governing the conduct of insurance within the state. Such statutes control the activities of insurers and their relationships with insureds. Similarly, Congress enacts statutes in areas of law entrusted to the federal government, such as interstate commerce and bankruptcy. Claim representatives should be familiar with statutory law that relates to insurance so that they do not violate it. Some policies are governed by statute—for example, workers' compensation insurance policies refer to state workers' compensation laws. Also, statutes might impose special requirements for certain types of losses, such as requiring that serious fire losses be reported to the state fire marshal's office. Auto coverages are governed by statutes requiring minimum auto liability coverage limits in some states.

Administrative Law

Administrative law

The body of law that is created by administrative agencies that are given power by the government.

In many specialized areas of law, Congress or a state legislature might create an administrative body or agency to assume the power to enact and enforce laws to govern its area of expertise. Such agencies enact **administrative law**. Decisions of these agencies can be appealed to the courts. This delegation of authority helps Congress and the state legislatures effectively regulate more situations and circumstances.

Congress grants this legislative power to administrative and regulatory agencies such as the Occupational Safety and Health Administration (OSHA), which creates regulations to govern workplace conditions. State legislatures can create agencies that enact administrative laws within that state. For example, many state insurance departments enact detailed regulations for insurance ratemaking. Administrative law is civil law.

Court Systems

Jurisdiction

A particular court's scope of powers or authority. A court must have jurisdiction over a case to hear and decide it.

In the U.S., the court system is divided into two systems: state and federal. State court systems are created by each state's constitution. The federal court system is created by the U.S. Constitution and acts of Congress. Whether a case is heard in state or federal court depends on the jurisdiction. **Jurisdiction** refers to a particular court's scope of powers or authority. A court must have jurisdiction over all three of the following aspects of a case to hear and decide it:

1. Parties involved in the case

2. Legal subject matter in question

3. Amount of money in dispute

In civil cases, courts generally have jurisdiction over a party only if that party resides in or does business in that state. As an exception, state courts extend jurisdiction over any person who operates a motor vehicle in that state. State courts have subject-matter jurisdiction over any legal dispute except disputes reserved for the federal courts by the U.S. Constitution, such as bankruptcy.

State Courts

Each state organizes its court system differently. For example, some states separate family-law cases (such as divorce, custody, and child support) from other civil cases. Each state has several levels in its court system. Each level is distinguished by the amount of money claimed and sometimes by the need for a jury. Because court names vary, claim representatives should become familiar with the names of courts in the jurisdictions where they handle claims. Exhibit 3-2 illustrates a typical state court system.

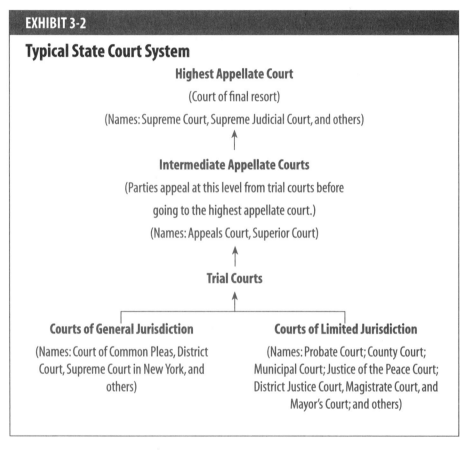

EXHIBIT 3-2

Typical State Court System

Highest Appellate Court

(Court of final resort)

(Names: Supreme Court, Supreme Judicial Court, and others)

↑

Intermediate Appellate Courts

(Parties appeal at this level from trial courts before

going to the highest appellate court.)

(Names: Appeals Court, Superior Court)

↑

Trial Courts

↑

Courts of General Jurisdiction	**Courts of Limited Jurisdiction**
(Names: Court of Common Pleas, District Court, Supreme Court in New York, and others)	(Names: Probate Court; County Court; Municipal Court; Justice of the Peace Court; District Justice Court, Magistrate Court, and Mayor's Court; and others)

The trial court system of a state consists of courts of general jurisdiction and courts of limited jurisdiction. The first type of trial court, a court of general jurisdiction, hears cases that have no dollar limit and might award equitable relief (nonmonetary relief such as an injunction or a court order to stop an action or compel an action). Courts of general jurisdiction have various names, including court of common pleas, superior court, and district court. A "superior court" can be a trial court in some states but an appellate court in others. Courts of general jurisdiction are the basic trial courts, and most lawsuits start there. These courts hear all felony cases. (A felony is a criminal act that involves significant moral fault on the offender's part and is punishable by lengthy confinement and fines.)

The second type of trial court, a court of limited jurisdiction, hears cases in only specific and limited situations. Examples are probate courts, county courts and municipal courts, and family or juvenile courts. A probate court hears primarily estate cases and wills; a municipal court might hear cases involving only limited amounts of money; and family or juvenile courts hear cases such as divorce, custody, child support, and juvenile offense cases. The lowest level of trial courts are certain courts of limited jurisdiction and might be called municipal, small claims, or mayors' courts, depending on local custom. Judges in these courts can be justices of the peace or magistrates.

Most states have an intermediate, appellate-level court. If one party to a dispute wants to challenge (appeal) the decision of a trial court, that party must take its case to an appellate court. One or two appellate courts could review the lower court's decision. Appellate courts make their decisions based on evidence presented in earlier trials; they do not hear new evidence, and they do not retry cases. Most appellate courts are restricted to examining the law as it applies to the facts determined by the trial court. Intermediate appellate courts hear appeals from trial courts before they can go to an appeal in the state's highest court.

The highest appellate court is the highest court in the state system and might be called a superior court or a supreme court; however, some states and the federal government also use those terms to describe trial courts. Matters decided by a state's highest court become the common law of that state and set a precedent for later decisions in lower courts in similar cases. A higher court can overturn a precedent, resulting in the evolution of common law.

Federal Courts

Every state has at least one federal district court that is part of the federal court system. The results of a trial conducted by a federal district court can be appealed to the appropriate circuit court of appeals. The federal court system is organized into circuits: eleven regional circuits that each serve a specific geographic region; the Washington, D.C., circuit; and the Federal Circuit. The U.S. Supreme Court hears appeals from federal courts. Unlike the highest state courts, which must hear all cases properly brought before them, the U.S. Supreme Court chooses the cases it reviews. Exhibit 3-3 illustrates the federal court system.

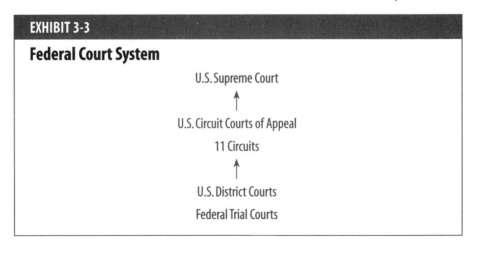

EXHIBIT 3-3

Federal Court System

U.S. Supreme Court

↑

U.S. Circuit Courts of Appeal

11 Circuits

↑

U.S. District Courts

Federal Trial Courts

Federal courts hear two main types of disputes: disputes about the interpretation of federal laws and disputes between citizens of different states. For example, a federal court would hear the dispute if persons who live in California and Texas were injured by the actions of a corporation headquartered in Florida and incorporated in Delaware. The federal court hearing eliminates any self-interests of a home state court and prevents problems with different laws among the states.

Because states regulate insurance, insurance cases generally do not receive U.S. Supreme Court consideration on appeal. However, insurance cases involving federal or constitutional questions or conflicts between state laws might be heard by the U.S. Supreme Court.

Forms of Dispute Resolution

Fortunately, not every claim results in a lawsuit; claim representatives use various forms of dispute resolution (formal ways for parties to resolve their differences). For example, claim representatives usually negotiate with insureds and third-party claimants to reach agreeable settlements. However, when a dispute arises about a proposed settlement and the insured or claimant disagrees with the claim representative, the dispute can be settled by negotiation, mediation, arbitration, or a lawsuit (litigation) or by other methods that are specified in the policy and apply to that type of coverage.

Negotiation

When a dispute over the settlement of a claim arises, such as a disagreement between the insured and the insurer on the settlement amount, claim representatives try to negotiate a solution first. Most often, they negotiate with insureds, claimants, or lawyers. Sometimes claim representatives negotiate with other insurance claim representatives, liable third parties, or civil authorities.

Many third parties who are responsible for causing an insured's loss have insurance to cover their liability. In such cases, claim representatives contact the liable party's insurer and negotiate a settlement. Negotiations with civil authorities may occur when, for example, an insurer and a civil authority disagree about the severity of damage to an insured's building and the civil authority wants to enforce its local ordinances or laws requiring the insured to demolish the building or rebuild it to meet current building codes. Negotiation is the most genial and least costly method of resolving disputes.

Arbitration/Mediation

When negotiation fails, alternative dispute resolution (ADR) methods might be used. Two common forms of ADR that may be used in most types of claims are arbitration and mediation.

Arbitration

A process that enables two opposing parties to present their cases to an impartial third party, the arbitrator. The arbitrator acts as a judge, weighing the facts of the case and making a decision based on the evidence presented.

Arbitration, which is one means of dealing with disputes, is a process that enables two opposing parties to present their cases to an impartial third party, the arbitrator. The arbitrator acts as a judge, weighing the facts of the case and making a decision based on the evidence presented. Arbitration is conducted by having the arbitrator(s) review written submissions of both parties. The insurer's arbitration file is based on the claim representative's claim file, usually with highlighted details or tabs on specific documents for the arbitrator's benefit. The file should be legible and in chronological order. A well-written arbitration statement that outlines the insurer's position in the case should accompany the file. The arbitrator reviews files from both parties to render a decision based on the credibility of each case. The arbitrator's decision is final and binding on both parties.

Parties in the dispute usually voluntarily submit the matter to an arbiter or arbitration panel; however, some state statutes require disputing parties to submit their disputes to arbitration. Claim representatives must be aware of the requirements in states where they handle claims.

Arbitration is used most often to resolve disputes between insurers about which insurer should pay the claim and for how much. One insurer usually settles the loss with the insured and then submits to arbitration with the other insurer so that insureds are not penalized by a delay in payment because of a dispute between insurers. Insurer trade associations offer arbitration services to member companies, or disputes may be submitted to the American Arbitration Association or Arbitration Forums, Inc.

Mediation

A process in which a neutral outside party helps participants to examine the issues and develop a mutually agreeable settlement.

In **mediation,** another means of resolving disputes, the opposing parties submit their dispute to an impartial third party, who is generally an experienced trial lawyer or a retired judge. The mediator has no binding authority but helps the parties analyze their dispute, consider possible solutions, and perhaps devise a compromise. Mediation is used most often in liability claims because many liability coverages recommend mediation for resolving disputes.

Lawsuits

Lawsuits are another method used to resolve disputes. When ADR methods fail, parties can settle their disputes through litigation by filing a lawsuit. A lawsuit is an action in court initiated by one party to recover whatever that party believes is owed (damages) from the allegedly responsible party.

Insurers engage in three types of lawsuits. In one type of lawsuit, an insurer provides a defense for an insured when a claim is made against that insured. This type of lawsuit ensues when, for example, an insured driver is sued for an auto accident and the driver's liability insurer provides a defense for the insured. The second type of lawsuit occurs when the insurer decides that no coverage exists for a particular claim, and the insured or the claimant (in some states) sues the insurer to provide coverage. The third type of lawsuit occurs when an insurer files a lawsuit to have a court decide whether coverage applies to a given set of facts.

In a lawsuit, the **plaintiff** is the party bringing the lawsuit and claiming to have suffered damages, and the **defendant** is the party allegedly responsible for damages. The box below shows how the parties who become the plaintiff and the defendant can change depending on the nature of the lawsuit.

Lawsuit Scenario	Parties in the Lawsuit
An insured driver is sued for an auto accident and the driver's liability insurer provides a defense for the insured.	The claimant is the plaintiff. The insured is the defendant.
The insurer decides that no coverage exists for a particular claim and denies the claim. The insured sues the insurer to provide coverage.	The insured is the plaintiff. The insurer is the defendant.
An insurer files a lawsuit to have a court decide whether coverage applies to a given set of facts.	The insurer is the plaintiff. The insured is the defendant.

The litigation process is divided into three phases: pretrial phase, trial phase, and post-trial phase.

In the pretrial phase, the lawsuit begins and each party has an opportunity to discover all of the facts and evidence that the other party has to support its position, called **discovery** (described subsequently). Two documents, called pleadings, are used to begin the pretrial phase of litigation. **Pleadings** are formal written statements of the facts and claims of each side in a lawsuit and include the complaint and the answer. The plaintiff files a **complaint** with the court that tells the plaintiff's side of the story and alleges that the defendant caused harm to the plaintiff. The plaintiff requests that the court issue a **summons**. An authorized person, such as a sheriff, serves the summons on the defendant, who has a certain amount of time, specified in the summons, to respond by filing an answer. The defendant's **answer** is a legal document that tells the defendant's side of the story and describes the defenses that the defendant will raise in response. If the defendant fails to respond by the summons' deadline, the court can enter a default judgment for the plaintiff. A **default judgment** is a final court decision automatically deciding in favor of one party. It can be awarded to either party any time the opposing party fails to respond as required by the rules governing litigation.

Each party to a lawsuit is generally represented by one or more lawyers. Lawyers observe the rules of civil procedure and statutes of limitations when planning a lawsuit. State-specific **rules of civil procedure** are patterned after Federal Rules of Civil Procedure and govern the litigation process and the form and substance (content) of all documents that must be filed with the court. After the harm has occurred, the injured party has a specific time period within which to begin a lawsuit. State statutes called **statutes of limitations** define that time period. After that time passes, no lawsuit can be pursued. These time limits force parties to act on their rights while the evidence is fresh and available.

Plaintiff
The party who starts a lawsuit and who claims to have suffered damages.

Defendant
The party to a lawsuit who is allegedly responsible for damages.

Discovery
The exchange of all relevant information between the plaintiff and defendant before the trial.

Pleadings
The formal written statements of the facts and claims of each side in a lawsuit.

Complaint
The allegations made by a plaintiff in a lawsuit.

Summons
A legal document issued by the clerk of the court and directed to the sheriff to issue to the person listed on the lawsuit compelling the person to respond.

Answer
A legal document that provides the defendant's initial response and defenses to the complaint.

Default judgment
A final court decision automatically deciding in favor of one party. It might result from a failure to file an answer to a summons and complaint or from a failure to appear in court at a specified time.

Rules of civil procedure
The conventions that govern the litigation process and the form and substance of all documents that must be filed with the court.

Statute of limitations
A law that limits the time during which a claimant can file a lawsuit.

Evidence

The information presented at trial by way of witnesses, records, documents, exhibits, or other concrete objects to persuade the court or jury to believe the arguments of the opposing parties.

Relevance

An indication of a relationship to the matter at issue.

Competence

A quality of evidence that suggests the source is reliable and the evidence is adequate to justify admission in court.

Materiality

A quality of evidence that tends to establish a particular element of the claim that has legal significance.

Hearsay

Secondhand information that a witness testifying in court heard from someone else but did not personally see or hear.

Counterclaim

A complaint brought by the defendant against the plaintiff.

Evidence is used to prove or disprove facts. It includes testimony, documents, or objects that demonstrate the truth or falsity of the facts at issue. Evidence must meet the court's standards for admissibility; if it does not, it is excluded from evidence and cannot be considered in the trial by the judge or the jury. Each state has its own rules of evidence, and the Federal Rules of Evidence specify what evidence is admissible in federal courts.

Generally, evidence must be relevant, competent, and material to be admissible. **Relevance** is an indication of a relationship to the matter at issue. For example, if a claim representative photographed the damaged front bumper of a third-party's car that jumped the curb and ran headlong into the insured's home, the photographs would be relevant because damage to the front bumper would be likely. **Competence** is a quality of evidence that suggests the source is reliable and the evidence is adequate to justify admission at trial. For example, testimony from a witness who observed an accident three months before the trial is competent. Conversely, testimony from a witness who observed an accident three years before the trial might not be competent unless it were supported by documentation taken shortly after the accident, because people's memories often fade over time. Likewise, testimony from an alleged witness whom the investigation determined was elsewhere at the time of the accident is not competent evidence. **Materiality** is a quality of evidence indicating that it is significant to the case and has consequences in the case. For example, testimony that a car involved in an accident was a 2004 model is immaterial unless a defect existed in that model year that contributed to the accident.

Generally, hearsay may not be admitted as evidence. **Hearsay** is secondhand information that a witness testifying in court heard from someone else but did not personally see or hear. Claim investigations often include hearsay. However, any statement made out of court and repeated by the claim representative at trial constitutes hearsay and is usually inadmissible.

In most states, the defendant can sue the plaintiff on a matter related to the claim in dispute if the defendant believes that the plaintiff has caused some harm. Such an action is called a **counterclaim**. Courts usually hear the original lawsuit and the counterclaim at the same time. For example, the defendant can raise a counterclaim that the plaintiff negligently damaged the defendant's car and that the defendant's actions were in response to the plaintiff's negligent driving. Also, if the defendant believes that a third party should bear some or all of the liability, the defendant can bring that third party into the lawsuit. For example, if the defendant caused an automobile accident, injuring the plaintiff, and alleged that the accident occurred because the defendant's newly installed brakes failed, then the defendant could bring the mechanic who installed the brakes into the lawsuit.

During the pretrial phase, discovery is used to gather facts and evidence about the other party's case. It also helps the lawyers decide what is likely to be used as evidence should the case go to trial so that they can prepare their own client's case. A lawyer can use many methods to discover his or her opponent's case. The following box explains these methods.

Methods of Discovery

Discovery is accomplished through the following methods:

- Interrogatories
- Requests for production of documents
- Independent physical and mental examinations
- Depositions
- Requests for admissions

One method of discovery, interrogatories are specific written questions about the claim or requests for documents that the opposing party must answer in writing within certain time limits. Interrogatories help identify specific facts and sources of information regarding the accident. Claim representatives work with the insured and counsel to draft answers to interrogatories.

Another method of discovery is requests for production of documents. These are requests for the opposing side of the lawsuit to provide all of the documents in its possession that relate to the facts at issue in the case, such as documents, photographs, visual recordings, diagrams, computer records, and any other media used to transmit or preserve information. Requests for production of documents might require that claim representatives produce claim documents from their claim files.

An additional method of discovery is independent physical and mental examinations. The opposing party in an injury claim can demand that the injured party submit to an independent medical examination (IME)—called a defense medical exam (DME) in some states—by another doctor or medical practitioner to assess the physical or mental injuries. The claim representative often facilitates scheduling the IME.

Another method of discovery is depositions. These are sworn statements made about the activities of or knowledge of a party or witness concerning the subject matter of the lawsuit. Depositions can be used as trial evidence of what a person saw, heard, or did in relation to the dispute between the parties to a lawsuit if the deposed person is not available to testify. Depositions can also be used to impeach (negate) the testimony of a person who changed his or her testimony. Parties who can be deposed include the plaintiff, the defendant, a representative of the plaintiff or defendant (such as a corporate representative), and any witnesses (other parties who have personal knowledge or opinions about some facts of the case). The claim representative usually does not attend depositions but will review deposition testimony to establish accuracy and credibility.

A final method of discovery is requests for admissions. Admissions are factual statements that, unless denied by the opposing party, cannot be contested later in the trial. Requests for admissions narrow the factual issues to those in dispute and reduce the number of facts that must be determined in the trial. Defense counsel will discuss admissions with the claim representative before they are made. Generally, insurers and others should admit any facts that are indisputable.

Some lawsuits are settled during the pretrial stage because of pretrial motions or pretrial conferences, which are meetings between the lawyers and a judge. A pretrial motion is a request that a lawyer makes to the presiding judge to dismiss the case before the trial begins, often for lack of sufficient evidence against the defendant.

The matter proceeds to the trial phase if no settlement has been reached after all discovery has been completed and pretrial motions have been heard and decided. A trial is a formal judicial examination of evidence and determination of legal claims in a court of jurisdiction. A trial demands that both sides to a case produce all of their witnesses and other physical evidence at a particular time and place. Claim representatives might attend trials to observe legal actions, become familiar with the trial process, and see how a claim file is used in a lawsuit. Some of these trials may be jury trials. Only certain civil trials are heard by a jury. The right to trial by a jury is determined by state laws and could depend on the amount of money in controversy or on the area of law that applies to the facts of the case. Trials that are not jury trials are called bench trials, meaning that the case is heard only by a judge.

Juries are selected from voter registration lists and the pool of driver's license holders within the court's judicial district, such as a county. Individuals who are called to serve are selected as part of a jury pool, and they may serve on one jury or several during a set time period or may not be called to serve at all. Potential jurors are called to a courtroom and questioned by the judge or lawyers about the parties to the lawsuit and the issues to be decided in the case to determine whether any potential jurors have a conflict of interest. Lawyers use this examination to select jurors whom they believe would be impartial. Lawyers can request that a set number of jurors, selected by the opposing lawyer, be excluded without stating a reason (called peremptory challenges). Friends, relatives, and acquaintances of the parties are typically excluded from juries.

When the trial begins, the judge and possibly the jury gather in a courtroom for a formal legal proceeding. Lawyers for each party can make an opening statement, which summarizes their case and the proof that the lawyers intend to present during the trial. No evidence or testimony is included in the opening statements. After the plaintiff's lawyer or both lawyers have presented their opening statements, the plaintiff's lawyer introduces evidence through witnesses' testimony. Courts allow several types of evidence to be presented at trial. The judge advises the jury that testimony about evidence might be misleading or inaccurate and is not necessarily true.

Opposing lawyers can test the truth of the witnesses' testimony through cross-examination and can question witnesses to uncover facts or opinions that can help their cases.

After the plaintiff's lawyer finishes presenting the plaintiff's case, the defense presents its case in the same manner. During a jury trial, if matters arise about the conduct of the trial that the judge must decide (such as whether a particular piece of evidence should be presented to the jury), the judge and lawyers might hold a bench conference. The jury is barred from hearing any evidence presented in a bench conference.

After all evidence has been presented, the lawyers for each side have an opportunity to address the jury through their closing arguments. Lawyers typically summarize the facts in a light most favorable to their client and attempt to influence the jury's decision. Next, the judge gives the jury instructions about the law to use in deciding the case (such as the principles of negligence and fault) and explains which party must prove the facts. Judges and juries are instructed to decide cases as though no insurance is involved; in other words, their decision should not be affected by the possibility that an insurer will pay the judgment and legal expenses. Then the jury retires to the jury room to decide the case. The jury deliberates until a unanimous verdict is reached and then returns to the courtroom. The judge asks for the verdict, which a court officer or jury spokesperson reads in open court. The judge usually accepts the jury's verdict and enters a judgment (an official decision on the case) to that effect. On rare occasions, the judge can overrule the jury's verdict and enter the opposite verdict, because the judge believes the jury's verdict was not based on the evidence presented at trial.

After the trial has concluded, the post-trial phase begins. Either a losing party or a winning party can appeal the verdict to a higher court (the latter party would do so to pursue a larger judgment). As mentioned, an appeals court will review the application of the law to the facts decided by the jury. An appeal might be based on issues such as a judge's faulty instructions to the jury or an outside influence that affected the jury's verdict. A state appeals court can overturn a lower court's decision, affirm the lower court's decision, or send the case back to the lower court for further hearing. The verdict, which may have been amended by a judge or an appellate court judge, resolves the dispute and is binding on all parties to an insurance policy.

Claim representatives can resolve disputes through negotiation or, if negotiation is not successful, through arbitration/mediation or a lawsuit. Litigation is the most complex and costly method of dispute resolution. Therefore, claim representatives should always use the other methods of dispute resolution when possible.

Claim representatives are influenced by many different laws while handling claims. These laws are enacted by states and the federal government and determine what licenses claim representatives might be required to obtain, how claims are investigated and handled fairly, how business must be conducted, and how private information must be obtained and handled. The following sections describe relevant state and federal laws.

State Laws That Influence Claim-Handling Practices

States enact several types of laws to protect the public from improper acts of claim representatives and insurers. These laws vary among states. Claim representatives must be aware of these laws to avoid any actions that might violate them. The following sections describe:

- Licensing laws (in general)
- Unfair trade practices laws
- Unfair claim settlement practices laws
- Privacy laws

Licensing Laws

Some states have adjuster licensing laws, and these differ among states. In certain states, only independent adjusters and public adjusters must obtain licenses. In other states, claim representatives, vehicle damage appraisers, and property appraisers must obtain licenses as well. Licensing laws might require claim representatives to pass an examination or meet continuing education requirements. Temporary licenses are often granted to out-of-state claim representatives for catastrophe claim handling.

Some insurers assign groups of claim representatives to specific territories. Those claim representatives obtain licenses from the states in their territories that require licensing. Claim representatives might obtain licenses in states outside their assigned territory if they help handle claims in those other states. If claim representatives handle claims in states where they are not licensed, those states can assess fines or penalties against the insurer.

Unfair Trade Practices Laws

Some insurance departments regulate claim practices through legislation enacted to prohibit unfair trade practices. Numerous unfair trade methods and deceptive acts are prohibited by these laws. Under the laws, individuals and organizations are barred from engaging in any trade practice that is determined to be an unfair method of competition or an unfair or a deceptive act or practice in the insurance business. These laws affect all aspects of the insurance business, and they may prohibit the following trade practices:

- Misrepresentations and false advertising
- Defamation of an insurer's financial condition
- Unfair discrimination
- Rebates and favors from insurers
- Unfair claim settlement practices

While insurers must avoid all of these prohibited trade practices, claim personnel are particularly concerned with the last one, unfair claim settlement practices.

Unfair Claim Settlement Practices Laws

Unfair claim settlement practices acts and similar state laws specify practices that, if committed as a general business practice of the insurer or if committed flagrantly, enable the state insurance department to impose penalties and sanctions on the insurer and possibly the claim representative. The federal and state laws are designed to back unfair trade practices laws. Conforming to the unfair claim settlement practices acts is discussed in a subsequent section of this chapter.

Privacy Laws

Various state laws are enacted to protect individuals' privacy. Claim representatives should be aware of the following three areas of privacy that are protected by these laws:

1. Public disclosure of private facts about a person—Claim representatives often have access to facts about insureds' and claimants' private lives. Disclosure or publicity of certain facts can be humiliating to these people; consequently, laws protect individuals from such disclosures.

2. False light—Publicity that places an individual in a false light in the public eye can be an invasion of privacy if that false light is highly offensive to a reasonable person. Claim representatives must be careful not to place insureds or claimants in a false light. For example, claim representatives should not tell medical providers that they suspect insureds or claimants of making fraudulent claims.

3. Appropriation of name or likeness—If a claim representative uses an individual's name or likeness, without that individual's consent, to imply endorsement of a product or service, such action breaches a privacy law. This law recognizes the personal property right connected with a person's identity and his or her exclusive right to control it. Although appropriation of name or likeness is less likely to occur in claim work, claim representatives must be aware of it.[2]

Federal Laws That Influence Claim-Handling Practices

In addition to being aware of state laws that protect individuals from the acts of claim representatives and insurers, claim representatives must be aware of the following three federal laws intended to protect insureds and claimants:

*   The Fair Credit Reporting Act
*   The Health Insurance Portability and Accountability Act of 1996 (HIPAA)
*   The Gramm-Leach-Bliley Act

Fair Credit Reporting Act

To ensure the accuracy and fairness of credit reporting and establish reasonable procedures, Congress passed the Fair Credit Reporting Act (FCRA). This act protects individuals from errors and invalid entries in consumer credit reports. The FCRA describes the rules of credit reporting, permissible uses of consumer credit reports, information that can legally be included, rules and restrictions for investigative credit reports, responsibilities of information providers, enforcements and penalties for failing to comply, dispute procedures, and other administrative instructions for obtaining and using consumer credit reports.[3]

Claim representatives sometimes check credit records when they suspect that an insured has submitted a fraudulent claim. A credit report might help confirm or deny such suspicions. For example, if the credit report demonstrates that the insured suffers financial hardships, then the insured could have a motive to commit fraud. Additionally, some insurers report information to credit bureaus, and some insurers report legal actions. In both cases, insurers and claim representatives must ensure the accuracy and proper handling and dissemination of information that is submitted to or collected from credit reporting bureaus based on the FCRA. Parties who use information from a credit report to make decisions have specific reporting requirements. For example, if a claim representative based a claim denial on information discovered in the claimant's credit report, by law the claim representative must notify the claimant that the decision was based, in part, on a credit report and must list the reporting bureau and its address in the claim denial letter.

Health Insurance Portability and Accountability Act of 1996 (HIPAA)

Congress passed the Health Insurance Portability and Accountability Act (HIPAA) in 1996. Among its provisions, this act includes privacy rights for all individuals, and claim representatives must respect those rights. HIPAA enables individuals to specify groups or persons with whom medical information may or may not be shared by completing appropriate forms in medical offices.

Claim representatives must obtain proper, signed authorization forms from the insured or claimant to obtain medical-file information. An authorization must specify several elements, including a description of the protected health information to be used and disclosed; the person authorized to use the information or make the disclosure; the person to whom the covered entity may make the disclosure; an expiration date; and, in some cases, the purpose for which the information may be used or disclosed.

Gramm-Leach-Bliley Act

The Gramm-Leach-Bliley Act, or GLB Act, also called the Financial Modernization Act of 1999, includes provisions that protect consumers' personal financial information held by financial institutions. Three principal parts to the privacy requirements are the following:

1. Financial privacy rule
2. Safeguards rule
3. Pretexting provisions

The GLB Act enables federal agencies and states to administer and enforce the financial privacy rule and the safeguards rule. These regulations apply to financial institutions, which include banks, securities firms, insurers, and other organizations that provide financial products and services to consumers.

The financial privacy rule governs the collection and disclosure of customers' personal financial information by financial institutions and applies to all organizations that receive financial information. Financial institutions must not disclose the nonpublic personal information of any consumer to any non-affiliated third party (with specific exceptions), unless that third party meets certain requirements. If the financial institution provides a privacy notice and a reasonable opportunity to opt out, and the consumer does not opt out, then the financial institution may disclose the consumer's personal information as described in the privacy notice.

The safeguards rule requires all financial institutions to design, implement, and maintain safeguards to protect customer information. Additionally, the safeguards rule applies to financial institutions that collect information from their customers and from other financial institutions.

The pretexting provisions of the GLB Act protect consumers from individuals and organizations that obtain their personal financial information under false pretenses, a practice known as "pretexting." Claim personnel must be careful not to release any private information about insureds or claimants.

REGULATORY REQUIREMENTS

Most aspects of the insurance business are regulated to some degree, and each state regulates the insurers doing business in that state. Some of the numerous regulatory requirements that insurers must meet affect claim handling. Most claim-practice regulations focus on complaints and unfair claim settlement practices.

Complaints

State insurance regulators investigate formal complaints against insurers and their claim representatives and enforce standards of conduct. Regulators document the number of consumer complaints made against insurers. If consumer complaints about a particular insurer are excessive or show a pattern of claim-handling abuses, regulators might conduct a claim audit to review a specific insurer's claim-handling procedures.

As mentioned, most states have laws addressing unfair trade and claim practices. Complaints reveal unfair practices, and these laws state penalties for failure to comply with the laws. Violation of the laws can result in license revocation for the claim representative and fines or penalties for the insurer. In severe cases, an insurer might lose its license to operate in the state.

Unfair Claim Settlement Practices

Most states' regulators establish or adopt standards for claim practices and monitor specific insurers' claim practices. For example, regulations might require claim representatives to respond to insureds or claimants within a specified number of days. The National Association of Insurance Commissioners (NAIC) promotes the uniformity of such standards. The NAIC is an advisory organization that influences the content and uniformity of state regulations by creating model laws and regulations. For example, the NAIC drafted the Model Unfair Claims Settlement Practices Act, which specifies fourteen wrongful claim settlement practices. Many states either adopted these unfair claim settlement practices as their own or model their own standard claim settlement practices after the NAIC model act. The following practices are commonly considered unfair claim settlement practices:

- Knowingly misrepresenting facts about coverage to insureds or claimants
- Failing to promptly acknowledge communications from insureds and claimants
- Failing to promptly investigate and settle claims
- Failing to settle claims in good faith, promptly, fairly, and equitably when liability is reasonably clear
- Offering insureds or claimants substantially less money than a claim is worth, thereby forcing them to sue to recover the rightful amount
- Refusing to pay claims without conducting a reasonable investigation
- Failing to affirm or deny coverage of claims within a reasonable time after completing a claim investigation
- When printed advertising material was included with the application, attempting to settle or settling claims for less than the amount that a reasonable person would expect the insured or beneficiary to be entitled to because of that advertising
- Attempting to settle or settling claims based on an application that was materially altered without the insured's notice, knowledge, or consent
- Making claim payments to an insured or a beneficiary without indicating the coverage under which each payment is made
- Unreasonably delaying a claim investigation or payment by requiring both a formal proof of loss form and a subsequent verification that duplicates the proof of loss information
- Failing to promptly deny a claim or to offer a compromise settlement without a reasonable and accurate explanation
- Failing to provide forms necessary to present claims within fifteen calendar days of a request
- When repairs are performed by a repairer that is owned by the insurer or that the insurer requires the claimant to use, failing to adopt and implement reasonable standards to ensure that repairs are performed in a workmanlike manner

GOOD FAITH CLAIM-HANDLING PRACTICES

Good faith claim handling is crucial to helping insurers meet their financial goals by avoiding bad faith litigation. **Good faith claim handling** requires an insurer to give consideration to the insured's interests that is at least equal to the consideration it gives its own interests. Good faith claim-handling practices focus on promptness, honesty, responsiveness, fair-mindedness, and even-handedness.

Proper attitude is the foundation of good faith. Insurance is a service industry. While claim representatives handle numerous claims, insureds and claimants are concerned only with their own claims, and they expect claim representatives to show similar concern and interest. If the claim representative seems rushed or impatient, insureds or claimants are likely to believe that they are not getting the attention they deserve and to find fault with the handling of their claims.

Claim representatives should be friendly and professional when communicating with the public. They should speak fairly and appropriately about lawyers, other insureds or claimants, and other insurers. Claim representatives should try to convey a positive attitude about their career, the insurer they represent, and the insurance business in general.

When insurers willingly pay what they owe on all claims, a positive attitude naturally flows down through management and affects claim representatives' communication with the public.

Positive attitudes must also be reflected in the insurer's claim-handling guidelines and in the insurer's approach to quality control. Supervisors and managers have criteria for quality control of claims, which might include how long the claim is open, how complex the claim is, or what dollar value the claim has. So that quality standards are met, supervisors or managers should note any delays in handling the claim and should correct any improper claim-handling practices to conform to the insurer's claim-handling guidelines.

Good faith is founded on proper attitude and is supported by the following:

- Training
- Efficiency
- Prompt and courteous communication

Training is one way of supporting proper attitude and good faith. Good training helps claim personnel handle claims fairly and with confidence. Education and training should occur continuously for all claim personnel. Personnel who are current on laws and procedures are less likely to make errors that result in customer complaints.

Good faith claim handling
The manner of handling claims that requires an insurer to give consideration to the insured's interests that is at least equal to the consideration it gives its own interests.

On-the-job training provides hands-on experience and is effective in teaching inexperienced claim representatives how to handle claims properly. Insurers often provide claim-handling guidelines and procedures that instruct claim representatives in handling almost every type of claim. New claim representatives can review these often to ensure that they handle claims in a manner consistent with established practices. Claim schools and other independent or company-sponsored courses can introduce the claim function and teach basic public relations and interpersonal skills, legal principles, and policy analysis.

Some states require claim representatives to complete coursework before they are granted an adjuster's license. Specialized claim seminars are offered by various organizations and associations throughout the U.S. Some training options focus on specific types of insurance claims and specialties and may be more appropriate for experienced claim personnel.

Efficiency is an additional way of supporting proper attitude and good faith. Claim departments can maintain efficiency through several measures. They can encourage specialization among claim representatives; provide well-trained support staff and modern equipment; and obtain assistance from insurance producers, such as allowing agents to issue agency drafts for small claims. Claim departments should establish contingency plans for sicknesses, disasters, and personal problems that might hinder claim representatives' efficient claim handling. Claim representatives can remain efficient by using common sense when handling claims. Sound judgment helps claim representatives determine the best way to handle specific claims, the amount of investigation and documentation needed, whether to involve experts and managers, and the best ways to prioritize tasks.

Prompt and courteous communication is another way of supporting proper attitude and good faith. Insureds and claimants (collectively, claimants) have questions that deserve prompt and accurate answers. Some of these claimants require special, frequent communication. Claim representatives must identify those claimants who need extra attention and meet their expectations. Common courtesy should guide claim representatives' actions. Good claim handling requires the claim representative to develop a relationship of trust with the claimant. Once that kind of relationship has been established, claimants will more willingly provide documentation, cooperate with policy requirements, meet with claim representatives, and accept fair settlements, and they are more likely to be satisfied with the claim handling.

REGULATORY COMPLIANCE

Insurers institute compliance measures, which are various guidelines that insurers ask personnel to use or other actions that they take to ensure that legal and regulatory requirements are met and to promote good faith claim-handling practices. This section describes compliance measures, and the next section explains the benefits of regulatory compliance.

Compliance Measures

Compliance measures include the following:

- Claim guidelines, policies, and procedures
- Controls, such as reports, access security, authority levels, and tracking
- Supervisor and manager reviews
- Claim audits

A combination of compliance measures helps insurers enforce good faith claim handling; encourages claim personnel to provide complete and accurate information to management, producers, reinsurers, lawyers, insureds, claimants, and others; and makes the insurer's operation run efficiently and with sound expense management.

Claim Guidelines, Policies, and Procedures

Some insurers have claim guidelines, which are policies and procedures that serve as a compliance measure. **Claim guidelines** specify how certain claim-handling tasks should be performed by setting policies and procedures for claim handling. For example, claim guidelines might specify when an independent adjuster should be assigned to a claim. Such a guideline helps ensure that the insurer pays an independent adjuster only when necessary and helps claim managers control claim department expenses so that they can help meet corporate goals. Exhibit 3-4 is a sample page from a hypothetical insurer's claim guidelines.

Claim guidelines
A set of guidelines and instructions that specify how certain claim-handling tasks should be performed by setting policies and procedures for claim handling.

EXHIBIT 3-4

Claim Guidelines Sample Page

WORTHY INSURANCE COMPANY CLAIM GUIDELINES

Subject:	Activity Log
Category:	File Documentation
Purpose:	The activity log is a chronological record of file development that describes the activities and analysis on the claim file.
Procedure:	The activity log form should be completed as events occur and include the day, month, year, time, and person making notes. The activity log should be a brief notation of file activities and analysis. Detailed explanations may appear in other documents and file reports.
Responsibility:	Anyone who conducts activity on the file must comply with this procedure.

Steps for performing some tasks can be clearly specified in claim guidelines so that claim personnel ensure that information is accurate and that claims are handled properly and in good faith. Claim departments can use guidelines in training new claim personnel because they provide instruction for performing tasks properly. They are also useful as a reference for performing infrequent tasks or when one employee must perform another employee's duties because of vacation, illness, or another absence.

Claim guidelines can be in electronic or paper form. Some electronic guidelines give specific online directions for handling the file to ensure that all pertinent claim issues are addressed.

Claim guidelines, policies, and procedures can also be useful when an insurer must defend a bad faith lawsuit. Evidence that good faith claim-handling procedures were prescribed and followed demonstrates that the insurer takes measures to help guarantee good faith claim handling. When claim personnel consistently follow company policies and procedures, insureds and claimants are less likely to find fault with the claim handling.

Supervisors and managers often use diaries as reminders to review claim files or perform another activity. Claim representatives usually have many claims to handle at the same time; therefore, a reminder system is essential to helping them handle all of them properly. A **diary**, or **suspense**, is a system to remind claim personnel to perform a particular task on a claim. A diary might be as simple as a note on the calendar to call an insured about her claim and a note in the file of that date. An automated diary system might send a computer message at set intervals to remind the claim representative to review the file or reserves; to make a payment; to contact the insured, the claimant, or witnesses; or to request additional information from service providers. Exhibit 3-5 shows what an automated diary might look like.

Diary, or suspense
A system to remind claim personnel to perform a particular task on a claim.

EXHIBIT 3-5

Sample Automated Diary

Claim # 12345678

Pol # 78-02-3359	**Ins** Brown, Jackie	**DOL** 12/12/X0	**TOL** Collision
Diary 12/14/X1	**Claim rep** Stone	**Date set** 12/12/X1	

Notes: Insured is to call today. Follow up if no response. Need vehicle location for inspection.

A claim information system might set an automatic diary entry when a claim is first reported. For example, an automatic diary of seven days might be set for each new claim. Claim representatives might modify that date, depending on the claim and their investigation plans.

Activity log
A record of all the activities and analyses that occur while handling a claim.

An **activity log** is a record of all the activities and analyses that occur regarding a particular claim. Exhibit 3-6 is an example of an activity log.

Because claim representatives handle a large volume of claims, the activity log is a crucial record of activity that has occurred on each claim. Claim representatives who rely on their memories to recall all the activity on a claim are likely to forget important information. A claim file should speak for itself so that anyone reading the activity log and other documents knows exactly what has occurred. Claim representatives should carefully document every activity on a claim. If insureds or claimants develop misunderstandings during the claim process, the claim representative can refer to entries in the activity log to remind himself or herself of previous conversations or other communications.

Many insurers use a team approach to claim handling and offer extended hours to provide better service to insureds and claimants. As a result, one claim representative might take an insured's statement during the day shift, and another claim representative might answer a question from the same insured during the evening shift. Without an accurate, complete activity log, the two claim representatives might give contradictory or confusing information to the insured. Especially when more than one claim representative might work on a claim, the activity log is crucial.

Activity logs are also useful in claim audits, described later in this chapter. Producers are sometimes interested in the details of how a claim was handled, and claim personnel can review activity logs to provide those details.

EXHIBIT 3-6

Sample Activity Log

Activity Log

Claim # 12345678

Date	Activity	Diary
12/12/X1	Rec'd claim from home office. Called insured— no answer. Left msg on answering machine.	12/14/X1
12/14/X1	No response from Mrs. Darlington. Called again. Spoke with 16-yr.-old daughter. She will have her mother (the insured) call me tomorrow.	12/15/X1
12/15/X1	Spoke with insured. Took recorded statement. Mrs. Darlington backed out of her driveway and hit the neighbor's mailbox across the street, which belongs to Mr. Bounds, of 1220 NW 84th Street, Anytown, PA 19344. His evening phone number is 111-123-4567. The mailbox was mounted on a concrete post that suffered no damage, and Mr. Bounds told Mrs. Darlington that he would not file an insurance claim for damages. Mrs. Darlington's car is at Sam's Auto Repair. Arranged for inspection. Explained claim process to Mrs. Darlington. Phoned Mr. Bounds to verify that his mailbox was not damaged and that he will not file a claim.	12/20/X1
12/20/X1	Estimates rec'd and differences analyzed to ensure fair comparison. Called Mrs. Darlington and reviewed repair estimate with her. Agreed on settlement amount. Processed payment today. Closed file.	

Controls

Claim departments can use various electronic controls as compliance measures, such as claim reports, access security, authority levels, and claim information tracking systems.

Most insurers' claim information systems can be used to generate periodic claim reports. Claim representatives, supervisors, and managers review those reports to ensure that claims have been entered correctly. Reports might include information such as the following:

- Claims with reserves above a specified amount
- Claims assigned to independent adjusters
- Claims in litigation
- Claims closed by agents
- Claims with reserve changes larger than a specified amount
- Claims closed without payment by a claim representative

Reports can help insurer personnel monitor claim practices by indicating possible errors. For example, managers might review a daily report listing all claims with reserves above $100,000. If claim personnel mistakenly entered a $10,000 reserve as a $100,000 reserve, the daily report would alert managers to the error. The error could then be corrected before it affected reports produced for parties outside the insurer and agents' commission calculations.

Reports of claims assigned to independent adjusters can help an insurer meet corporate goals for expense management. If the reports indicate that many claims are assigned to independent adjusters, the insurer can examine the reasons for those assignments and determine whether a staff claim representative should be assigned to a different territory to reduce independent adjusting expenses. Similarly, claims in litigation can be reviewed to ensure that legal expenses are managed properly.

Access security
A security setting that controls an individual computer user's ability to review, enter, and change information in a claim information system.

Access security refers to an individual's ability to review, enter, and change information in a claim information system. These systems limit access to claim information using three methods.

The first method of access security requires a person attempting to access claim information to enter a password maintained by the information systems department. The system will deny access to any person who does not have the password, thereby preventing unauthorized persons from reviewing or modifying claim information.

The second method of access security restricts access to certain data in the claim information system to managers only. For example, information provided by a lawyer might be considered highly confidential. Therefore, support staff would not be allowed to access that portion of the electronic claim file.

The third method of access security prevents unauthorized individuals from changing crucial information in the claim information system, such as reserve amounts or claim codes, and can prevent them from requesting payments. For example, a newly hired support person might be prohibited from requesting claim payments until that person has completed appropriate training.

These three methods of access security dictate which claim personnel can review or modify claim information. Authority levels restrict claim personnel from making changes to claim information that exceed their authority and are described next.

Authority levels refer to the reserve amounts and payment amounts that claim personnel are allowed to set and make. Claim information systems might be designed to allow different authority levels for different types of employees. For example, experienced personnel might be allowed to set reserves and request payments for larger amounts than inexperienced personnel. Supervisors might have an authority level that is higher than that for experienced claim personnel.

Authority levels help control claims in several ways. First, if a claim requires high reserves or payments, authority levels ensure that experienced, qualified personnel handle those reserves or payments. Second, if inexperienced claim personnel enter a reserve amount or payment inaccurately and the inaccurate amount exceeds their authority level, the claim system prevents the error.

While authority levels prevent claim personnel from exceeding their authority to review and modify claim information, claim information tracking systems capture details of changes that were made to prevent fraud and help identify claim personnel training needs.

Claim information tracking systems can be designed to automatically capture information such as the date a reserve was changed, the name of the individual who made the change, the date a payment was requested, and the name of the individual who made the request. Such information is stored in the claim information system and cannot be altered. Tracking systems discourage fraud and are useful for identifying training needs. For example, if claim personnel often make unintentional errors, tracking systems can identify which employees might need additional training.

Authority level
A designated dollar amount assigned to claim personnel to limit the reserve amounts they can set and the payment amounts they can make.

Supervisor and Manager Reviews

In addition to the various claim guidelines and controls, supervisor and manager reviews are another type of compliance measure that insurers can use. Supervisors and managers use diary systems as reminders to review claims. During a review, they might check the claim codes, reserves, and payments entered for the claim. They might review the claim representative's reports to the file; the activity log; and other file documentation, such as police reports, physician reports, and damage estimates. During the review, supervisors and managers might detect errors that can be corrected.

The review also allows supervisors and managers to coach claim representatives on how to handle claims, on additional investigation that might be needed, and on negotiation or settlement approaches. Supervisor and manager reviews are essential to helping claim personnel learn how to improve job performance.

Claim Audits

Claim audit

A review of claim files to examine the technical details of claim settlements; ensure that claim procedures are followed; and verify that appropriate, thorough documentation is included.

Internal claim audit

A review of claim files conducted by an insurer's staff to examine the technical details of claim settlements; ensure that claim procedures are followed; and verify that appropriate, thorough documentation is included.

Most insurers use claim audits as a type of compliance measure. **Claim audits** are a review of claim files, both paper and electronic, to ensure that claims are being handled properly. Claim audits can be conducted by an insurer's internal personnel or by others.

An **internal claim audit** is a review of claim files conducted by an insurer's staff to examine the technical details of claim settlements; ensure that claim procedures are followed; and verify that appropriate, thorough documentation is included. Generally, internal claim audits are conducted by claim personnel, but they might also be conducted by personnel from other departments, such as accounting, underwriting, or human resources and training.

Internal claim audits can be conducted by managers, supervisors, technical support staff, or other claim representatives. The reason for the audit determines which claim files are audited. For example, to ensure that claim representatives comply with procedures and policies, a random sample of claim files might be appropriate as a routine, regularly scheduled audit. If a specific catastrophe generated many claim complaints, managers might audit claims only from that catastrophe. A supervisor might audit a specific claim representative's claims to prepare for a performance review. Technical support staff might audit a sample of files involving only subrogated or only litigated claims.

An actuary might review claim files to examine how reserves are set, how frequently they are changed, and how accurate the initial reserves were, compared to the final settlement amount. If reserves are habitually lower than the amount of the final claim settlement, the actuary might increase total reserves beyond the amounts set by the claim department. Such a change would help ensure that total reserves for all claims are adequate to maintain the insurer's financial condition.

The underwriting department might audit claim files to see the kinds of claims that are being reported; how much is being paid for those claims; and what, if any, coverage or underwriting standards should be changed to address those claims. For example, if an underwriter notices many claims for damage from sewer backup, the underwriter might decide that underwriting standards should be made more strict for properties likely to experience sewer backup.

Human resources and training might audit claim files to identify training needs for the claim department. For example, a trainer might discover that a claim code for a particular kind of loss is often entered incorrectly. Based on that finding, the trainer might develop a short class to teach support staff about that type of loss and how to code it correctly.

Internal claim audits might also be conducted to ensure that employee fraud is not occurring. In addition, if employees know that claims will be audited, it might deter them from committing fraud.

External claim audits are claim file reviews conducted by someone other than an insurer's own employees. External claim audits are conducted to review overall claim-handling practices; to review reserves and other technical details of claim settlements; to investigate consumer complaints; to ensure that claim procedures were followed; and to verify that appropriate, thorough documentation was included.

State insurance regulators might conduct a claim audit to review an insurer's claim-handling practices. The purpose of the review is to determine whether an insurer is violating any unfair claim settlement practices acts or laws and whether the insurer routinely engages in any illegal claim-handling practices.

Many state insurance regulators are interested in insurers' reserving practices because adequate reserves are crucial to insurers' financial condition. Regulators can evaluate reserves based on an insurer's annual financial statement. However, if regulators need additional information, they might conduct a claim audit to review reserves and reserving practices. Regulators might find that an insurer routinely sets claim reserves lower than necessary and then increases the reserves in steps. On the other hand, regulators might find that an insurer routinely sets claim reserves higher than necessary so that the insurer owes fewer taxes. (Insurers do not pay taxes on premiums they have not yet earned, as described earlier in this text.) Regulators would take action to correct either of these situations.

Insurance advisory organizations such as Insurance Services Office (ISO) and the American Association of Insurance Services (AAIS) are also interested in insurers' reserves but rarely conduct a claim audit to study reserves or reserving practices. Instead, such organizations rely on the information provided in insurers' Annual Statements.

In summary, insurers use a combination of compliance measures to meet legal and regulatory requirements and promote good faith claim-handling practices. The next section examines the benefits of regulatory compliance to insurers and others.

Benefits of Regulatory Compliance

Insurance contracts differ from other types of contracts because they involve the public interest and, usually, unequal bargaining power between insurers and insureds. This public interest is a major concern for insurance regulators, who scrutinize insurers to protect the public from irresponsible, unwise, or dishonest activities that could leave consumers with insurance policies that will not respond to their needs. The possibility that an insurer might not be able to pay legitimate claims to or for its policyholders is the primary concern of insurance regulators, who monitor the financial condition and operations of insurers.

Insurers are corporations that generally have greater bargaining power than insureds. This bargaining power stems from the fact that the insurer develops the insurance policy and settles claims. Insureds generally must accept the

External claim audit
A review of claim files conducted by organizations other than the insurer that involves reviewing overall claim-handling practices; reviewing reserves and other technical details of claim settlements; investigating consumer complaints; ensuring that claim procedures were followed; and verifying that appropriate, thorough documentation was included.

policy terms as the insurer writes them. When claims occur, insureds cannot choose to deal with another insurer; they must deal with the insurer that provides their coverage. Additionally, insurers have greater control over claim investigations and settlements than insureds, as described in insurance policy provisions. Therefore, courts hold insurers to high standards of conduct to ensure that they do not abuse their position, and courts hold insurers responsible for the outcome of their claim handling if they have acted in bad faith.

The measures that insurers take to comply with state regulations benefit them in the following ways:

- Recording accurate information
- Fulfilling reporting requirements
- Detecting and preventing fraud
- Ensuring adequate reserves
- Preserving insurer solvency
- Encouraging good faith and fair claim handling

Recording Accurate Information

One benefit insurers realize from compliance measures is recording accurate information. Many opportunities exist for inaccuracies in handling claims. Claims can be complex and can take months or years to settle. During that time, claim representatives gather large amounts of information about the claim, contact many people (such as insureds, witnesses, experts, lawyers, and managers), and request reserve changes or payments. All of these actions require changes to the claim file and introduce the possibility of inaccurate entries in the file.

Office distractions, interruptions, and other events might cause individuals to enter data incorrectly in the insurer's claim information system or to make other errors, such as inserting a report in the wrong claim file. Compliance measures help point out such inaccuracies and enable insurers to correct them.

When insurers record accurate information, they can correctly monitor their financial standing and increase or decrease rates to simultaneously cover their expenses and compete for policyholders. Regulatory compliance measures help ensure accurate recording, which helps the insurer remain solvent and satisfies regulators that the insurer will be able to meet its obligations to its policyholders.

Fulfilling Reporting Requirements

Another benefit insurers realize from compliance measures is fulfilling reporting requirements. The loss information that claim departments gather is used to fulfill reporting requirements for the following parties:

- Insurer management
- Associations and insurance advisory organizations
- State insurance departments

Insurers spend more money on loss payments than on other expenses. Therefore, insurer management monitors losses and claim handling. To monitor claims, management reviews reports that summarize losses in various ways: by state, by date of loss, by type of loss, by claim representative, or by claim supervisor, for example. Management uses such information to determine what business is profitable and to evaluate claim representatives' or supervisors' productivity. In addition, management might study reports on specific claims that are expected to exceed a certain dollar amount. Management depends on useful information, and these reports give them the types of information they need to make wise decisions for the insurer.

Many associations and insurance advisory organizations rely on claim information. NAIC, ISO, AAIS, and the National Council on Compensation Insurance (NCCI) use information that originates in claim departments. For example, if an insurer writes workers' compensation insurance, that insurer is likely to report its workers' compensation losses to the NCCI. The NCCI collects detailed loss information on workers' compensation claims and uses that information to assist insurers in developing rates for workers' compensation policies. Reporting requirements ensure that associations and insurance advisory organizations receive information that contains enough detail to be useful for their purposes.

Insurers might be required to submit rates, forms, and underwriting guidelines, through reports to state insurance departments for approval or review. One report that insurers are required to submit to state insurance regulators is their financial Annual Statement. An **Annual Statement** includes detailed information about losses by year, by type of loss, and by type of policy, and about premiums, expenses, assets, and liabilities. Reporting requirements ensure that state regulators receive annual statements and that all insurers' information is reported completely and in a consistent format. Regulators use these statements to help evaluate insurers' financial condition and operations.

Annual Statement
A report to the state insurance department on the insurer's financial results, including premiums, losses, expenses, assets, and liabilities.

Detecting and Preventing Fraud

Another benefit insurers realize from compliance measures is detecting and preventing fraud. Although special investigation units (SIUs) are effective in teaching others how to detect and prevent fraud, other compliance measures are required to combat the high cost of fraud. Fraud costs insurers billions of dollars annually, which is passed on to policyholders through increased premiums. One source estimates that increased premiums due to fraudulent medical, auto, and life insurance claims cost the average U.S. family $1,030 in insurance premiums per year.[4] Compliance measures that detect and prevent fraud can generate tremendous savings for insurers that, in turn, result in lower premiums for insureds.

Sometimes claim representatives may suspect fraud on the part of insureds, claimants, and service providers because of fraud indicators or red flags. For example, an insured might claim that his auto was stolen and never recovered, when in fact the insured has colluded with a body shop to dismantle the auto and sell the parts for a share of the profits. After observing fraud indicators, claim representatives should alert support staff and SIU staff that further investigation is required.

Many insurers have their own fraud unit (such as an internal affairs department) to detect fraud by employees. One example of such fraud is support staff creating fictitious claims for small amounts and requesting claim payments payable to themselves, members of their family, or friends. Also, claim representatives might own or be affiliated otherwise with an auto repair business and refer insureds and claimants to that business for auto repairs—a situation making conflicts of interest and fraud very likely. Compliance measures should be designed to detect and prevent employee fraud.

Ensuring Adequate Reserves

Another benefit insurers realize from compliance measures is ensuring adequate reserves. Claim personnel influence an insurer's financial stability by setting adequate claim reserves. Collectively, adequate reserves accurately depict an insurer's financial condition. For example, if an insurer sets reserves too low, it could lead the insurer to charge less for coverage than what is required to pay claims and expenses. Over time, inadequate reserves could lead to the insurer's insolvency.

Compliance measures reduce reserving errors that can increase claim costs and ensure that reserves accurately reflect the amounts needed to pay claims. Insurers benefit from having adequate reserves because they help guarantee insurers' financial stability. Policyholders also benefit because a financially stable insurer can meet its policy obligations.

Preserving Insurer Solvency

Another benefit insurers realize from compliance measures is preserving insurer solvency. Compliance measures help insurers preserve their solvency through the following actions:

- Monitoring expense management
- Managing claims properly

Insurers attempt to control their expenses in many ways, such as by using technology to increase productivity, to eliminate unnecessary tasks, and to streamline processes for maximum efficiency. Some compliance measures provide instructions for handling tasks so that they can be completed as efficiently and economically as possible. Other compliance measures can generate reports on the claim department's expenses so that the insurer can look for ways to improve operations in that department.

Finally, compliance measures such as claim audits help ensure that claims are managed properly. For example, if an inexperienced claim representative overpaid a claim by $5,000, a claim audit might catch the overpayment and enable a supervisor to instruct the claim representative in properly calculating the claim and avoiding future overpayments.

Insurers must conscientiously fulfill their contractual promises to their insureds, but they must not pay for claims that are not covered or pay excessive amounts for claims that are covered. Compliance measures support proper claim management by helping to ensure that reserves are adequate, claim investigations are proper, and claims are paid accurately, all of which help preserve the insurer's solvency.

Encouraging Good Faith and Fair Claim Handling

Another benefit insurers realize from compliance measures is encouraging good faith and fair claim handling. Insurers use compliance measures to reduce their exposure to bad faith claims and to satisfy the requirements of unfair claim settlement practices acts. If claim representatives mishandle claims, the state insurance department might impose fines or revoke an insurer's license to operate. Compliance measures such as supervisor and manager reviews and claim audits reduce the possibility that claims will be mishandled.

SUMMARY

Many types of laws affect the work of claim representatives. Criminal law protects the interests of the public. Civil law protects the personal and property rights of individuals and organizations, and it protects and enforces contract rights. Common law is based on court decisions and evolves at different paces in different areas of the country. Most contract law is based on common law. Because insurance policies are contracts, claim representatives should be aware of insurance-related common law in the states where they handle claims. Local, state, and federal legislatures enact statutory laws. All states have statutes governing the conduct of insurance. Congress or a state legislature might create an administrative body or agency to assume the power to enact and enforce administrative laws.

The U.S. court system is divided into two systems: state and federal. Whether a case is heard in state court or federal court depends on the jurisdiction. Each state has several levels in its court system that are distinguished by the amount of money claimed and sometimes by the need for a jury. Every state has at least one federal district court that is part of the federal court system.

Claim representatives use various forms of dispute resolution. When a claim settlement dispute arises, claim representatives try to negotiate a solution first. If negotiation fails, claim representatives might use alternative dispute resolution (ADR) techniques, such as arbitration and mediation. When ADR methods fail, parties can settle their disputes through litigation by filing a lawsuit.

Lawsuits include three phases of litigation: pretrial, trial, and post-trial. Claim representatives should be familiar with the phases of litigation so that they can prepare claim files in anticipation of possible litigation.

Claim representatives comply with state laws that can include adjuster licensing laws, unfair trade practices laws, unfair claim settlement practices laws, and privacy laws. Claim representatives and insurers must also comply with federal laws, including the Fair Credit Reporting Act, the Health Insurance Portability and Accountability Act of 1996 (HIPAA), and the Gramm-Leach-Bliley Act.

Most claim-practice regulations focus on complaints, unfair trade practices, and unfair claim settlement practices. Insurers who violate these laws might pay fines or penalties, and the state might revoke their license to operate.

Good faith claim handling requires an insurer to give consideration to the insured's interests that is at least equal to the consideration it gives its own interests. Good faith is founded on proper attitude and is supported by training, efficiency, and prompt and courteous communication.

Insurers use compliance measures to help meet state compliance regulations. Compliance measures include claim guidelines, policies, and procedures; controls such as claim reports, access security, authority levels, and claim information tracking systems; supervisor and manager reviews; and internal and external claim audits. States enact legislation to protect the public from insurers' irresponsible or dishonest actions; therefore, courts hold insurers to high standards of conduct and hold insurers responsible for the outcome of their claim handling if they act in bad faith.

Insurers realize benefits from compliance measures that include recording accurate information, fulfilling reporting requirements, detecting and preventing fraud, ensuring adequate reserves, preserving insurer solvency, and encouraging good faith and fair claim handling.

A good understanding of claim legal and regulatory environments, good faith claim-handling practices, and compliance measures prepares claim professionals for a close examination of claim handling. The next chapter examines the claim-handling process and describes specific investigative issues for various types of claims.

CHAPTER NOTES

1. Contract law is not common law when it has been modified or replaced by statutory or administrative law. All contracts for the sale of goods are governed by statutory law rather than common law—in particular by the Uniform Commercial Code (UCC).

2. James A. Barnes, Thomas Bowers, Arlen W. Langvardt, Jane P. Mallor, and Michael J. Phillips, *The Legal Environment* (New York: The McGraw-Hill Companies, Inc., 2000), p. 97.

3. "An Introduction to the Fair Credit Reporting Act and Its Purpose in Protecting Consumers' Credit Rights," Fair Credit Reporting.com, www.fair-credit-reporting.com/Fair-Credit-Reporting-Act/fair-credit-reporting-1681.html (accessed February 1, 2005).

4. "South Carolina Legislature Faces Increasing Insurance Fraud; NAMIC Comments," National Association of Mutual Insurance Companies, November 30, 2004, www.namic.org/newsIssues/Fraud.asp (accessed December 1, 2004).

Chapter 4

Direct Your Learning

The Claim Process

After learning the content of this chapter and completing the corresponding course guide assignment, you should be able to:

■ Describe what is involved in each of the following activities in the claim-handling process.

- Acknowledging and assigning the claim

- Identifying the policy

- Contacting the insured or the insured's representative

- Investigating and documenting the claim

- Determining the cause of loss and the loss amount

- Concluding the claim

■ For auto physical damage, property damage, and bodily injury claims:

- Describe the cause of loss investigation.

- Describe how the loss amount or damages are determined.

■ Describe the purpose of subrogation and how it is pursued in auto physical damage and property damage claims.

■ Describe the compensability investigation in a workers' compensation claim.

■ Identify the benefits payable in a workers' compensation claim.

■ Describe the elements of a fraud scheme and the means of detecting them.

■ Define or describe each of the Key Words and Phrases for this chapter.

Develop Your Perspective

What are the main topics covered in this chapter?

This chapter discusses the claim-handling process, including each of the claim-handling activities. The claim-handling activities for both auto physical damage claims and property damage claims include determining the cause of loss, damages, and subrogation potential of the claim. Claim-handling activities for workers' compensation claims also include determination of the cause of loss (compensability) and of the amount of damages (benefits), valuation of benefits, conclusion of bodily injury claims, and documentation of the claim file. Fraud must be investigated regardless of the type of claim presented.

Review your company's claim-handling guidelines.

- What investigation is recommended for an auto physical damage claim, a property damage claim, a bodily injury claim, and a workers' compensation claim?
- What method(s) does your employer use to determine the value of a bodily injury claim?

Why is it important to learn about these topics?

For some claims, claim representatives spend much of their time investigating the cause of loss (or compensability, for a workers' compensation claim) and the extent of damages (or benefits, for a workers' compensation claim) in a given claim. A thorough investigation into the cause of loss and damages (appropriate benefits) enables the claim representative to properly determine whether a claim is covered and the amount that should be paid for a covered claim.

Contrast a closed auto physical damage claim, property damage claim, bodily injury claim, and workers' compensation claim.

- How do the investigations in each of these claims differ?
- How does the determination of damages in each of these claims differ?

How can you use what you will learn?

Analyze a closed claim of any type.

- Do you agree with the coverage determination? Why or why not?
- Would you have conducted any activities as part of the investigation that weren't completed?
- Are any indicators of possible fraud present?

Chapter 4
The Claim Process

A primary function of insurers is to pay the claims of their insureds and other parties who are entitled to payment under the insurance policy. Consequently, handling claims is a crucial part of an insurer's business. The insurer is obligated to properly handle all claims submitted and to pay the insured for covered losses. By introducing insurance concepts, parties to the insurance policy who help provide insurance products and services and who are involved in claim handling, and the legal environment, the first three chapters laid a foundation for understanding the claim-handling process. This chapter expands on the claim-handling process that was introduced earlier in this text to give claim personnel a fuller understanding of the intricacies of handling claims. This chapter also describes unique investigative issues and causes of loss that claim representatives should consider to properly handle auto physical damage claims, property damage claims, and bodily injury claims, and it explains settlement options for bodily injury claims. The chapter examines unique investigative issues for workers' compensation claims, and it examines investigative issues for fraud claims to help claim personnel know how to proceed when they discover fraud indicators.

THE CLAIM-HANDLING PROCESS

As mentioned in previous chapters, different types of claims, such as auto physical damage, property damage, and bodily injury claims, require unique treatment, but, despite these differences, claim representatives can perform the same basic activities to handle any type of claim. These claim-handling activities appear in the following box and are described in the sections that follow. These activities are not always sequential but instead can begin and end at any point in the process and can overlap. Depending on the severity and complexity of the loss, claim handling can be quick, completed within hours or days of receiving a loss notice, or it can extend over many months. These activities provide a guideline for handling all types of claims and help claim representatives take a logical, systematic approach to properly preparing claims for settlement.

Claim-Handling Activities

- Acknowledging and assigning the claim
- Identifying the policy
- Contacting the insured or the insured's representative
- Investigating and documenting the claim
- Determining the cause of loss and the loss amount
- Concluding the claim

Certain activities occur before a claim representative begins to handle the claim. When a loss occurs, the insured reports the loss to the producer or directly to the insurer's claim department. If the loss is reported to the producer, the producer typically enters the loss information into the agency information computer system and then transmits the appropriate loss notice to the insurer. If the producer prepares a hard copy of the loss notice, he or she might fax it to the insurer. If the loss is reported directly to the insurer, insurer claim personnel enter the loss information into the insurer's claim information system.

The loss notice form varies for different types of losses. One of the most commonly used loss notice forms is the ACORD form. ACORD forms include basic information about the loss, such as the loss date and time, policy number, insured name and address, covered property, and loss description. The loss notice also includes the accident location and the names and addresses of any witnesses or injured persons. The loss notice is the starting point for a claim representative's loss investigation. After a loss notice has been received and the information has been entered into the insurer's claim information system, the insurer begins the claim-handling process.

ACORD

ACORD (Association for Cooperative Operations Research and Development) is a global, not-for-profit insurance association that assists in the development and use of standards for insurance, reinsurance, and related financial services. ACORD serves as an independent advocate for sharing information. ACORD standards and services improve efficiency and expand market reach for insurers, reinsurers, producers, and other financial service providers.[1] Many insurance organizations use standardized forms provided by ACORD.

Acknowledging and Assigning the Claim

The first activity in the claim-handling process is acknowledging receipt of the claim and assigning the claim to a claim representative. Some insurers acknowledge claims by contacting the insured immediately upon receiving the loss notice—through a phone call, an e-mail message, a letter, or a postcard from claim personnel. Others acknowledge the claim after it has been assigned to a claim representative. These acknowledgments advise the insured that the claim has been received, who the assigned claim representative is, and what the claim number and claim representative's contact information are.

Some insurers transfer claim files to a claim manager for assignment to a claim representative. This transfer can occur manually or via an automated system. The claim manager may add comments to the file, such as coverage questions to investigate, and then transfer the file directly to the assigned claim representative.

Insurers use different methods of assigning claims to claim representatives. Insurers might assign claims based on territory, type of claim, or extent of damage, or by the insurer's internal company guidelines. The goal is to assign the claim to a claim representative who possesses the skills needed to handle that claim. In some states, claim representatives are required to have an adjuster license to handle claims in that state. Such state requirements must also be considered when assigning a claim to a claim representative. Also, once the claim representative begins the investigation, the facts of the claim might make it necessary to reassign the claim to a different claim representative or specialist. For example, a claim with complex liability issues might be reassigned to a more experienced claim representative or specialist.

Upon receiving a claim assignment, the claim representative should contact the insured, and possibly the claimant (if it is a third-party claim), to acknowledge the claim assignment and explain the claim process. As mentioned, for insurers who do not make early contact, this contact serves as the claim acknowledgment. For some types of losses, the claim representative might offer instructions to the insured to help avoid any further loss, such as covering roof damage with a tarp. If the claim involves property damage, the claim representative might arrange a time with the insured to inspect the damage or the damage scene. This inspection is part of the claim investigation, which is described later in this chapter. As an alternative, the claim representative may advise insureds or claimants that an appraiser will contact them to inspect the vehicle or that an independent adjuster will contact them to inspect their property damage. If the claim involves bodily injury, the claim representative should get information about the nature and extent of the injury.

Identifying the Policy

Another activity in the claim-handling process is identifying the policy. Upon receiving the assignment, the claim representative identifies coverages that were in force on the date of loss. This identification might take place before the claim representative acknowledges the claim, but it certainly takes place before the investigation begins. In either case, the claim representative should thoroughly read the policy forms to determine whether coverage is provided for the loss. The following box lists some of the questions that a claim representative should consider when reviewing a policy for this purpose.

Questions for Identifying Coverage

- Does the loss fall within the policy's effective and expiration dates?
- Who is the insured in the policy?
- What is insured by the policy?
- Is the location covered?
- What caused the loss, and is that cause of loss covered by the policy?
- Do any exclusions, limitations, or endorsements apply to the loss?
- How is the loss valued?
- What are the policy limits and deductibles?

The claim representative performs a more thorough coverage identification by checking coverage based on the policy terms. The claim representative should review the policy as described in the first chapter, while considering any obvious coverage issues, such as no coverage existing for the type of loss specified. Any limitations or exclusions that may apply to the claim should be investigated. Any policy or coverage conditions that the insured has not met should be noted and communicated to the insured, because some violations of policy conditions can result in claim denial. However, the claim representative should remain open-minded while conducting the investigation and make a final coverage determination only after a thorough investigation has been completed.

If it is apparent from the loss notice that the loss might not be covered—because of, for example, a loss date outside the policy period or a claim involving a location not named on the policy—the claim representative should notify the insured of these concerns through a nonwaiver agreement or a reservation of rights letter. Both of these documents reserve the insurer's and policyholder's rights under the policy and are explained more fully later in this chapter.

Individual reserve method
A method to determine the amount estimated and set aside by insurers to pay claims for losses based on the judgment of the claim representative handling the claim.

Average reserve method
A method that uses a predetermined dollar amount set aside for each claim when it is reported.

In conjunction with identifying the policy, claim representatives establish initial claim reserves. A reserve is the amount the insurer estimates and sets aside to pay claims for losses that have not been settled. Insurers might use the **individual reserve method** for each claim or type of loss (such as property damage or bodily injury), based on the judgment of the claim representative handling the claim, even before any investigation has begun. Some insurers use an average reserve method or a formula reserve method to establish claim reserves. The **average reserve method** establishes predetermined dollar amounts set aside for each claim when it is reported, usually based on past claim payments for each different type of loss. For example, an insurer might set an average reserve of $3,000 for hail claims to roofs. Claim representatives can override an average reserve if they expect to pay more than the standard dollar amount for a claim. In such a case, they set individual reserves based on their experience with similar claims.

The **formula reserve method** uses mathematical formulas to establish reserves for different types of loss. Some insurers use a combination of average reserves and individual reserves. For example, they might use average reserves for most auto physical damage claims, but they might set an individual reserve for damage to an expensive, late-model auto.

Formula reserve method
A method to determine a reserve amount based on mathematical formulas.

The insurer's claim information system often determines the types of reserves that are established, such as one reserve for property damage and another for bodily injury. Some insurers have computer system requirements for separate reserves for each claimant in a claim and other requirements for separate expense reserves for the costs of handling the claim. Claim representatives can consult claim guidelines or supervisors to learn how expense reserves are set in their organization.

As claim representatives proceed with claim investigations and evaluations, they should increase or decrease the reserve amounts to reflect new information that might change the value of the claim, such as the property damage amount or the extent of injuries. Establishing and maintaining adequate reserves is important for the insurer's financial health because reserves affect the insurer's ability to maintain and grow its business.

Contacting the Insured or the Insured's Representative

Another activity in the claim-handling process, which occurs soon after the loss has been assigned to a claim representative, is contacting the insured or the insured's representative. For insurers who do not acknowledge claims before they are assigned to a claim representative, or for certain types of claims as specified in an insurer's claim guidelines, this contact occurs at the same time as the claim acknowledgment. Generally, the claim representative reviews the initial loss report and policy and then contacts the insured, although for many claims no contact other than acknowledgment is required. When contacting the insured, the claim representative often schedules a time to meet with the insured or a party representing the insured, possibly at the loss location, either on the same day or within a few days, or this can be a telephone discussion. If the loss involves a third-party claimant, then the claim representative also contacts the claimant and often schedules a time to meet with the claimant or a party representing the claimant.

The first meeting or discussion with the insured sets the tone for the claim. For the insured, the loss creates a disruption and can be an emotional event. The insured might never have filed an insurance claim, in which case the insured might be apprehensive or confused about how the claim will be handled. The claim representative should consider all of these factors when meeting or speaking with the insured for the first time, to set a positive tone for the settlement discussions.

Most insureds do not fully understand the details of their insurance coverages. The claim representative should explain the policy terms and what they mean in relation to the loss. Most important, the claim representative should explain any possible policy violation, exclusion, or limitation that might affect coverage. The claim representative should honestly convey such concerns. Withholding such information could be considered a breach of the claim representative's or insurer's duties. The claim representative must protect the insured's interests and be careful not to give the insured or claimant the impression that a claim will be paid if there are possible grounds to deny it. If there is a chance that insurance will not cover the loss, the insured or claimant can take other measures to protect his or her financial interests.

During this initial contact with the insured, the claim representative should explain how the claim will be handled by doing the following:

- Telling the insured what is required to protect the insured's damaged property and documenting the discussions with the insured

- Describing the inspection, appraisal, and investigation that the claim representative will be conducting

- Telling the insured what additional investigation is needed to resolve any potential coverage issues

- Explaining potential coverage questions or policy limitations or exclusions, and obtaining a nonwaiver agreement when necessary

- Estimating and explaining the time needed to process and conclude the claim

- Supplying the insured with a blank proof of loss form and any necessary written instructions if property damage is involved

- Obtaining the authorizations necessary to get medical and wage loss information if it is part of the claim

The claim representative might take a recorded statement from the insured for investigation purposes during this initial meeting.

Legal Issues in Contacting the Insured

Claim representatives should be aware of the legal implications of their words and actions when contacting insureds. Whenever claim representatives investigate claims, they should be careful not to mislead insureds or claimants about the potential coverage for the claim or the amount of the claim payment. Three legal concepts—good faith, waiver, and estoppel—affect whether a claim should be paid or denied. This section describes these three concepts, as well as nonwaiver agreements and reservation of rights letters.

Good faith is the first legal concept that claim representatives should consider when contacting insureds. When conducting a good faith investigation, a claim representative should attempt to correctly and promptly resolve coverage issues. Many situations that present coverage questions require further investigation to determine whether the claim should be paid or denied. While attempting to resolve the coverage issues, claim representatives should continue to look for facts that will both confirm or deny coverage.

Claim representatives should also continue to work on determining the loss amount so that payment will not be delayed, should coverage be confirmed. Until the coverage issues have been resolved, the claim representative and the insurer should avoid actions that would lead insureds or claimants to believe that their claim will be paid. Otherwise, the insurer might waive its right to legitimately deny coverage.

Waiver is the second legal concept that claim representatives should consider when contacting insureds. **Waiver** involves voluntarily or intentionally relinquishing a known right, such as rights contained in a policy condition or exclusion. A claim representative can waive these rights by telling an insured that a loss is covered before checking the policy. The claim representative waives the insurer's right to deny the claim when he or she tells the insured that a loss is covered.

Waiver
Actions taken by the insurer that relinquish a known right, such as the right to deny coverage.

> ### Example of Waiver
>
> Anne, an insured, had water in her basement that resulted from a covered cause of loss, and her basement carpet and other property were soaked. Everett, a claim representative for Worthley Insurance, told Anne to get rid of the soaked carpeting and other property before it became moldy, without first checking the policy for water damage coverage. Anne tore out the carpet and discarded it along with the other waterlogged property. Everett later discovered that coverage did not exist for water damage to the carpeting or other property, but because he told Anne to get rid of it, he waived Worthley's right to deny coverage for the water damage.

Estoppel is the third legal concept that claim representatives should consider when contacting insureds. **Estoppel** prohibits a party to a contract from enforcing certain conditions of the contract because that party's behavior or words caused a breach of the contract. Estoppel results when one party's behavior or words cause another party to detrimentally rely on that behavior or those words. An example of estoppel is a claim representative telling an insured that the insured can throw out damaged goods before inspection, and then the claim representative later trying to deny the claim because the goods were not available for inspection. The claim representative would be estopped from denying the claim on that basis because his or her words worked to the claimant's detriment.

Estoppel
The prohibition of an insurer from enforcing certain conditions of the policy when one party's behavior or words cause another party to detrimentally rely on that behavior or those words.

Claim representatives use nonwaiver agreements or reservation of rights letters to avoid waiver and estoppel. Nonwaiver agreements and reservation of rights letters both serve the following two general purposes:

1. To advise the insured that any action taken by the insurer in investigating the claim or in ascertaining the amount of loss is not intended to waive or invalidate any policy provisions
2. To clarify that the intent of the agreement or letter is to permit an investigation of the claim and that neither the insured nor the insurer will thereby waive any of their respective rights or obligations

Nonwaiver agreement
A document that presents an agreement indicating that, during the course of investigation, neither the insurer nor the insured waives rights under the policy. The agreement becomes effective when signed by both parties to the agreement.

A **nonwaiver agreement** is a document that presents an agreement indicating that, during the course of investigation, neither the insurer nor the insured waives rights under the policy. The agreement becomes effective when signed by both parties to the agreement. This agreement protects the insurer from estoppel by reserving the right to deny coverage based on the investigation. This agreement also alerts the insured to a potential coverage problem. The nonwaiver agreement is usually used when the claim representative is concerned about spending time and money investigating a claim before the insured has substantially complied with the duties after a loss that the policy requires (such as notifying police after an auto accident when parties were injured), or when the claim representative becomes aware of a specific coverage problem or defense. The claim representative may uncover these concerns in the loss notice, during initial contact with the insured, or at any point during the claim investigation. A nonwaiver agreement might be used, for example, when the insured reports the theft of an auto but refuses to make a police report about the theft.

A nonwaiver agreement requires the insured to agree to its terms by signing the agreement. Often, insureds will refuse to do this. In such situations, the claim representative can use a reservation of rights letter to protect the insurer's rights. A **reservation of rights letter** is a document that reserves the insurer's and policyholder's rights under the policy without the need for the insured's signature or consent when the insurer delivers the letter to the insured. A reservation of rights letter serves the same purpose as a nonwaiver agreement, but it is in letter form and does not require the insured to sign or agree to the letter's contents.

Reservation of rights letter
A document that reserves the insurer's and policyholder's rights under the policy without the need for the insured's signature or consent when the insurer delivers the letter to the insured.

Example of Nonwaiver Agreement or Reservation of Rights Letter

In the water damage claim cited previously, if, before Everett told Anne to get rid of the carpeting and wet property, he had explained that coverage for the damage had not yet been verified and had asked Anne to sign a nonwaiver agreement, then Anne would have accepted the risk that coverage might not exist, and Worthley's right to deny the claim would have been preserved. If Anne refused to sign the agreement and Everett issued her a reservation of rights letter, then Worthley's right to deny the claim would have been preserved.

Nonwaiver agreements and reservation of rights letters are used only with the insured. They are not used with third parties because third parties have no rights under the policy and they are not parties to the contract. Both nonwaiver agreements and reservation of rights letters can be used with any type of first-party claim.

Representation by Others

Insureds sometimes hire other parties, such as public adjusters or lawyers, to work with their insurer and represent the insured's interest in a claim. This section describes representation by public adjusters and lawyers.

One type of representative for insureds is a public adjuster. Some insureds hire **public adjusters** to handle claims on their behalf. In exchange for a fee, they help insureds present claims to insurers. Insureds request that the public adjusters act as their representatives for the purpose of the claim. The claim representative should respect that request and discuss claim-related issues with the public adjuster until advised not to do so by the insured. Public adjusters are most often used in complex property damage claims.

Public adjuster
An outside organization or person hired by an insured to represent the insured in a claim in exchange for a fee.

Public adjusters perform many of the tasks of a claim representative, such as investigating and documenting claims, except that they do so for the insured and not for the insurer. They analyze the scene and assess the damage. They prepare inventories of damaged or destroyed property for insureds and obtain repair or replacement estimates for damaged property. They assist commercial insureds in documenting and presenting claims for lost earnings, business income losses, or lost rent. Finally, they assist in settlement negotiations and sometimes serve as appraisers when disputes occur related to valuation. All of these functions are described in subsequent sections of this chapter. A public adjuster's goal is to handle the insured's claim properly to achieve the best possible result for the insured.

Claim representatives for insurers complete their investigations independently from the public adjuster. The claim representative's goal is to handle the claim properly to achieve a fair resolution for all parties. At times, public adjusters and claim representatives for insurers disagree; however, generally, public adjusters present complete and organized claims that are used to help reach a satisfactory settlement for the insured and the insurer.

Another type of representative for insureds (or claimants) is a lawyer. Sometimes, insureds or claimants hire lawyers to represent them in their claims. If the insured or claimant hires a lawyer, the claim representative must direct all communication to that lawyer, and it is against the insured's or claimant's intent for the insurer to contact the insured or claimant directly when the lawyer is not present or without the lawyer's permission. Additionally, the claim representative must conduct all negotiations with the lawyer who represents that insured or claimant, who then relays information to the client.

Claim representatives should be aware of the legal issues presented when contacting insureds and of the issues that exist when insureds or claimants are represented by either public adjusters or lawyers. They should adapt their claim-handling activities when insureds or claimants are represented by others.

Investigating and Documenting the Claim

Another activity in the claim-handling process occurs when the claim representative investigates and documents the claim. Investigation and documentation continue throughout the life of the claim. The investigation can take many different forms, and all aspects of the investigation should be documented to avoid duplicate work within the claim department and to create a complete claim file.

Claim representatives begin investigating a claim as soon as it is assigned. They can develop an outline or notes at the onset of the investigation to logically organize it and to ensure that information that might be available for only a short time is investigated first, such as an accident scene or any damaged property that might be destroyed or discarded. Claim representatives should plan to contact any third-party claimants early in the investigation. Such contact can help claim representatives establish rapport with claimants, which could facilitate the investigation of the claim and promote a timely settlement. Claim representatives should also gather information about coverage, liability, and damages, and as much information about the loss as they need to make an appropriate decision. Insurers may have claim-handling guidelines established by claim managers that help claim representatives determine the types and extent of investigation needed for a satisfactory claim settlement.

No textbook can address all of the different situations that a claim representative may face. However, this section provides a basic outline for the claim representative to follow in any type of investigation. Claim representatives should follow good faith claim-handling practices and their company guidelines to ensure a thorough investigation. Many claims require the same basic investigation; however, the information discovered in the basic investigation will tell the claim representative what additional investigation is needed to conclude the claim.

Claim representatives also have to know when their investigation and documentation are sufficient. Investigations should be geared toward discovering information that helps to determine the cause of loss and the amount of damages. Once sufficient information has been obtained to reasonably determine the cause of loss, liability, and the amount of damages, the claim representative does not need to continue the investigation unless the determination is disputed. Additionally, claim representatives should know when to ask for help. For example, while asking an expert for an opinion on an electrical fire in a commercial building is usually a good investigation technique, asking for an expert opinion on the cause of a small trash-can fire that did little damage is probably not a good use of the insurer's resources.

Considering these investigative issues sets the stage for a successful claim investigation, but different types of investigations should follow a common pattern. A claim representative conducts appropriate investigations for a given claim to properly determine the cause of loss and help determine damages. For some claims, a single investigation is appropriate, but for complex claims and most third-party claims, multiple investigations are needed to determine the insured's degree of liability, as well as the cause of loss and damages.

Claim representatives conduct different investigations based on the type of claim and the circumstances. Several different investigations are common across the following various types of claims:

- Insured/witness investigation
- Claimant investigation

- Accident scene investigation
- Property damage investigation
- Medical investigation
- Prior claim investigation
- Investigation of and recovery from subrogation

Claim representatives should know when and why each investigation is important and how to conduct each investigation. The next section describes these common claim investigations, explains when and why they are important, and provides details about how to conduct them. Subsequent sections describe the use of experts in investigations and file documentation and reports.

Insured/Witness Investigation

One common investigation that a claim representative might conduct is an insured/witness investigation. Insureds and witnesses can provide valuable information about the circumstances surrounding the loss. Insured parties are always named or defined in the policy. Under a workers' compensation policy, the insured is the employer. Witnesses are any persons who have personal, firsthand knowledge of the incident that resulted in the claim.

In some claims, such as third-party claims, the claim representative investigates the insured and any witnesses to secure their versions of the incident. To obtain their versions, claim representatives often take statements from the insured and witnesses. In first-party and third-party claims, these statements permanently document the facts of the loss. The witness investigation could support or refute an insured's or a claimant's version of an incident, which may be important in determining liability.

Claimant Investigation

Another common investigation that a claim representative might conduct is a claimant investigation. Claim representatives conduct a claimant investigation to learn the claimant's version of the incident that led to the claim. Often, this is accomplished by taking the claimant's statement to determine the extent of injury or damage and to confirm whether the injury or damage was likely caused by the incident. For example, the claimant under an automobile policy or some other liability coverage might be a third party who was injured in an accident or whose property was damaged. Under a workers' compensation policy, the claimant is an injured worker.

Accident Scene Investigation

Another common investigation that a claim representative might conduct is an accident scene investigation. The accident scene offers crucial clues in automobile, third-party liability, and workers' compensation claims. The accident scene investigation tells the claim representative whether accounts of the accident are plausible or questionable. Details such as tire tracks, curves in the roadway, and objects or conditions that could interfere with a driver's view or cause an accident (such as a pothole in the road) can be discovered and verified through an accident scene investigation. Claim representatives also consult weather or traffic reports in certain accident scene investigations to confirm or deny weather or traffic factors that may have contributed to the loss.

Property Damage Investigation

Another common investigation that a claim representative might conduct is a property damage investigation. An investigation of the scene of a loss where property was damaged can be useful in automobile and property coverage claims to confirm the extent of damage to the property and the cause of the damage.

A property damage investigation is also useful in business income claims for lost income or loss of use of equipment or property because of covered property damage. This investigation can confirm the extent of the damage to property or equipment, which could result in lost profits. It can also help confirm the need to move operations to an alternate site or to temporarily replace damaged equipment with rented equipment while repairs are being made.

Medical Investigation

Another common investigation that a claim representative might conduct is a medical investigation. Claim representatives conduct medical investigations in all bodily injury claims, such as auto bodily injury and other liability claims, and workers' compensation claims. A medical investigation helps the claim representative determine the costs of the medical treatment, the expected duration of medical treatment and disability, the need for rehabilitation, and whether the medical care that is provided is appropriate for the injuries that the claimant suffered.

Prior Claim Investigation

Another common investigation that a claim representative might conduct is a prior claim investigation. Claim representatives conduct prior claim investigations on all claims to avoid paying for damages or injuries that have been paid through prior claims by the same insurer or by other insurers. Although it defeats the purpose of insurance and drives up insurance costs, many claimants submit claims to different insurers or different types of insurers to obtain multiple payments for the same loss. For example, an insured might claim a neck injury resulting from an auto accident that occurred as an occupational injury or in a previous auto accident. By conducting a prior claim investigation, the claim representative ensures that the insurer pays damages on only new claims for which the insurer has a duty to pay.

Some organizations, called index bureaus, compile loss information submitted by subscribing insurers of all types and provide service to subscribers. Claim personnel can enter loss information for submission to the index bureau to which they subscribe. The bureau checks the loss information against its database to locate any similar claims made by that insured or claimant within a specific time period. The bureau then reports any matching loss information to the subscribing insurer who submitted the loss. Claim representatives can use this reported information as part of their prior claim investigation. However, further investigation of the prior loss is usually required.

The prior claim investigation might be used to reduce a claim payment for a previous injury that may have been aggravated in the accident under investigation, to deny payment for a loss paid under another insurance policy, or as a basis of a fraud investigation.

Subrogation Investigation and Recovery

Another common investigation that a claim representative might conduct is a subrogation investigation and recovery. Subrogation rights are established by insurance policies and by law. When an insurer pays a claim to an insured for a loss that was caused by a negligent third party, the insurer can recover that payment amount from the negligent third party through the right of **subrogation**. When claim representatives investigate any loss, they should be alert to any subrogation possibilities. Claim representatives investigate subrogation possibilities concurrently with the other investigations. The thoroughness of the claim representative's investigation helps determine the success of subrogation efforts. The following examples describe losses for which a claim representative should investigate subrogation possibilities while investigating the claim:

Subrogation
An insurer's right to recover payment from a negligent third party.

- Losses caused by the negligent operation of an automobile or a piece of construction equipment by a third party
- Fire, explosion, or water losses caused by the negligence of tenants
- Fire, explosion, or water losses caused by construction workers at a building site
- Losses that result from poor workmanship of contractors after the work has been completed
- Losses caused by defective or poorly designed products

The subrogation clauses in most insurance policies require the insured to cooperate with the insurer by assigning the rights of subrogation to the insurer through a subrogation agreement. The subrogation agreement could be included in another form, such as a proof of loss form that the insured completes for a property damage claim. Most subrogation agreements require the insured to give testimony and appear in court, when necessary, so that the insurer can establish the legal basis to recover from the negligent third party.

An insured might breach (violate) the subrogation condition by impairing or interfering with the insurer's right of subrogation, by failing to cooperate in preserving evidence, by giving or failing to give testimony, or by releasing the responsible party from any liability following the loss. If an insured breaches the subrogation agreement, the insurer has the right to collect damages from the insured that could have been recoverable from the responsible third party.

The insurer has the right to recover through subrogation only the amount that it has paid for the claim. The insurer has no right of recovery for losses that the insured retains because of lack of coverage, exclusions, or limitations of coverage under the policy. Therefore, both the insurer and the insured might have rights to recover damages from responsible third parties. When the insured retains only the deductible amount, the insurer usually pursues recovery of the deductible amount as well, on the insured's behalf, and then pays the insured when the deductible amount has been recovered.

Claim representatives should consider the costs required to pursue subrogation and the likelihood of success in collecting subrogation. For example, a single parent with several children might not have the means to pay subrogation. Claim representatives must also consider that some contracts (such as some lease agreements) deny the right of subrogation. Additionally, subrogation can be costly to pursue if litigation is required. The insurer may decide that pursuing subrogation is not cost-effective. However, the insurer's decision does not affect the insured's right to subrogate, on his or her own behalf, against the responsible party for the unpaid portions of the claim.

When a negligent third party who is responsible for a loss has liability insurance, the first-party insurer who has paid a loss can present a subrogation claim for payment to the third party's liability insurer. Usually, the liability insurer pays the entire loss or offers a compromise settlement on the claim, depending on the assessment of liability. When the two insurers cannot agree on the liability, they can use intercompany arbitration to resolve the dispute.

Intercompany arbitration is conducted by having the arbitrator(s) review written submissions of both parties. The insurer's arbitration file is based on the claim representative's claim file, usually with highlighted details or tabs on specific documents for the arbitrator's benefit. The file should be legible and in chronological order. A well-written arbitration statement that outlines the insurer's position in the case should accompany the file. The arbitrator reviews files from both insurers to render a decision based on the credibility of each case. The decision of the arbitrator(s) is final and binding on both insurers.

In summary, claim representatives conduct different investigations that are appropriate to each claim and consider the various issues presented. Claim representatives can complete many investigations independently. However, some claims might require consultation with an expert to determine liability or the amount of damages. The next section examines different experts who might assist claim representatives with investigating claims.

Use of Experts in Investigation

During the claim investigation, claim representatives sometimes require the services of experts to properly evaluate the cause or value of a loss, to investigate the possibility of fraud committed by an insured or a third-party claimant, or to provide legal advice. The box below lists experts who may be consulted in property or liability claims. The list is not exhaustive; it identifies some of the experts used most frequently. These experts can assist a claim representative in claim investigations according to their expertise.

Experts Consulted in Property Claims

- Special investigation units (SIUs)
- Origin and cause experts
- Private investigators
- Accountants
- Restoration specialists
- Salvors
- Lawyers
- Professionals needed to rebuild
- Appraisers

Experts Consulted in Liability Claims

- Special investigation units (SIUs)
- Accident reconstruction specialists
- Accountants
- Lawyers
- Private investigators
- Medical experts

A claim representative should refer a claim to the insurer's special investigation unit (SIU) when a claim appears to be fraudulent and meets the insurer's guidelines for such referral. Claim representatives might also consult with SIU personnel to discuss possible fraud indicators in a claim investigation. SIU personnel may be consulted or engaged on any claim in which fraud is suspected.

Claim representatives might consult origin and cause experts to investigate auto or other property fire losses and to determine where and how a fire began. Origin and cause experts use their background in fire science and arson investigation to determine whether a fire started accidentally or was set deliberately. Claim representatives consult these experts for fires of suspicious origin or when the cause of loss is known and they believe that the expert can help prepare the case for subrogation.

Claim representatives may contract for services from a private investigator in a property loss when fraud is suspected, in potential arson cases in which an insured has allegedly directed another party to commit arson, or to work with origin and cause experts. Private investigators are professionals who have the knowledge and skills required to obtain information from witnesses, public records, and law enforcement agencies. When a claim representative is suspicious of a claimant's injuries under a liability or workers' compensation claim, the claim representative may hire a professional private investigator. The private investigator can conduct surveillance and help determine whether a claimant feigns or exaggerates injuries by documenting any activity that is inconsistent with the reported injury. The claim representative can use the information that the private investigator gathered to reach coverage decisions, determine claim value, determine whether insurance fraud is being attempted, and document potential subrogation opportunities.

Claim representatives might consult an accountant who specializes in claims and legal matters to resolve financial issues related to property claims. These claim accountants are often used to verify the extent of business merchandise or stock losses and business income losses. An accountant can help resolve cases in which the insured might have overstated the amount of the loss. An accountant can also determine the financial condition of the insured's business and whether the insured actually had the financial means to purchase property that was allegedly stolen or destroyed. Claim representatives may consult accountants or other financial or economic analysts in liability or workers' compensation injury claims to determine the value of a claimant's pre-accident ability to earn a living over the course of a working lifetime and to place a value on such loss of earnings capacity.

Claim representatives might consult or contract with restoration specialists when windstorms, fire, smoke, or water damages property. Restoration specialists clean structures (including carpeting, walls, and floors), equipment, stock, merchandise, and personal or business property to preserve value after property has been damaged and to avoid further damage from mold or other causes. Claim representatives contact restoration specialists immediately to stop subsequent damage.

Claim representatives contact salvors on business property losses. Salvors separate damaged from undamaged merchandise, supplies, and equipment; prepare inventories of damaged and destroyed property; and establish values of damaged or destroyed business property. Claim representatives might also employ salvors to sell salvage or, by special arrangement, to purchase salvage.

Claim representatives may consult lawyers on all types of losses for legal advice and counsel on coverage issues and on investigations of complex claims. A lawyer's services might be required to gain access to information relevant to the claim. Claim representatives also consult lawyers to help resolve coverage and settlement disputes or to provide legal opinions, recommendations, or defense for the insurer when a legal action has been filed against the insured.

Claim representatives might consult with professionals who rebuild damaged property, such as engineers, architects, and contractors, to determine the cause of loss and the costs to repair or rebuild, or for related services. Claim representatives may consult engineers to help determine whether defects or malfunctions were the root cause of a loss and thereby determine whether subrogation is a possibility. Architects sometimes draw plans or provide specifications for partial or complete reconstruction of structures or for specialized equipment. Architects also provide specifications needed to obtain remodeling or building permits. Claim representatives might consult building contractors about emergency repairs to structures damaged by fire, water, windstorm, or other causes of loss. These various professionals use their expertise to try to restore the insured's property to its pre-loss condition and value.

Appraisers help establish the value of personal property, merchandise, and equipment, and, for real property settlements, they resolve disputes over the amount of the loss. Claim representatives contact appraisers when investigating real and personal property losses from all causes of loss. Some specialized appraisers assist claim representatives; for example, auto appraisers inspect vehicle damage and prepare damage estimates for claim representatives.

In auto and other liability injury claims when injuries are serious and liability cannot be determined conclusively, claim representatives contact accident reconstruction specialists. Accident reconstruction specialists use information from an accident scene to make scientifically and mathematically accurate conclusions on details such as the speed and direction of a vehicle and what the parties saw before the accident. Their findings can be used to assess negligence or comparative negligence (as described in a subsequent chapter).

Claim representatives work with medical experts such as medical consultants, rehabilitation nurses, and other medical providers. These medical experts help insurers assess the medical requirements in injury claims. Medical consultants arrange independent medical examinations (IMEs) or defense medical exams (DMEs), review medical reports, and audit bills from physicians and other medical providers to determine whether the treatment being provided follows the physician's treatment instructions. Rehabilitation nurses help claim representatives assess whether rehabilitation is possible for the claimant and, if so, to what extent. Other medical professionals help by providing opinions on the medical necessity of treatments, sometimes through IMEs or DMEs.

File Documentation and Reports

Claim representatives prepare two types of documentation as part of the claim-handling process. Claim representatives should document their files through file status notes (also called adjuster activity logs and reports). File status notes describe all of the claim representative's activities in handling the claim. Insurers notify others within and outside the company of claim activity through two types of formal reports: internal reports and external reports. Described next are file status notes and documentation and internal and external reports, whom they are produced for, and how they are used.

The first type of documentation is file status notes and documents. File status notes should accurately reflect and document claim representatives' investigations, their evaluation of claims and their decisions to deny them, and the settlement or other resolution of claims. Other claim personnel should be able to read the file status notes and know exactly what has been done toward settling the claim. Because lawyers and state regulators can obtain copies of claim files and, therefore, see everything in the file that may either help or hurt the insured, file status notes and other file documentation should reflect the following:

- Clear, concise, and accurate information
- Timely claim handling

- A fair and balanced investigation considering the insured's and the insurer's interests

- Objective comments about the insured or other parties associated with the claim

- A thorough, good faith investigation

The second type of documentation that claim representatives prepare is reports. One kind of report that insurers prepare is an internal report. Claim representatives prepare and distribute internal reports to parties within the insurer who have an interest in large losses. Most insurers require internal reports such as large loss reports and file status reports when applicable.

Large loss report
A formal written document that informs senior management of claims that exceed a specified reserve amount and therefore have the potential for high loss payments.

One internal report is a large loss report. A **large loss report** is a formal written document that informs senior management of claims that exceed a specified reserve amount and therefore have the potential for high loss payments. Insurers set criteria for which large losses should be reported to management. For example, large loss reports might be required for claims with reserves that exceed $500,000. Large loss reports summarize all of the file status information for management.

File status report
A written document that summarizes activity on a claim that is open beyond a certain time period.

Another internal report is a file status report. A **file status report** is a written document that summarizes activity on a claim that is open beyond a certain time period. Generally, claim representatives write four types of file status reports: preliminary, status (or interim), summarized (or captioned), and underwriting. Often, these reports are typed directly into a claim entry system (the electronic claim file) using an electronic template; distributed electronically to claim supervisors, managers, or underwriters; and then printed for any necessary outside distribution (such as to lawyers). These reports might have attachments such as estimates, police reports, diagrams, photos, statements, and correspondence. These attachments might already be included as images in the electronic claim file or included in the paper claim file.

Preliminary reports are internal reports that acknowledge that the claim representative received the claim assignment; informed the insurer about initial activity on the claim; suggested reserves; noted coverage questions; and requested assistance, if needed. Preliminary reports might be required within the first twenty-four hours, within seven days, or only if the file remains open after thirty days. For small, uncomplicated claims that claim representatives settle quickly, such as claims in which liability is clear, the preliminary report might be the only report in the claim file.

Status reports are internal reports that tell anyone reviewing the claim how it is progressing and are usually produced periodically, such as every fifteen to thirty days. In these reports, claim representatives update claim progress, recommend reserve changes, and request assistance and settlement authority when the amount payable exceeds their authority. Status reports confirm that the claim representative is progressing through the claim-handling activities in a timely manner.

Another internal report is a summarized report. Summarized reports are usually detailed narratives of claim activity that follow an established format. Claim representatives usually file a summarized report within thirty days of the claim assignment date to inform managers of the progress of claims that are open for more than thirty days. Insurers might require summarized reports when a claim should be reviewed by managers at regional or home offices. For example, managers might review a file when the reserve exceeds a specified amount. Some insurers require summarized reports on certain types of claims because they want to track trends in certain types of business. Typically, suspected arson and insurance fraud claims are reported to the regional and home offices because of their serious and sensitive nature. A summarized report has captioned headings that give structure to the report. Exhibit 4-1 is an example of a summarized claim report.

A less formal internal report is a diary entry. Claim representatives can set a diary entry (a computer-generated reminder system) to flag a file for review or reporting within the specified time frames. Some workflow systems create automatic diary entries that list the claim files that need attention in the claim representative's work queue. (A work queue is an on-screen list of files that contains links to open and modify the corresponding electronic files on the computer.)

The last internal report is a closing or final report. When concluding a claim or transferring a claim to another claim representative, the claim representative should complete a closing or final report. He or she might include recommendations on subrogation, advice to underwriters, and other suggestions in these reports. For example, when transferring the file to another claim representative, the current claim representative might suggest some additional investigations to pursue.

The second kind of report that insurers prepare is external reports. External claim reports inform parties who have a financial interest in the claim, and they inform the public of the insurer's financial standing. Many external reports compile data from all of an insurer's claims, rather than reporting on individual claims as is often the case with internal claim reports. Insurers are required to complete external reports, which consist of claim information collected by claim representatives, such as year-end reporting of the amounts of open reserves, closed reserves, and reserves that were closed without payments; claims paid for which reinsurance recoveries are expected; and similar information that is appropriate for the report recipient.

These reports are prepared for parties such as producers, for some states' advisory organizations, for potential investors, and for others who might have a financial or another interest in the insurer's results. Because insurers often write business through producers, losses are reported to the producer who sold the insurance. In addition, in some states, insurer financial departments might be required to report premium and loss information to an advisory organization. Finally, insurer financial departments file premium and loss information

EXHIBIT 4-1

Summarized Claim Report

Claim #:_____

Insured: _____   Date of report: _____

Policy #: _____   Adjustment firm: _____

Date of loss: _____   Claim representative: _____

Producer:_____

1. **Assignment Date**
   Give date notice of loss received and how. Give date insured first contacted and how (phone or personal).

2. **Enclosures**
   List items attached (photos, estimates, fire/police reports, etc.).

3. **Activity Requested**
   List special requests (expense payments, coverage questions, etc.).

4. **Suggested Reserves**
   Show suggested net reserves, by coverage, after any advances.
   Show scheduled items separately.
   Ex.   Collision $22,000
         Medical Payments $10,000

5. **Abstract of Coverage**
   List forms applicable and amounts; state deductibles; identify other contributing insurance, if any; identify any limiting clauses.

6. **Ownership/Encumbrances**
   List title holder, mortgagee, loss payables, additional named insureds, contract sellers, and liens. Indicate source of information. Also include opinion as to current solvency, cash flow, receipts.

7. **Location and Cause of Loss**
   Give date, time, and place of loss. Relay cause as determined by authorities. If an outside expert has been employed, identify and give his or her findings. State claim representative's opinion.

8. **Insured/Employee Version of Loss**
   Give insured version—indicate whether statement was secured. Indicate manager, guards, or service personnel on premises at time of loss.

9. **Witness Version of Loss**
   Give witness version—indicate whether statement(s) secured. Indicate whether patrons were present at time of loss.

10. **Scope of Loss/Estimates of Damage**
    Describe property insured. Detail extent of damage. Cover any problems that might be encountered in reaching a settlement. List estimates received. Indicate whether an agreement has been reached with the insured as to scope and procedures.

11. **Salvage/Subrogation**
    Identify salvage and give an estimate of worth. When appropriate, give details of the likelihood of successful subrogation and what steps have been taken to protect the right of subrogation.

12. **Work Done to Date**
    Itemize work done to date.

13. **Work to Be Done/Forecast of Closing**
    Itemize work to be done. Give claim representative's forecast of closing. Estimate hours needed for completion of each activity.

14. **Remarks**
    Provide comments on assistance of insured and employee in completing investigation. Identify attorney or public adjuster if involved.

DATE OF NEXT REPORT: _____

through financial statements with state insurance departments and insurance trade organizations. Information from these financial statements becomes public and indicates an insurer's solvency through reserve adequacy. State insurance departments use the information to evaluate an insurer that requests licensing and to examine the solvency of insurers in order to safeguard policyholders.

Claim representatives use the documented information collected through the various claim investigations and use of experts to determine the cause of loss and the loss amount for the claim. The next section describes how claim representatives determine cause of loss and loss amount.

Determining the Cause of Loss and the Loss Amount

Another activity in the claim-handling process is determining the cause of the loss and the loss amount. Although every activity in the claim-handling process is important, claim representatives find that on some claims, such as bodily injury or liability claims, they spend most of their time determining the cause of the loss and the loss amount (or damages in liability claims). Investigation involves determining how, when, where, and why a loss has occurred and how that information may or may not affect coverage. The activities required to investigate and determine the cause of the loss and the loss amount (or damages) depend on the type of claim. Subsequent sections of this chapter provide detailed descriptions of the investigations required to determine the cause of loss and loss amount in auto physical damage, property damage, and bodily injury claims; and to determine compensability and benefits in workers' compensation claims.

Concluding the Claim

The culminating activity in the claim-handling process is concluding the claim. Once the investigation has been completed, all documentation has been prepared, and the cause of loss has been determined, the claim representative should decide whether to pay the claim or deny it.

Should a dispute arise between the parties, they may use negotiation or alternative dispute resolution methods, or the case might be resolved through litigation. Once the claim is settled, the claim department should explore any reinsurance recovery. The following sections describe these activities that could occur in concluding the claim:

- Payments
- Claim denial
- Alternative dispute resolution
- Litigation
- Reinsurance

Payments

When the claim representative concludes a covered claim through negotiation or other means, the claim representative or other claim personnel should issue a payment to the insured or claimant. However, for some claims, the claim representative must request a signed general release from the insured or claimant before payment can be made. A release is a form of settlement agreement, which is an oral or a written agreement by which the parties compromise a disputed matter. A general release usually includes the following information:

- Names and addresses of the parties involved
- Date of the accident
- Amount of the settlement
- Statement that the release applies to all claims related to this accident that the claimant now has or will have in the future, whether or not they are known
- Statement that the parties understand and agree to the release's terms
- Signatures of the parties, dated and witnessed

Once any required, signed release has been secured, the claim payment can be made. Claim payments can be made by check, draft, or electronic transfer of funds.

Draft
A document similar to a check written on the insurer's checking account, but requiring authorization from the insurer before a depositing bank can advance the funds.

A check creates a demand for payment on the insurer's bank account and can be endorsed and presented at a bank for payment without further insurer authorization. A **draft** is similar to a check, but when a claimant presents the draft to the insurer's bank, that bank must verify that the insurer has authorized payment of the draft before disbursing any funds. Because of this required authorization, a claimant can deposit a draft in a bank account, but the funds will not be available for withdrawal until the bank has confirmed the authorization. An electronic transfer of funds creates a credit in the payee's bank account and is available immediately, with no further authorization from the insurer.

When issuing claim payments, claim personnel should ensure that the proper parties are being paid. For example, many other parties can have a financial interest in property, such as mortgagees on homes and loss payees on autos and personal property. These parties that are named in the policy have rights, described in the policy, to be included as payees under certain circumstances, such as when property has been destroyed. The claim representative is responsible for including all required payees when issuing a claim payment to conclude the claim. Insurers and other claim payors have systems in place to ensure compliance with various state and federal laws regarding claim payments, such as child support enforcement lists. A general release ensures that all claims by all parties who have a financial interest in the property have been settled.

Claim Denial

When claim investigations reveal that a policy does not provide coverage for a loss, that the insured is not liable for damages, that the insured failed to meet a policy condition, or that the claim is fraudulent, the claim representative should deny the claim. Insurers often have strict guidelines that claim representatives should follow when denying claims, and some insurers require that claim representatives obtain a claim manager's approval to issue a claim denial as a last opportunity to review the claim file for a proper claim investigation and cause of loss determination.

Before denying a claim, the claim representative should investigate the loss thoroughly, analyze the coverage carefully, and evaluate the claim fairly and objectively. Courts often rule in favor of insureds when they present a lawsuit against the insurer and the claim denial fails to meet these requirements. The court might assess penalties against the insurer, in addition to the loss amount.

Once the claim representative has determined that the loss should be denied and (if required by the insurer) the claim manager has authorized a claim denial, the claim representative should prepare and send a denial letter. The denial must be communicated in a timely manner. Some denial letters are drafted by lawyers to ensure that they comply with the jurisdiction's legal requirements. For example, a denial letter should usually state all the known reasons for the claim denial. Specific policy language supporting the reasons for denial should be quoted, and the location of the language in the policy should be cited. The policy provisions should be described in relation to the facts of the loss. An insured who disagrees with the denial should be invited to submit additional information that would give the insurer cause to reevaluate the claim. The denial letter should be signed and sent by the claim representative, even if it is drafted by a lawyer; the denial must be signed by the insurer's claim representative to be valid.

Insurers usually send denial letters by certified mail with a return receipt requested, to be signed by the addressee. Doing so verifies that the proper party has received the denial letter and the date on which he or she received it. The return receipt is added to the claim file as documentation of good faith claim handling. Some insurers also send a copy of the letter by regular mail, marked "personal and confidential," in case the certified mail is not claimed.

Alternative Dispute Resolution

Most claims are resolved through negotiation. However, when a dispute arises, claim representatives might use other alternative dispute resolution (ADR) methods to settle the claim. The most common methods of ADR that could be used for any type of claim include mediation, arbitration, mini-trials, summary jury trials, and pretrial settlement conferences.

Mediation is a process in which an impartial intermediary, usually selected by the parties, assists them in settling the dispute by listening to the case presented by both sides and reviewing the evidence presented. The process is private, voluntary, informal, and nonbinding. The goal of mediation is to bring the parties together to more realistically value their case and ultimately reach a settlement.

In arbitration, legal counsel representing the parties present the facts and evidence to an impartial third party, the arbitrator, who acts as a judge, weighing the facts of the case and making a decision based on the evidence presented. Arbitration can be binding or nonbinding.

Mini-trial
An abbreviated version of a trial that allows parties to present evidence and arguments to a panel or an advisor. The advisor has no authority to make a binding decision but can pose questions and offer an opinion on the outcome of a trial based on the evidence.

Mini-trials involve the lawyers for the parties presenting an abbreviated version of their case to a panel or an advisor. The advisor has no authority to make a binding decision but can pose questions and offer an opinion on the outcome of a trial based on the evidence. A mini-trial enables the parties to see the strengths and weaknesses of their cases, thereby facilitating settlement negotiations.

Summary jury trials are often used when specific claim issues must be resolved, such as with claims involving a question of coverage or causation. A summary jury trial is staged like a regular jury trial except that only a few witnesses present the case. Mock jurors weigh the evidence presented and decide the case based on the limited information presented.

During pretrial settlement conferences, the presiding judge attempts to get the parties to settle the case to avoid a trial. While the judge's role is similar to that of a mediator, the judge may express opinions about the parties' respective cases. Parties can use the judge's opinions to examine whether litigation may or may not be successful.

Litigation

Litigation is often a last resort when other methods of dispute resolution fail, but it can occur at almost any point during the life of a claim. If a claimant has retained the services of a lawyer, it does not necessarily mean that the claim will result in litigation. Litigation occurs most often when the parties to the claim are unable to reach an agreement by negotiation. Litigation ultimately settles the claim either by encouraging the parties to continue to negotiate or by going to trial and resulting in a judgment. A trial is almost always expensive, and most claim representatives and lawyers try to resolve the claim before trial. However, some claims must be resolved by a trial.

Reinsurance

Once a claim has been concluded through a claim payment, the insurer should recover payment amounts using any available resource—for example, subrogation, salvage, or reinsurance. Subrogation and salvage were described in a previous chapter. Reinsurance is a type of insurance in which one insurer transfers some or all of the financial consequences for certain loss exposures from policies written for its insureds to another insurer. An insurer buys reinsurance for the same reasons that individuals and organizations purchase insurance. Reinsurance protects insurers from the financial consequences of large losses by reimbursing the insurer for a portion of the claims paid to insureds and claimants. Claim representatives should be aware of claims that should be referred to reinsurers and should complete claim reports to reinsurers based on the insurer's reinsurance agreements and the insurer's guidelines.

The conclusion of any claim depends on the information gathered through investigation of the loss, the determination of the cause of loss and loss amount (or damages), and the application of available coverages to the loss. The claim representative should apply all of the information gained through all claim-handling activities to reach an appropriate conclusion to the claim.

This section concludes the description of the activities in the claim-handling process. The next sections describe the specific investigations needed for the following types of losses:

- Auto physical damage
- Property damage
- Bodily injury
- Workers' compensation
- Fraud

INVESTIGATING AUTO PHYSICAL DAMAGE CLAIMS

One type of claim that claim representatives investigate is auto physical damage claims. Auto claims are usually divided among several different types of claim representatives. Some claim representatives handle only the auto physical damage resulting from a loss, while others handle the bodily injury that may result from an accident. This section discusses only the investigation needed to handle an auto physical damage claim; the investigation of bodily injury claims is discussed in a subsequent section.

Cause of Loss Investigation

Generally, a claim representative asks for either a written or recorded statement from the insured or the insured driver; obtains a copy of the police report of the accident; and obtains witness statements and an estimate of damages before determining the cause of loss and the amount of the damages. But not all claims are so straightforward; some claims may require more in-depth investigation. If the cause of loss is not clear, the claim representative may also have to obtain photos of the accident location or ask an expert to reconstruct the accident. If fraud is suspected, the claim representative involves the SIU.

Initial Contact and Statements

After receiving a loss report for damage to an insured vehicle, a claim representative contacts the insured to obtain the loss details. This contact is usually made by phone. Depending on the insurer's guidelines, the claim representative may be required to take a recorded statement from the insured at this time. The recorded statement is used to obtain the details of the loss or accident in the insured's own words. As part of the recorded statement, the claim representative asks the insured to verify ownership, describe the circumstances surrounding the accident, and describe any injuries sustained. The claim representative also learns the extent of damage to the vehicle and where the vehicle is located. During the recorded statement, the claim representative learns whether any witnesses saw the accident and, if so, how they might be contacted. The claim representative learns whether police went to the accident scene and whether the officers completed an accident report. The claim representative may also take a recorded statement from the insured driver (if different from the owner) and any passengers or witnesses. These statements help to confirm the insured's version of how the accident occurred.

Some insurers send out statement forms rather than have claim representatives take recorded statements. These forms ask for details about the accident (including the same questions as those presented in a recorded statement) and often ask for a diagram of the accident scene showing the paths of each auto. Insurers send these forms to the insured, the insured driver, and any passengers or witnesses.

Inspection

The claim representative might arrange for a physical damage appraiser to inspect the damaged vehicle and prepare an estimate of damages. Alternately, the claim representative might ask the insured to obtain a couple of competitive estimates from local body shop appraisers. The physical damage appraisal could occur concurrently with taking the recorded statements. The appraiser often takes photos of the vehicle, which helps confirm the statements taken.

Vehicle identification number (VIN)
A unique number that is assigned to each vehicle and that identifies certain vehicle characteristics.

The appraiser verifies the **vehicle identification number (VIN)**, which is a unique identifier on the vehicle. The VIN identifies the exact make and model of the vehicle so that the proper repair parts can be obtained. The VIN is sometimes stamped into certain vehicle parts, such as the engine.

Verification of the VIN is particularly important if a vehicle has been stolen or mostly destroyed, because many fraudulent claims are attempted by burning a vehicle, by dumping the vehicle into a body of water, or by dismantling the vehicle entirely. Location of the VIN on recovered auto parts can uncover such fraud attempts.

Regardless of whether the auto damage is inspected by a physical damage appraiser or a local body shop, the appraiser prepares an estimate of the damage that includes the items to be repaired or replaced, the amount of labor involved, and the parts involved. This estimate is costed out (the price of materials and labor is determined) and sent to the claim representative, the insured or claimant, and the repair facility. If the insured obtains competitive estimates, the claim representative must verify that the estimates describe the same damaged parts and, if so, base the claim payment on the lowest repair estimate.

Documentation and Use of Experts

The file documentation for an auto physical damage claim might include the following items:

- Statements from the insured, drivers, and witnesses
- Photos of the damaged vehicle(s)
- Police report
- Fire marshal report (when fire is the cause of loss)
- Estimates of the damages
- Any expert reports

The file also contains any reports that the claim representative has prepared, the file status notes, and copies of any related correspondence sent or received. Much of this documentation is contained in the electronic claim file. If the vehicle is a total loss, whether from damage or from theft, the claim representative should include an explanation in the file of how the total loss was calculated. He or she might also include the vehicle title and a statement about how the vehicle was disposed of.

Fire Claims

For fire claims, the claim representative may assign an origin and cause expert to inspect the damaged vehicle and determine how the fire started. The cause of the fire may determine whether the loss is covered under the policy. Fires are caused by accident, intent (arson), or negligence. If the origin and cause expert determines that the fire started by accident, the claim representative may not need any further information to conclude the claim. If the origin and cause expert determines that the fire was set intentionally, the claim representative works with the SIU to determine whether the insured was involved. If the origin and cause expert determines that the fire was caused by a faulty part, the claim representative investigates who put that part into the vehicle and whether that person or party was negligent and, therefore, responsible for the loss. Subrogation possibilities would exist for such negligence and would also exist if the damage were caused by any other third party's negligence.

Theft Claims

If a vehicle is allegedly stolen, the claim investigation has the following four possible outcomes:

1. Vehicle not recovered
2. Vehicle recovered and repaired

3. Vehicle recovered and a total loss
4. Claim denied because of fraud or another coverage defense

When assigned a total theft claim, the claim representative should immediately verify the existence of the vehicle and the circumstances of the loss by taking a recorded statement from the insured. When questioning the insured about the loss, the claim representative should consider all possible scenarios. For example, the police may have impounded the vehicle, or the vehicle may have been repossessed. The statement should also cover when and where the vehicle was acquired, the VIN, whether the vehicle was financed, and whether it was recently repaired. The claim representative should ascertain the vehicle's overall condition, the vehicle's optional features, and the vehicle's mileage.

When a vehicle is stolen, the insured has a duty to report the theft to police. The claim representative should obtain a copy of the police report to verify the loss. If the insured did not report the theft to police, so no police report exists, the claim representative should begin to look for fraud indicators, such as the following:

-   Domestic problems
-   Significant debt
-   Invalid VIN
-   Leased vehicle with excessive mileage
-   Major repair work needed for vehicle
-   Unusual amount of personal property in the vehicle at the time of the loss

Actual cash value (ACV)
A value of property that is calculated by determining the cost of repairing property or replacing it with property of like kind or quality and then subtracting depreciation.

If the vehicle is recovered, some damage will probably require repairs. Once the vehicle has been recovered, the claim representative should have it inspected and the damage appraised. If the vehicle has not been recovered within thirty days, most insurers declare it a total loss. Once a total loss has been declared, the claim representative determines the vehicle's **actual cash value (ACV)** at the time of the loss. ACV is the replacement cost (the cost to repair or replace the property with new property of the same type) minus depreciation. The insured completes an affidavit of vehicle theft, an odometer statement, and sometimes a power of attorney, so that the claim can be paid. As part of the claim payment process, the insured also gives the insurer the title to the vehicle. Some insurers might pay only half of the loss before securing the title, and then pay the final half after receiving it.

Damages

Salvage value
An amount that an insurer can recover by selling or otherwise disposing of insured property for which the insurer has paid a total loss or a constructive total loss.

Whether a vehicle is declared a total loss because it is not recovered or because of damage (caused either during a theft or an accident), the claim representative should determine the vehicle's value at the time of the loss and any salvage value. **Salvage value** is the amount that an insurer can recover by selling or otherwise disposing of insured property for which the insurer has paid a total loss or a constructive total loss.

Claim representatives can use one of two methods of determining the auto's value: ACV or market value. For most vehicles, claim representatives determine ACV by using valuation guides, such as the *Kelley Blue Book* or the National Automotive Dealer Association (NADA) *Official Used Car Guide*. These guides supply the claim representative with the vehicle's pre-accident value (the auto's value before the accident occurred and damaged it). To correctly determine the ACV and calculate a fair value, the claim representative should know the vehicle's make, model, and year, along with the vehicle's optional features and its mileage.

For antique autos or older specialty autos (such as a Jaguar that is more than ten years old but not an antique), claim representatives might base the auto's value on the fair market value. The **fair market value** (or market value) is the amount at which a knowledgeable buyer, under no unusual pressure, would be willing to buy property, and a knowledgeable seller, under no unusual pressure, would be willing to sell it. The fair market value is based on the assumption that a number of buyers and sellers are available for such property. In some cases, the number of buyers and sellers in the market is limited; in those cases, the ACV gives a more accurate valuation of the property than fair market value.

Fair market value
The amount at which a knowledgeable buyer, under no unusual pressure, would be willing to buy property, and a knowledgeable seller, under no unusual pressure, would be willing to sell it.

Regardless of which valuation method claim representatives use, they must deduct any salvage value from the ACV or market value. Claim representatives determine salvage value by obtaining bids from various salvage dealers, either through a salvage pool or a bid process.

Insurers specify a waiting period before paying total auto theft claims. Once the waiting period has expired or a damaged vehicle is declared a total loss, the claim representative calculates the claim payment based on ACV as follows:

Claim payment = ACV − deductible.

A deductible is the portion of the loss that the insured pays. If the insured elects to retain the car, the calculation includes a salvage figure, as follows:

Claim payment = ACV − deductible − salvage value.

Calculations for market value are the same, except that the current market value would replace ACV in these formulas.

If a vehicle is simply damaged during an accident, the claim representative concludes the claim by paying the insured the amount required to repair the damage, minus the deductible. In some cases, repairing the vehicle may not be cost-effective. Therefore, the vehicle is determined to be a total loss and the claim payment is calculated in the same manner as if the vehicle were stolen and not recovered.

To determine whether a vehicle is worth repairing, the claim representative should know the vehicle's value, the cost of the repairs, and the salvage value. Each insurer sets the threshold for a total loss, such as 75 or 85 percent. If the cost to repair the vehicle (including salvage value) exceeds 75 or 85 percent of the ACV, then the vehicle is determined to be a total loss and the claim is paid accordingly.

When an insurer has paid the insured for a total loss, the insurer can leave the salvage with the insured or take the salvage. If the insured keeps the salvage, the insured is responsible for repairing or disposing of it. The insurer has no obligation to dispose of the salvage, but it has the right to take the salvage after paying for a total loss and is likely to take it, if the value is considerable. If so, the insurer takes title to the auto with the salvage and generally sells the salvage to a salvage buyer.

Subrogation

During the investigation, the claim representative may determine that a third party is responsible for the damage to the vehicle. After the insured has been paid, the claim representative tries to recover the amount of the claim payment (and usually the insured's deductible) from the responsible third party through subrogation. Usually, the claim representative notifies the third party that he or she is considered responsible for the damage, and the third party's insurer negotiates a settlement. In some cases, such as when the other party does not agree with the allegations, subrogation claims are decided through arbitration.

Claim representatives must consider numerous issues when investigating auto physical damage claims, including issues that affect the cause of loss investigation and the valuation of the damaged auto. Additionally, they must consider subrogation if a third party might be responsible for the damage. The next section examines issues that claim representatives must consider when investigating property damage claims.

INVESTIGATING PROPERTY DAMAGE CLAIMS

Another type of claim that claim representatives investigate is property damage claims. Investigating property damage claims is similar to investigating auto physical damage claims because the damage is usually physical damage to a building or property or theft of property from a building. Buildings and their contents can also be total losses. Property theft claims are investigated a little differently from property damage claims; therefore, they are discussed in a subsequent section.

Cause of Loss Investigation

A home or a commercial building can suffer damage from various causes of loss. The claim representative should investigate the cause of loss and amount of damage, in light of the policy, before any claim payment can be made or the claim can be denied. Causes of loss are described in the property policy as either covered causes of loss or excluded causes of loss. The policy also describes how claims should be handled.

Buildings and contents can be damaged by the actions of a third party, such as when a sprinkler system has been installed incorrectly and floods the premises. Such losses are usually covered by the third party's liability policy.

Residential and commercial buildings can be damaged by numerous causes of loss, such as fire, lightning, windstorm, hail, vehicles, vandalism or malicious mischief, sprinkler leakage, and many others. The contents of a building can be stolen or can suffer damage from these and other causes.

Initial Contact and Statements

On receipt of the claim, the claim representative contacts the insured to get information about the cause of the loss and the extent of the damage. Unless the loss involves a theft, in which case the insured's statement might help determine how the theft occurred, the claim representative does not usually take a recorded statement. The damaged property provides enough evidence of the loss. Often during this initial contact, the claim representative discusses emergency repairs or temporary re-location with the insured, because one of the insured's duties, as described in the policy, is to protect the property from further damage. During these conversations, the claim representative should be careful not to waive any rights available through policy provisions.

Inspection

After initially contacting the insured, the claim representative often goes to visit the insured and inspects the building or assigns an outside claim representative or an independent adjuster to do so. During the on-site inspection, the claim representative obtains detailed facts about the cause of the loss. Usually the claim representative photographs or otherwise visually records the damage, and sometimes he or she draws diagrams to clearly depict the damaged areas.

During or after the visit with the insured, the claim representative creates a scope of the loss. The **scope** is a list of the areas damaged in a loss and includes the type of damage (such as fire, smoke, or water), a description of the proposed type of repairs (such as repair, replace, remove, or demolish), and measurements of the area. An example of a scope is shown in Exhibit 4-2.

Scope
A list of the areas damaged in a loss, which includes the type of damage, a description of the proposed type of repairs, and measurements of the damaged areas.

The claim representative uses the scope to create the estimate of damage. The claim representative can prepare the estimate, or the scope can be sent to contractors who bid on the job. The estimate includes the quantity and price for materials and labor needed to complete the repairs.

Documentation and Use of Experts

Depending on the type of loss, the claim representative may obtain a fire marshal's report or a police report. In the event of a fire, the claim representative may want to interview and take statements from witnesses, neighbors, and the police or fire personnel who were on the scene.

EXHIBIT 4-2

Example of a Scope Sheet

Property Loss Worksheet

Page No. _____1_____

Preliminary Estimate ___10/19/XX___
                              Date

Final Estimate _____   _____M. Boyer_____
                              Date   Claim Representative

Claim No. _____524 BL 101_____

Insured _____J. Smith_____

Claimant _____Insured_____

1 Item	2 Description	3 Quantity	4 Units / Age	5 Unit price / Orig. cost	6 Cost / Repl. cost	7 Deprec.	8 A.C.V.	9 Loss & Damage
1.	Permit (if required)							

2.	Demolition
	  Remove range hood
	  Remove cabinets (4 LF)
	  Remove drywall
	  (above cabinet)
	  (5′ x 10′ = 50 SF)
	  Remove Formica countertop (12 LF)
	  (est. 2 men x 5 hrs. = 10 hrs.)							

3.	Cartage 1 pickup & driver (1.5 hrs.) Dump fee ($10.00)							
4.	Clean range (est. 1.5 hrs.)							
5.	Install new range hood (Lowe's 30″, est. 1 hr.)							

6.	Install upper cabinets
	  Paint grade plywood of 4 LF x 3′ tall
	  (est. 1.5 hrs.)							

7.	New Formica countertop							
8.	Drywall (above range) 5′ × 10′ = 50 sq. ft. Tape and texture (splatter finish)							

9.	Painting
	  Kitchen—wash and paint
	  (14′ x 8′) x 2 = 224 SF
	  (20′ x 8′) x 2 = 320 SF
	
	  1 coat high-gloss latex
	  2 coats on new cabinets
	
	  Living Room—wash and paint
	  1 coat flat latex (20′ x 8′) x 2 = 320SF
	  (24′ x 8′) x 2 = 384 SF
	
	  Entrance Hall (4′ x 8′) = 32 SF
	  (14′ x 8′) x 2 = 224 SF							

10.	Shampoo carpets LR and halls (200 sq. yds.)							
11.	Clean vinyl tile in kitchen (280 SF)							
12.	Clean furniture (per estimate)							
13.	Contractor overhead & profit (OH/P 15% or 20%)							

While most claims are straightforward, some require additional investigation and the use of experts. If a claim representative suspects that a claim is fraudulent, he or she enlists the help of the SIU to further investigate the claim. The SIU investigates the insured's background to determine whether the insured had a motive to cause the damage. Usually such a motive is financial, but the insured could cause a loss for personal reasons, such as revenge. The SIU investigation also determines whether the insured had an opportunity to cause the damage—for example, if there is no way to verify the insured's location at the time of the loss.

If the loss involves fire, the claim representative may consult an origin and cause expert to determine the cause of the fire. If it appears that an appliance or a piece of machinery malfunctioned and caused the loss, that appliance or piece of machinery should be examined by an expert (usually an engineer) to determine the cause of the malfunction. If the loss involves a weather-related condition such as hail, lightning, windstorm, or heavy rain, the claim representative often requests confirmation of the weather condition from a weather tracking source or a local television station. If the loss involves water from an internal source, the claim representative contacts a plumber to help locate the source of the leak and determine its cause. If the loss involves a large amount of inventory at a retail or manufacturing site, the claim representative may retain an accountant to verify the value of that inventory. The claim representative may also hire a professional salvor to inventory the damaged items, place a value on them, and then sell them for the insured.

Fire Claims

When identifying the cause of a fire that damages property, claim representatives should determine the following:

- Property's history and condition
- Mortgages or liens that exist
- Insured's claim history
- Any personal details about the insured, such as a pending divorce or recent financial difficulties

Combined with other documentation from the investigation, this information might suggest that the fire resulted from arson rather than an accident. When factors exist that suggest arson, and depending on the property value and the extent of the damage, the claim representative might consult an origin and cause specialist to determine the likelihood of arson.

Theft Claims

Claim representatives obtain or create an inventory of missing property and its value when a theft or burglary has occurred. For a business, inventory records show what was in stock and how much it was worth. For a home, people do not often keep such inventories of their property. Claim representatives should be flexible in accepting the proof of ownership that insured homeowners can provide to document their claims. Receipts for items may no longer exist, but the insured may have photos or other visual recordings showing the items. The claim representative weighs the personal property claimed by the insured against the insured's circumstances and reasonable conditions. For example, if an insured claims that six sets of golf clubs were stolen from the trunk of his car, the claim representative should consider whether the trunk would actually hold six sets of golf clubs and why an insured would have so many sets of clubs.

Loss of Income Claims

Commercial entities are also subject to another type of loss: They can lose business income as a result of physical damage to their buildings or contents that renders them unable to be used during the period of reconstruction or until repairs have been completed. Depending on the policy, loss of business income may be covered. Adjusting business income losses is complicated. Usually, only very experienced claim representatives handle business income losses, and they often request an accountant's assistance to determine the value of lost income, which is based on current economic factors.

Damage

Claim representatives determine the value of damaged property that is covered by property insurance policies by using actual cash value (ACV) or replacement cost. In addition, some policies pay a stated value for an item that cannot easily be replaced, such as a piece of artwork.

Actual Cash Value (ACV)

The definition of actual cash value for a building corresponds with the definition of ACV for auto physical damage, except for how ACV is determined. No valuation guides comparable to auto valuation guides exist for buildings to provide the ACV of a specific building. Determining the ACV for a repair estimate requires the claim representative to know the useful life of building components as well as court decisions about ACV in the jurisdiction. To determine ACV, the claim representative examines each item for repair and quantifies the extent of betterment. Betterment is another way of expressing depreciation. The depreciation amount for an item is the difference between the value of a new object and that of an older object. The item's age, condition, obsolescence, and actual use affect the depreciation amount. If an entire building must be replaced, the ACV may be the fair market value.

Replacement Cost

Replacement cost
The cost to repair or replace property using new materials of like kind and quality with no deduction for depreciation.

Replacement cost of a building or personal property is somewhat easier to calculate than ACV. **Replacement cost** is the cost to repair or replace the property using new materials of like kind and quality with no deduction for depreciation. Claim representatives can estimate replacement cost by using a software package. Alternately, a general contractor who is bidding to perform the work can provide a replacement cost estimate for the building.

Subrogation

If the investigation into the cause of the loss determines that a third party is responsible for the damage, then the claim representative subrogates against that party for the amount of the claim payment and the insured's deductible. For example, an art museum contracts for sidewalk maintenance around the museum, but the maintenance contractor performs poorly and fails to correct large cracks and holes in the sidewalks. If an exhibitor trips on a crack and drops an expensive sculpture that shatters on the sidewalk, and then files a lawsuit against the art museum because of the poorly maintained sidewalks, that contractor could be held responsible for the loss. If a thief is caught and convicted, the thief can be required to pay restitution for the items stolen that were not recovered or that were damaged.

Claim representatives must consider numerous issues when investigating property damage claims, including issues that affect the cause of loss investigation and the valuation of the damaged property. Additionally, they must consider subrogation if any third party might be responsible for the damage. The next section examines issues that claim representatives must consider when investigating bodily injury claims.

INVESTIGATING BODILY INJURY CLAIMS

Another type of claim that claim representatives investigate is bodily injury claims. People can be injured in numerous ways. They can be injured in car accidents or in a fall while visiting a grocery store or a neighbor's backyard. They can be injured by a faulty product or suffer food poisoning from food served at a restaurant. While each of these losses might be covered under a different type of policy, such as an auto policy or a general liability policy, the investigation of the cause of loss and the amount of damage is generally the same. The only bodily injury claims that are handled differently are workers' compensation claims, because those claims are strictly regulated by state governments.

Cause of Loss Investigation

Bodily injury investigations to determine cause of loss focus on how the accident happened and who was at fault. The investigation is the same whether the insured or a third party was injured, except that the insurer cannot subrogate against its own insured. Most often, a claim representative receives a first report of loss that includes basic information about how the loss occurred and who was injured. However, sometimes the first notice that an injury has occurred is the insured's notice of a lawsuit alleging that someone was injured as a result of the insured's negligence.

When a lawsuit is the first notice of an injury, the claim representative assigns the lawsuit to defense counsel while completing the investigation into the cause of loss. Insurers have procedures in place dictating how these lawsuits should be handled, and claim representatives should follow those procedures.

Initial Contact and Statements

When an insurer receives a loss report that indicates someone was injured on the insured's premises or as a result of an auto accident with the insured, the claim representative's first action is to contact the insured and take a statement about the circumstances of the loss. If the claim concerns an auto accident, the statement covers details such as who was in the car; how fast the insured was driving; where the insured was coming from and going; whether there were traffic controls, such as a stop sign or a traffic light; when and where the other vehicle was first seen; and whether either driver took action to try to prevent the accident. The claim representative also takes statements from any witnesses and from the injured party, provided the injured party is not represented by a lawyer. If the injured party has retained a lawyer, the claim representative must direct all contact to that lawyer. The statements taken establish what each party was doing at the time of the accident and assist the claim representative in determining who was at fault.

Documentation and Use of Experts

The claim representative should obtain a copy of any police report of the accident and may also request copies of any police photos and diagrams. The claim representative should also obtain a copy of the report of any emergency or rescue personnel who responded to the accident scene. Using a signed medical authorization from the claimant, the claim representative requests copies of medical treatment records to compare them to the various descriptions of the accident or injury. The claim representative may request copies of any toxicology reports to determine whether the parties to the accident had any drugs, toxins, or alcohol in their body at the time of the accident.

Claim representatives learn details about a claimant's injuries and/or disability through medical records. These records include emergency room reports; physician bills and reports; hospital records that contain nurses' notes; results of lab tests, X-rays, and other diagnostic procedures; and reports from rehabilitation services. However, the claim representative must obtain a signed medical authorization from the injured party before obtaining these records.

In cases in which death results from an accident or from a cause that is not readily apparent, an autopsy is usually performed. An autopsy is a scientifically detailed examination of the deceased person's body to determine the cause of death, and an autopsy report is usually obtained from the medical examiner's office for a fee. Autopsy reports are important in cases in which there is a possibility that the person's death may have been caused by a factor other than the accident. Autopsy reports also help to determine whether the deceased person suffered for any time period before death. When evaluating damages, the more a claimant has suffered before death, the greater the award to the deceased's family for pain and suffering.

The claim representative may want to hire an expert to assist with some investigations. For example, a vehicle accident might be particularly complex or involve an allegation that some part of a vehicle malfunctioned. An accident reconstruction expert can determine how a vehicle accident occurred using photos of the scene, witness accounts, measurements of the damage to the vehicles involved, and the nature of the injuries sustained. An engineer specializing in vehicles can inspect a vehicle and determine, for example, whether the brakes malfunctioned. A different type of engineer might inspect a product to see whether it malfunctioned. A chemist might be asked to check for the presence of bacteria or other contaminants in food or beverages.

Liability Determination

Once the cause of the loss has been determined, the claim representative can determine liability. Determining liability is an art rather than a science; the claim representative determines liability based on experience, case law, and the facts of the claim. The liability determination is the claim representative's opinion about who was at fault for the accident and for what amount of damages. If the facts show that a third party failed to stop at a red light and hit the insured, who was legally crossing the intersection, then the third party may be 100 percent at fault for the accident. If the facts show that the insured and a third party both lost control of their vehicles because of an ice patch, then they may each be assigned 50 percent of the fault. Ultimately, the final apportionment of liability is often negotiated among the claim representatives and/or lawyers representing the various parties. This negotiation finalizes the percentage of negligence apportioned to each party and determines the damages that each party must pay.

Damages

While investigating the cause of the loss in a bodily injury liability claim, the claim representative also investigates the amount of the damages. Bodily injury liability claims have two types of damages: special damages and general damages.

Special damages, or "specials," are monetary awards to compensate a victim or his or her family for specific out-of-pocket expenses incurred because of a loss, such as medical expenses, wage loss, or funeral expenses. When determining special damages, the claim representative should do the following two things:

1. Verify the amount of the damages claimed
2. Verify that the special damages are related to the insured's accident

Claimants also make claims for general damages. General damages are more difficult to measure than special damages because they are subjective. **General damages** are monetary awards to compensate a victim for covered losses, such as the value of the injured party's pain and suffering, inconvenience, disfigurement,

Special damages
A monetary award to compensate a victim for specific, out-of-pocket expenses incurred because of a covered loss, such as medical expenses, wage loss, funeral expenses, or repair bills.

General damages
A monetary award to compensate a victim for covered losses, such as pain and suffering, that do not involve specific, measurable expenses.

and certain intangible factors that do not involve specific, measurable expenses. Claim representatives use their experience and the experience of other claim representatives and lawyers to value general damages appropriately.

Valuation of Damages

To consider all aspects of a claim, claim representatives who are evaluating bodily injury should consider the following elements of damages, among others:

- Medical expenses
- Injury type
- Injured person's wage loss or loss of earning capacity because of the injury
- Pain and suffering resulting from the injury
- Extent of any disability or impairment
- Injured person's loss of enjoyment as a result of an injury
- Any disfigurement resulting from the injury
- Whether preexisting conditions contributed to the injury

Valuation of a particular injury differs by person for a number of reasons. First, not all people respond in the same way to an injury. A similar accident and injury can create different levels of pain and disability depending on the person. Additionally, the jurisdiction in which the claim is made affects the claim valuation. Juries in one state may value an injury higher than do juries in another state. A jury's probable award in a given case affects the claim value. Factors such as the injured person's age, gender, and occupation and the lawyers' reputations affect a jury's perception of the injured person and the insured. Such differences can even occur among different jurisdictions in the same state.

Valuation of Special Damages

Many types of special damages are compensable, meaning that the insurer is responsible to pay them. Incurred and future doctor and hospital bills are examples of medical expenses that are compensable as special damages in bodily injury liability claims. Travel expenses incurred going to and from healthcare providers are also compensable. Medical expenses should be reasonable and necessary to be compensable. Claim representatives often work with independent medical reviewers to determine whether medical expenses are reasonable and necessary. Wage and income losses refer to the economic loss caused by an inability to perform a specific job because of the injury suffered. Wage loss is used to describe the loss of earnings from the date of the injury to the time recovery is complete. Loss of earning capacity, which is also compensable, is based on future estimated losses resulting from a permanent disability.

Valuation of General Damages

When evaluating general damages in a bodily injury liability claim, claim representatives should answer the following questions:

- What are the specific injuries, and what type of pain is associated with them?
- Are the injuries consistent with the accident?
- Did symptoms (and pain) exist before the accident?
- Do other causes contribute to the pain?
- Is pain severe, and is it temporary or chronic?
- What is the resulting disability and how does it affect the claimant's daily activities and ability to work and enjoy life?
- How significantly do the claimant's age, occupation, and gender affect the pain and suffering?

When evaluating pain and suffering claims, claim representatives should consider three elements: physical pain, mental suffering, and mental anguish. Physical pain can result from the accident itself, from aftereffects of the healing process, from undergoing physical therapy, and from painful diagnostic procedures. Mental suffering includes fear, anxiety, depression, grief, despair, and anger related to a physical injury. Mental anguish is the unpleasant mental consequence resulting from an injury. It is often used to describe the psychic injuries not directly related to physical pain. Anguish over a scar and embarrassment from being unable to perform normal activities are examples of mental anguish.

Damages for pain and suffering are established by the testimony of medical providers; the individual's own testimony; and the testimony of others, such as employers, clergy, family members, or friends. These parties can testify about the expressions of the severity, intensity, and duration of pain that they have observed.

A claim representative should evaluate whether the injury will result in a permanent impairment or disability. The following are some issues to consider regarding permanent injuries:

- Have the job, family, and recreation been changed for the worse as a result of this permanent injury?
- Does chronic pain accompany the injury?
- Does disability or disfigurement accompany the injury?
- Has the person's personality been affected?

Claim representatives can contact medical experts to help evaluate the potential losses resulting from a permanent impairment or disability.

Most jurisdictions treat loss of enjoyment as a compensable general damage, distinguishable from pain and suffering. Loss of enjoyment claims are based on the claimant's reduced capacity to enjoy certain activities, and they can include the loss of physical and intellectual gratification and other lifestyle losses. Loss of enjoyment damages have two components. The first component is a medically determined, permanent injury. The second component is a comparison of what the person could do before the accident and what the person can do after the accident.

Other types of bodily injury liability claims are pure mental injury claims, such as post-traumatic stress disorder, or claims involving fatalities. Evaluating these claims usually requires knowledge of the jurisdiction and settlement amounts on similar claims. These claims often involve litigation.

Compensation for pain and suffering frequently constitutes the largest part of a bodily injury liability settlement. Claim representatives consider future as well as past pain and suffering in determining this compensation.

Methods to Evaluate a Bodily Injury Claim

Claim representatives may use one or more of the following methods to help evaluate a bodily injury claim (including special and general damages):

- Individual case method
- Roundtable method
- Formula method (not recommended)
- Expert systems

The individual case method allows the claim representative to determine the value of the claim based on all of the claim's circumstances and the claim representative's experience in similar cases. Because of the numerous factors that go into this valuation, the individual case method may yield valuations that vary by claim representative. Generally, the following four factors are considered in determining a value for a bodily injury claim:

1. Likelihood that the insured will obtain a favorable verdict
2. Insured's proportionate share of liability in the event of an unfavorable verdict
3. Numerous variables that affect a jury's likely award
4. Reasonable estimate of damages that the claimant is likely be able to prove in court

The roundtable method involves two or more claim representatives evaluating the claim file and each suggesting a value. After discussing the suggested values, the parties reach a consensus on the range of values or they calculate an average of all of the values.

With the formula method, a mathematical formula is used to set the value. This formula might be based on the assumption that a certain ratio exists between medical expenses and general damages. Although it was commonly used in the past, the formula method of calculating general damages has been the subject of bad faith litigation and should be avoided.

An expert system is computer software that uses artificial intelligence to identify and simulate the thinking pattern of experts in order to perform a given task. Claim evaluation expert systems, in theory, simulate the thought process of experienced, knowledgeable claim professionals. An expert system can be calibrated to value claims based on specific insurer guidelines and specific jurisdictions, so that the values match comparable claim values in those areas.

Concluding Bodily Injury Claims

Concluding bodily injury claims includes settling the claim and making the claim payment or denying the claim. Bodily injury claims can be settled in three different ways: by negotiation with the injured party, by ADR methods, or through litigation. This section examines insurers' claim payment options.

Once a claim has been settled, the claimant must usually sign a release of all claims, and the insurer must make a payment. As an alternative to a lump-sum payment, claims can be paid through a structured settlement. **Structured settlements** provide some immediate payment and defer the remaining payment to the future. The future payments are usually disbursed over a period of time rather than in a lump sum. The insurer arranges a structured settlement by purchasing an annuity from a life insurer and naming the claimant as the beneficiary so that the claimant will receive periodic payments over a set number of years. Structured settlements are often used when a claimant needs ongoing medical treatment or is unable to return to working at his or her original job. Structured settlements provide a flow of income to the claimant, which is especially helpful if the claimant is a minor. Insurers benefit by making a smaller payment overall, because the annuity generates earnings that are considered in the ultimate settlement value. Therefore, structured settlements benefit both the insured and the insurer.

Structured settlements
Periodic and guaranteed payments made for damages over a specified time period; an alternative to lump-sum payment for claim settlement.

Claim representatives must consider numerous issues when investigating bodily injury claims, including issues that affect the cause of loss investigation and determination of liability, types of damages that can be claimed, and the valuation of those damages. They must also be aware of special issues for concluding bodily injury claims. The next section examines issues that claim representatives must consider when investigating workers' compensation claims.

INVESTIGATING WORKERS' COMPENSATION CLAIMS

Another type of claim that claim representatives investigate is workers' compensation claims. Workers' compensation claims all involve bodily injury, disease, or death. However, the investigation into the cause of the loss and the amount of damages is distinguishable from other bodily injury claims because of the difference in the coverages. This coverage difference is discussed in a subsequent chapter. This section explains how workers' compensation claims differ from other bodily injury claims.

Compensability

In contrast to bodily injury claims, workers' compensation investigations focus on compensability and the payment of statutorily defined benefits. Compensability determination is very similar to the determination of the cause of the loss, but workers' compensation investigations involve additional issues. To determine whether a claim is compensable, the claim representative should investigate whether the injured party is an employee under the workers' compensation statute, whether the injury is covered under the statute, and whether the injury arose out of and in the course of employment.

Generally, the claim representative conducts the compensability investigation at the employer's location or at the accident scene, if the accident did not occur at the employer's location. The claim representative takes statements from the injured worker, witnesses to the injury, and the injured worker's supervisor. These statements focus on what the injured worker was doing at the time of the injury and whether the activity that caused the injury was employment-related. The claim representative requests records from the employer, such as payroll records, to determine employment status and wage loss amounts. The claim representative may request copies of pre-employment physical reports, safety training records, and other pertinent documents from the human resources department. The claim representative may also photograph the area in which the worker was injured or the piece of machinery that caused the injury, in the event that a third party may be responsible for the injury.

While most injuries are covered by the state workers' compensation statutes, some are not. The claim representative should know which injuries are and are not covered by the specific state statute and should conduct the investigation appropriately. For example, some states do not cover injuries arising out of a willful failure to use a safety device.

Finally, the claim representative should investigate whether the injury arose out of and in the course of employment. Workers can suffer injuries at work that are unrelated to employment, such as an office worker who faints from dehydration while at work. Although the accident or injury occurs at work, it is unrelated to the office worker's job duties. The injury also must occur in the course of the worker's employment. This requirement means that the claim representative should investigate whether the injury occurred as a result of a work-related activity or was incidental to work. For example, if an office worker is struck by a co-worker's car in a parking lot that is not owned by the employer as they are arriving for work, the resulting injury would generally not be considered to have occurred during the course of employment, because "employment" does not begin until employees are on the premises.

Benefits

A workers' compensation claim representative determines what benefits the injured worker is entitled to receive and how much to pay for those benefits. The benefits payable under workers' compensation are as follows:

- Medical benefits
- Disability benefits
- Rehabilitation benefits
- Funeral expense benefits
- Survivors' benefits

A workers' compensation insurer pays the medical expenses of the injured worker. Workers' compensation claim representatives should have a working knowledge of medical terminology and procedures to effectively review the medical expenses and determine whether they are related to the injury and are medically necessary for the injury. Alternately, the claim representative uses a medical expert's services to help make this determination. The claim representative also reviews medical records and, with the help of experts, determines whether the injured worker has suffered a permanent disability from the injury or can return to work, either at the same job or another type of job.

The claim representative uses the medical records and the treating doctor's records to determine how long the injured worker will be unable to work and then to calculate the appropriate disability benefit payment. The claim representative may also pay funeral expenses or survivors' benefits if the injured worker has died.

Documentation and Use of Experts

When documenting a workers' compensation claim file, the claim representative often includes statements from the injured party, the injured party's supervisor, and any witnesses to the accident. The claim representative may include photos of the area where the accident occurred or photos of the piece of equipment that caused the injury. Claim representatives may obtain wage statements from employers and medical reports from the emergency room, hospital, and treating doctor to document the injury. Depending on the nature of the injury, claim representatives may also obtain rehabilitation and training reports to include in the claim file. Additionally, claim representatives include in the claim file medical bills submitted for payment, wage loss calculations, and an explanation of how any final settlement was determined.

Claim representatives must consider unique issues and concepts when investigating workers' compensation claims. Rather than determining the cause of loss and loss amount (or damages) as in other types of claims, claim representatives must determine compensability and the benefits payable to the injured worker. Because workers' compensation is governed strictly by laws, claim representatives and insurers must comply with reporting regulations for workers' compensation claims. The next section examines issues that claim representatives must consider when investigating fraud claims.

INVESTIGATING FRAUD

Claim representatives should be alert for facts and circumstances that might signal a fraudulent claim. Fraudulent claims can involve one person or many people. Fraudulent schemes usually involve one or more of the following elements:

- Deliberately causing an accident or a loss
- Claiming that a loss or an event occurred when it did not
- Exaggerating the amount of the claim or the extent of injury

When investigating a claim, a claim representative might notice one or two indicators of fraud that may or may not mean that the claim is fraudulent. The claim representative should use common sense. For example, if a home has been burglarized and the insured produces receipts showing that all of the items stolen were purchased within the last year, this could indicate fraud. Common sense would dictate that some of the items stolen would have been obtained in other years as well. If a business has been burglarized and the business owner has few receipts or invoices for the stolen items, this also could indicate fraud. Common sense would dictate that a business owner would keep business receipts for tax and other purposes.

Some insurers use technology to detect fraud and enhance the fraud-screening process. They use software packages that screen claim data for specific indicators and then assign them a weight or score. A particular weight or score designates a claim as potentially fraudulent. Insurers subscribe to information services that help claim representatives determine whether arson was likely or whether a claimant has filed similar claims.

When a claim appears to be suspicious, a claim representative should involve the SIU. Early involvement preserves the integrity of the investigation and facilitates additional investigation. It also allows the claim representative to continue to work on the claim while the parallel SIU investigation is conducted.

Many different fraud indicators exist, and most are specific to a type of loss. Comprehensive lists of fraud indicators are too extensive to include in this chapter. However, most insurers provide such lists to their claim representatives so that they are familiar with the fraud indicators to consider.

SUMMARY

Handling claims is a crucial part of an insurer's business, and understanding the intricacies of claim handling helps claim representatives process claims properly. The activities in the claim-handling process are as follows:

- Acknowledging and assigning the claim
- Identifying the policy
- Contacting the insured or the insured's representative
- Investigating and documenting the claim
- Determining the cause of loss and the loss amount
- Concluding the claim

Claim representatives must perform a good faith investigation on every claim. When dealing with an insured or a claimant, claim representatives should be careful not to mislead the insured or claimant about potential coverage, and they should be careful not to waive any of the insurer's rights or cause the insurer to be estopped from enforcing a policy provision. Claim representatives use nonwaiver agreements and reservation of rights letters to inform insureds that a coverage issue exists and that the continuation of the investigation does not waive any policy provisions.

Claim representatives should document their investigations, consult appropriate experts, and prepare reports for internal and external use.

On some claims, claim representatives spend the majority of their time determining the cause of the loss and determining the loss amount (or damages). Investigation involves determining how, when, where, and why a loss occurred and how that information affects coverage.

When ready to conclude the claim, the claim representative determines whether the claim should be paid or denied. Disputes should be resolved using appropriate alternative dispute resolution (ADR) methods; litigation provides a last resort to settle disputes. Reinsurers should be notified of claim activity as required by the insurer's and reinsurer's guidelines. If reinsurance applies to the claim, the reinsurer should be notified of the outcome.

In this chapter, investigations are discussed as they apply to the following categories of claims:

- Auto physical damage claims
- Property damage claims
- Bodily injury claims
- Workers' compensation claims
- Fraudulent claims

For each of these different types of claims, claim representatives should complete investigations. The investigation provides the claim representative with enough information to determine the cause of the loss and the loss amount (or damages). For a workers' compensation claim, the claim representative investigates to determine compensability and benefits payable. Claim representatives use fraud indicators and common sense to recognize fraudulent claims and refer them to SIU personnel.

The remaining chapters of this text examine the coverages associated with automobile first-party claims, property first-party claims, liability claims, and workers' compensation claims, and they describe claim-handling issues related to these coverages.

CHAPTER NOTE

1. Association for Cooperative Operations Research and Development (ACORD), "Mission," ACORD Global Insurance Standards, January 21, 2005, www.acord.com/about/mission.aspx (accessed January 21, 2005).

Chapter 5

Direct Your Learning

Automobile First-Party Claims

After learning the content of this chapter and completing the corresponding course guide assignment, you should be able to:

- Explain how the following policy provisions and coverages affect automobile first-party losses:
  - Insured persons
  - Automobile physical damage coverages
  - Other first-party coverages
  - Exclusions
  - Conditions
- Describe the following endorsements that can apply in automobile first-party losses:
  - Personal injury protection (PIP) endorsement
  - Uninsured motorists (UM) and underinsured motorists (UIM) endorsements
  - Customizing equipment endorsement
  - Electronic equipment endorsement
- Describe the following types of automobile physical damage losses:
  - Partial losses
  - Total losses
  - Diminished value losses
- Identify common forms of dispute resolution for automobile physical damage claims.
- Define or describe each of the Key Words and Phrases for this chapter.

Develop Your Perspective

What are the main topics covered in the chapter?

Building on the claim-handling process described in the previous chapter, this chapter describes automobile policy provisions, coverages, and endorsements that relate specifically to automobile first-party physical damage losses. First, the chapter describes the named insureds, the coverages provided for automobile first-party losses, other first-party coverages, exclusions, conditions, and endorsements. Next, the chapter describes types of auto physical damage (APD) losses and common forms of dispute resolution used for APD claims.

Review your automobile policy or a friend's automobile policy.

- Is the policy a standard automobile policy?
- What types of first-party losses are covered under this policy? Where did you find this information?

Why is it important to learn about these topics?

An effective claim representative must be able to properly investigate and pay losses. On an automobile loss, this investigation begins with the claim representative's review of the covered insureds and vehicles and the applicable first-party coverages. Claim representatives must know how to determine whether an APD loss is a partial loss or a total loss and whether diminished value loss should be determined.

Examine the automobile policies that your organization uses.

- What types of first-party physical damage losses would your organization decline based on the automobile coverages?
- Which first-party endorsements are used with policies for the various states in which your organization writes auto insurance?

How can you use what you will learn?

Analyze an automobile physical damage claim.

- What coverage issues are documented in the claim file?
- Was the loss a partial loss or a total loss, and how was the value determined?
- If the claim was disputed, what form of dispute resolution would be applicable and why?

Chapter 5
Automobile First-Party Claims

Automobile insurance protects policyholders and others who qualify as insureds from the financial losses that they might suffer as a result of covered auto accidents. Automobile insurance typically includes auto physical damage (APD) coverage, auto liability coverage, and coverage for other financial losses (such as limited medical, funeral, and rehabilitation costs and lost income).

As described in previous chapters, first-party property losses are losses to the insured's own property or, in this case, the insured's auto. First-party losses also include bodily injury and related losses that would be covered under medical payments coverage, personal injury protection (PIP) coverage, and uninsured motorists (UM) or underinsured motorists (UIM) coverages.

Auto insurance policies use the term "automobile" or "auto" to describe passenger autos, sport utility vehicles, vans, and pickup trucks.

To successfully handle auto first-party physical damage and bodily injury claims, claim representatives must understand the types of property losses and bodily injuries and the related losses that auto policies cover. The first section of this chapter describes coverages that are provided for auto first-party losses by examining the various concepts and parts of auto policies that relate to first-party losses, including insured persons, APD coverages, other first-party coverages, exclusions, conditions, and endorsements. The second section of the chapter examines auto physical damage losses, and the third section examines forms of dispute resolution that are commonly used for auto physical damage claims. The chapter concludes with a case study illustrating an auto first-party physical damage claim.

COVERAGE PROVIDED FOR AUTOMOBILE FIRST-PARTY LOSSES

Owners or leaseholders (called "owners" hereafter) can suffer large financial losses because of loss exposures created by owning, operating, or maintaining an auto. For example, the owner could be held responsible for the injuries of passengers in the insured auto if the passengers are injured in an accident involving that auto. Common coverages for auto loss exposures include the following:

- Personal auto policies
- Business auto policies

- Garage policies
- Truckers policies
- Motor carrier policies

Auto insurance policies and endorsements typically include the following types of policy provisions and coverages:

- Insured persons
- Auto physical damage (APD) coverages
- Other first-party coverages
- Exclusions
- Conditions
- Endorsements

Subsequent sections of this chapter offer a general description of these provisions. Insurance Services Office (ISO) policies provide the basis for these descriptions, and the coverage descriptions apply broadly to many personal and commercial policies. As described in the first chapter, claim representatives must read the insurance policy closely to determine whether coverage exists for a loss.

Standardized Versus Insurer-Specific Auto Policies

Insurance Services Office (ISO) provides standardized auto policies that some insurers use. However, many insurers develop their own insurer-specific auto policies. Because policies have been carefully developed and phrased to provide the intended coverage, claim personnel should refer to the policy language when handling claims.

Insured Persons

Most auto insurance policies list the named insured and other persons who are insured at the beginning of the policy or coverage form. Generally, the named insured on an auto policy is the policyholder or the person(s) or entity whose name appears on the policy declarations and who pays premiums, receives any returned premiums, cancels the policy, and receives any notice of cancellation or nonrenewal. Exhibit 5-1 shows a sample personal auto policy (PAP) declarations.

In addition to covering the named insured, most personal auto policies cover the named insured's family members and anyone driving the covered auto with the owner's permission (subject to certain exceptions). Consequently, if the insured allowed his neighbor to drive the insured auto one day, and the neighbor had an accident, the policy would cover the neighbor's damages because the owner gave permission for the neighbor to drive the auto.

EXHIBIT 5-1

Sample Personal Auto Policy Declarations

Personal Auto Policy Declarations

POLICYHOLDER: (Named Insured)	David M. and Joan G. Smith 216 Brookside Drive Anytown, USA 40000
POLICY NUMBER:	296 S 468211
POLICY PERIOD:	**FROM:** December 25, 20X0
	TO: June 25, 20X1

But only if the required premium for this period has been paid, and for six-month renewal periods if renewal premiums are paid as required. Each period begins and ends at 12:01 A.M. standard time at the address of the policyholder.

INSURED VEHICLES AND SCHEDULE OF COVERAGES

VEHICLE	COVERAGES	LIMITS OF INSURANCE		PREMIUM
1	2000 Ford Taurus	ID #1FABP3OU7GG212619		
	Coverage A—Liability	$ 300,000	**Each Occurrence**	$ 201
	Coverage B—Medical Payments	$ 5,000	**Each Person**	$ 36
	Coverage C—Uninsured Motorists	$ 300,000	**Each Occurrence**	$ 60
			TOTAL	$ 297
2	2004 Toyota Corolla	ID # JT2AL21E8B3306553		
	Coverage A—Liability	$ 300,000	**Each Occurrence**	$ 201
	Coverage B—Medical Payments	$ 5,000	**Each Person**	$ 36
	Coverage C—Uninsured Motorists	$ 300,000	**Each Occurrence**	$ 60
	Coverage D—Other Than Collision	Actual Cash Value Less $100		$ 40
	—Collision	Actual Cash Value Less $250		$ 230
			TOTAL	$ 567

POLICY FORM AND ENDORSEMENTS: PP 00 01, PP 03 06

COUNTERSIGNATURE DATE: December 1, 20X0

AGENT: A. M. Abel

The persons insured can vary by the type of auto coverage. For example, a PAP may have different definitions of "insured" for its APD coverage, medical payments coverage, and uninsured and underinsured motorists coverages. Auto policies define "insured" in terms of both the persons or entities insured and the autos insured. For example, if an insured rents an auto while on vacation and that auto is involved in an accident, the insured's auto policy might provide some coverage, as might the auto owner's (the rental firm's) policy.

The claim representative should determine whether the person or entity making an auto claim meets the definition of an insured according to the policy terms, and then determine whether coverage exists for the loss.

Automobile Physical Damage Coverages

Auto insurance policies provide first-party coverage called auto physical damage coverage to pay for damage to insureds' covered autos. **Auto physical damage (APD) coverage** is a coverage for damage to or theft of a covered auto that includes both collision coverage and other than collision (comprehensive) coverage. Policies define covered autos differently. For example, APD coverage in personal auto policies applies to autos listed in the declarations, some newly acquired autos, and certain nonowned autos. Business auto policies might cover one or more of several categories of autos, such as any auto, owned autos only, hired autos only, or nonowned autos only; therefore, claim representatives should check the policy to determine the types of autos covered by that policy.

Some insurers' policies provide APD coverage in the policy or coverage form without an endorsement. However, for APD coverage to apply, other insurers might require a policy endorsement to describe the persons or entities insured and the autos insured.

Claim representatives must verify that the auto listed in the loss notice is a covered auto under the policy terms. The auto for which a loss is reported must match an auto described in the declarations or must be a newly acquired covered auto, as specified in the policy terms. To verify that the auto matches the description, the claim representative should compare the vehicle identification number (VIN) of the auto listed in the loss notice to the VIN(s) listed in the declarations. If the numbers do not match, then further investigation is required. Additionally, auto manufacturers often stamp the VIN on various parts of the auto. When the VINs on the various parts do not match, the claim representative should investigate the reason.

Sometimes, fraud is indicated when the VINs do not match, or an incorrect VIN might be listed in error. As described in the box on the next page, the VIN indicates the exact make and model of an auto, along with other details. When the reported VIN does not match a covered auto and other fraud indicators are present, the claim representative might consult a physical damage appraiser who specializes in autos to help with the investigation. The appraiser will be able to decode the reported VIN and determine whether it is valid.

Once the claim representative has determined that the persons and vehicle involved in the accident are covered by the policy, the claim representative must determine whether coverage applies to the loss. As mentioned in previous chapters, when investigating coverage, claim representatives must consider all first-party coverages that might apply to the loss. Claim representatives must also determine whether a loss is covered under collision or other than collision (OTC) coverage. If the insured has selected specified causes of

---

Auto physical damage (APD) coverage

Coverage for damage to or theft of a covered auto that includes both collision coverage and other than collision (comprehensive) coverage.

loss, then the claim representative must verify that the loss is covered as one of those specified causes or coverage must be denied. Claim representatives must be familiar with the laws of the state where the accident occurred to determine how any conflicting coverages, such as medical payments and PIP coverage, should be resolved.

Decoding Vehicle Identification Numbers (VINs)

The VIN is made up of seventeen numbers and letters. The following is an example:
7M9HL32Y588456789.

The first three digits are the World Manufacturer Identifier, unless the manufacturer builds fewer than 500 vehicles per year. If the manufacturer builds fewer than 500 vehicles per year, the third digit is always a "9," and the digits in the twelfth, thirteenth, and fourteenth positions are used to identify the country and the manufacturer. Digits four through eight are the Vehicle Descriptor section. These digits are used by the manufacturer to identify various vehicle attributes. The digits are codes for body style, engine type, model, series, etc. The ninth digit is an accuracy check digit that is created by a mathematical formula. The last eight positions are the Vehicle Identifier section, the last four of which are always numeric. These digits are the identifier for the specific vehicle. They indicate the sequence of the vehicle in production when it came off the assembly line. If the vehicle manufacturer uses a year code, it will be in the tenth position. If the manufacturer uses a factory or plant code, it will be in the eleventh position. Because of the specific information contained in the VIN, it is useful for obtaining the proper replacement parts when the auto requires repair.

APD coverage often includes the following coverages:

- Collision coverage
- Other than collision or comprehensive, or specified causes of loss coverage
- Transportation coverage
- Towing and labor coverage

The first two coverages relate to the cause of loss—whether it was a collision or some other cause. The second two coverages pay additional costs related to the loss. Each of these coverages is described next.

Collision Coverage

The first type of APD coverage is collision coverage. Auto insurance policies provide **collision coverage** to pay for direct and accidental physical damage that occurs when a covered auto is upset and/or overturned or when a covered auto collides with another auto or object. Following are some examples of collision losses that many auto insurance policies can cover:

- An insured driver loses control, and the auto overturns.
- An insured driver loses control and drives into a tree.
- An insured auto that is parked is damaged when someone strikes it.

Collision coverage
Coverage for direct and accidental auto physical damage to a covered auto resulting from collision with another object or by overturn.

Insurers pay collision losses regardless of whether the insured or someone else caused the damage. When making a claim payment, the insurer subtracts the collision deductible (that is specified in the policy declarations) from the amount of the loss. If the insurer pays an insured for a loss under collision coverage and a party other than the insured is legally liable for the damage, the insurer tries to recover its loss payment and the insured's deductible from the responsible party through subrogation.

PAPs specify that some losses are not collision losses. PAPs provide coverage for those losses under another coverage called other than collision coverage or comprehensive coverage, or through specified causes of loss coverage.

Other Than Collision (OTC) or Comprehensive Coverage, or Specified Causes of Loss Coverage

Other than collision (OTC) coverage
Coverage for direct auto physical damage to a covered auto resulting from any cause of loss except collision or a cause of loss specifically excluded.

Comprehensive coverage
Coverage for direct auto physical damage to a covered auto under a commercial auto policy resulting from any cause of loss (except collision) or a cause of loss specifically excluded.

Another type of APD coverage is other than collision coverage. Many PAPs provide **other than collision (OTC) coverage**, which is a coverage for direct auto physical damage to a covered auto due to any cause of loss except collision or a cause of loss specifically excluded. Business auto policies often call this coverage **comprehensive coverage**. To simplify the discussion for the remainder of this chapter, the term OTC will mean either OTC or comprehensive coverage. OTC coverage is not usually specifically defined in the policies. Instead, some PAPs list a few examples of losses that are covered and state that OTC coverage applies to all non-excluded causes of loss other than collision. Business auto policies may not provide examples of covered causes of loss but instead state that the insurer will pay for losses from any cause except collision with another object or overturn; however, exclusions apply. Causes of loss that are typically covered as OTC include missiles or falling objects; fire; theft or larceny; explosion or earthquake; windstorm; hail, water, or flood; malicious mischief or vandalism; riot or civil commotion; contact with a bird or another animal; and glass breakage.

OTC coverage pays for damage resulting from all causes of loss, except collision, that are not excluded. For example, if an insured driver takes a bleeding person to the hospital in an insured auto, and blood stains the upholstery, OTC coverage would pay for that damage (if it exceeds the deductible). Although this kind of loss is unusual, the policy would cover it because it is not excluded. However, the policy excludes damage resulting from wear and tear, such as upholstery that the sun has faded or a window control motor that fails after many years of use.

Some insureds purchase OTC coverage but not collision coverage because collision coverage is more expensive, especially for young drivers and drivers who have had recent motor vehicle violations or auto accidents. Insurers generally offer a lower deductible for OTC coverage than for collision coverage, which can be an important factor in calculating glass breakage claims. For example, if the insured has only OTC coverage and an incident other than collision causes the windshield to break, the insurer will pay for glass breakage under that coverage and subtract the appropriate deductible. A high deductible might preclude claim payment for a new windshield. If glass breakage results from a collision, the insured can elect to claim the glass damage under collision coverage, and then only the collision deductible applies. In that case, no separate OTC deductible would apply.

Under some business auto policies, insureds can purchase **specified causes of loss coverage** as another option. Specified causes of loss coverage pays only for damages that result from the causes of loss specified in the policy. This coverage usually includes the more common causes of loss that are usually covered by other than collision coverage.

Specified causes of loss coverage
Coverage for damage resulting from fire, lightning, theft, windstorm, hail, earthquake, flood, vandalism, and other specifically listed causes of loss.

Transportation Coverage

Another type of APD coverage is transportation coverage. Personal and business auto policies provide limited coverage for transportation expenses in several situations. For example, under a PAP, if the insured's auto is damaged in a collision, the policy pays up to a stated limit for auto rental fees, taxi fares, or other replacement transportation expenses. If the loss results from theft, special time limits apply, and the insured's duties must be met to help establish that the theft actually occurred, when it occurred, and under what circumstances. Claim representatives must read the policy provisions to properly evaluate available transportation coverages.

Towing and Labor Coverage

A final type of APD coverage is towing and labor coverage. Towing and labor coverage might be included in the PAP, or an endorsement might be required for the coverage to apply. Towing and labor coverage pays a small amount of the costs for labor at the site of the disablement (such as the labor to jump-start a battery) and of the expenses of moving a disabled auto from the place of disablement. The coverage provides a low limit, such as $25, $50, or $75.

Towing and labor coverage is often included in business auto policies without a separate endorsement when the insured pays an additional premium for the coverage. In those policies, the coverage is described in the APD coverage section.

In summary, claim representatives handling auto physical damage claims should check the policy definition of an "auto" and determine whether the vehicle involved in the accident fits that definition. They should next determine whether the damage is covered under collision, OTC, or specified causes of loss coverage, and determine whether transportation and towing and labor coverages apply. The claim representative should also determine whether other first-party coverages apply to the loss, as described in the following section.

Other First-Party Coverages

In addition to including the APD coverages, auto insurance policies might provide medical payments coverage. **Medical payments coverage** pays medical expenses for the named insured, family members, and others who are injured as a result of an accident while occupying a covered auto. The policy defines "occupying" broadly so that it covers injuries for people getting into or out of the covered auto. For example, if a child's hand is shut in the car door and requires medical treatment, this coverage pays the related medical expenses. Medical payments coverage provides payment for medical and funeral expenses regardless of who is responsible for the injury. Some exclusions apply to medical payments coverage.

Medical payments coverage
An optional accident benefit that pays for reasonable and necessary medical expenses incurred by persons who are injured as a result of an accident, while occupying a covered auto, regardless of legal liability.

Medical payments coverage is generally included under a specific section of a PAP, but business auto policies often require an endorsement to provide medical payments coverage. This coverage defines insureds differently from other coverages within the same policy. As always, claim representatives should read the policy carefully to verify coverage.

Exclusions

All first-party coverages in personal and business auto policies have exclusions; these policies are not intended to cover every loss exposure. Exclusions can serve several purposes, as presented in the first chapter. Some loss exposures are more appropriately covered by other policies, such as a homeowners or a workers' compensation policy. Therefore, exclusions eliminate coverage for those loss exposures. Exclusions can also eliminate coverage for uninsurable causes of loss, such as wear and tear, nuclear disaster, or war. Finally, exclusions sometimes eliminate coverage for unusual exposures; insureds who need coverage for those exposures can add it by endorsement. These exclusions help reduce the premium that the insurer would otherwise have to charge to cover those unusual exposures. A partial list of exclusions under some of the first-party auto coverages is shown in Exhibit 5-2.

Conditions

Policy conditions describe the insured's duties after a loss and contain general provisions that apply to the entire policy. Conditions are similar among auto policies. For example, one common provision states that the insured must notify the insurer promptly when an accident has occurred and cooperate with the insurer in the accident investigation. General provisions also specify the policy period and territory, and some provisions describe what happens if the insured becomes bankrupt or commits fraud. Conditions can affect losses by eliminating coverage if the insured does not comply with those provisions.

EXHIBIT 5-2

Partial List of Exclusions for First-Party Auto Coverages

Coverage	Exclusion	Purpose
Collision	Damage caused by fire, theft, hail, and vandalism	Likelihood of coverage duplication reduced—covered under OTC
Collision, OTC, comprehensive, and specified causes of loss coverage	Damage caused by wear and tear, road damage to tires, and freezing	Uninsurable loss exposures—normal deterioration and exposure to weather
	Damage caused by war or radioactive contamination	Uninsurable loss exposures—war and pollution
Medical payments	Bodily injury sustained while occupying any auto while competing in organized races	Special treatment (such as special underwriting and rating) required for coverage

Endorsements

As described in the first chapter, endorsements can add to, delete, replace, or otherwise modify coverages that exist in a policy. Claim representatives should be familiar with the following common endorsements that provide additional coverages and that can affect APD claims:

- Personal Injury Protection (PIP)
- Uninsured motorists (UM) and underinsured motorists (UIM)
- Customizing equipment
- Electronic equipment

Some of these endorsements, such as for PIP, UM, and UIM coverages, may be required by state laws. PIP coverage replaces other coverages in personal auto policies when the endorsement is added. The following sections describe the coverage that each of these endorsements provides and any limitations that apply.

Personal Injury Protection (PIP)

One common first-party coverage endorsement is personal injury protection. **Personal injury protection (PIP) coverage** provides medical expenses, income loss, and other benefits to the insured and auto occupants for bodily

Personal injury protection (PIP) coverage
Coverage for medical expenses, income loss, and other benefits stipulated in an auto no-fault plan.

injuries sustained in covered auto accidents in an auto no-fault state, subject to specified coverage limits. In some states, most injured parties seek medical benefits from their own PIP coverage, except any party who is uninsured. An uninsured passenger injured in an auto accident could seek medical benefits from the PIP coverage applicable to the auto. PIP coverage varies by state but usually includes payment for the following:

- Medical expenses, including rehabilitation
- Funeral and burial expenses
- Loss of income up to a percentage of the insured's wages
- Loss of services, such as child care, household cleaning, or home maintenance
- Survivor's loss of the deceased's income and the services that the deceased would have provided

PIP coverage pays regardless of who was at fault in the accident. Many states have laws that either require auto owners to carry PIP coverage or require insurers to offer optional PIP coverage to all drivers. Other states do not have PIP coverage and generally use medical payments coverage to pay first-party bodily injury claims for insureds and to provide the first payment for bodily injury claims of other persons in the covered auto (depending on liability, bodily injury liability might cover the remaining costs above the medical payments limits). State laws that require PIP coverage might restrict the rights of injured drivers, passengers, and pedestrians to sue for certain injuries.

In states requiring PIP, personal or business auto policyholders must purchase a PIP endorsement to add this coverage. Because state law prescribes what losses are covered under PIP, these endorsements are state-specific.

PIP endorsements contain several exclusions, such as payment to any insured who intentionally caused a bodily injury. The insured must fulfill specific duties, such as cooperating in the investigation and submitting a written proof of loss if the insurer requests one. Claim representatives subtract a PIP deductible from any loss payments, if a deductible is specified in the endorsement.

Claim representatives must be familiar with PIP coverages in the states where they handle claims. They must also understand how the PIP coverage relates to other policy coverages and be knowledgeable about medical terminology, medical treatments, and medical billing codes. Therefore, PIP claim representative is usually a specialized position.

Uninsured Motorists (UM) and Underinsured Motorists (UIM)

Uninsured motorists (UM) coverage
Coverage for medical expenses, income loss, and other benefits stipulated for an insured who is injured in an auto accident by an uninsured motorists; also covers property damage in some states.

Underinsured motorists (UIM) coverage
Coverage for medical expenses, income loss, and other benefits stipulated for an insured who is injured in an auto accident caused by a negligent driver when that driver has liability insurance at the time of the accident but has limits lower than those of the victim's coverage.

Two other common first-party coverage endorsements are uninsured motorists coverage and underinsured motorists coverage. **Uninsured motorists (UM) coverage** and **underinsured motorists (UIM) coverage** protect insureds if they are injured by uninsured or underinsured drivers, respectively, who were responsible for the damages, subject to specified coverage limits. UM and UIM coverages protect insureds against the following losses:

- Medical expenses, including rehabilitation
- Funeral and burial expenses
- Loss of income up to a percentage of the insured's wages
- Loss of services, such as child care, household cleaning, or home maintenance
- Survivor's loss of the deceased's income and the services that the deceased would have provided
- Pain and suffering
- Loss of enjoyment of life
- Inconvenience

UM and UIM coverages are available because some drivers do not have auto insurance and some drivers are insured but do not purchase limits high enough to pay for all of the damages incurred in an accident. UM coverage also applies in hit-and-run accidents because the responsible person and his or her insurer (if the person is insured) are unknown and cannot cover the loss. Some states require these coverages, and others give insureds the option to purchase them.

Insurers generally provide UM coverage as a separate coverage in a PAP but add the coverage by endorsement to business auto policies at the insured's request. Insurers can generally add UIM coverage to both personal and business auto policies when the insured requests it. In some states, insurers provide one endorsement that includes both coverages and that replaces any UM coverage portion of a PAP.

As with PIP endorsements, UM and UIM coverages contain several exclusions, such as payment to any party who uses an auto without a reasonable belief that he or she is entitled to use it. Also, the insured must fulfill specific duties. Because UM and UIM coverages vary by state, claim representatives should be familiar with state requirements where they handle auto claims.

Customizing Equipment

Another common first-party coverage endorsement is coverage for customizing equipment. If an insured owns a van with awnings, height-extending roofs, sleeping facilities, or furnishings, the insured might purchase a customizing equipment endorsement to add coverage for that equipment to the PAP. Similarly, the insured might purchase this endorsement with a PAP to cover special carpeting, cooking facilities, or custom decals or graphics that might be applied to a van or pickup truck.

Damage to custom equipment is excluded in some PAPs, so insureds can purchase this endorsement to add coverage for it. Customizing equipment is not excluded in some business auto policies; therefore, customizing equipment coverage applies in those policies without adding an endorsement.

Electronic Equipment

Another common first-party coverage endorsement is electronic equipment. Personal and business auto policies exclude coverage for a variety of electronic equipment and media, such as tapes and compact discs used with that equipment. However, an insured can purchase an electronic equipment endorsement to add limited coverage to a PAP for such equipment and media.

Claim representatives who handle auto first-party claims should be familiar with these common types of policy provisions and coverages so that they can skillfully handle such claims. Once coverage has been identified for the claim, the claim representative can handle the claim following the process described in previous chapters. The next section examines auto physical damage losses in relation to the extent of damage to the auto.

AUTOMOBILE PHYSICAL DAMAGE LOSSES

As with all claims, claim representatives who handle APD losses begin their investigation with the loss notice and then perform the activities in the claim-handling process. Exhibit 5-3 shows an ACORD Automobile Loss Notice that insurers use to establish an auto claim and that claim representatives use as the basis of their coverage determination and loss investigation for APD and auto liability losses.

Because values are significant for new autos and depreciate rapidly in a short time, and because the popularity of owning autos in most parts of the U.S. creates a broad market for new and used autos, claim representatives must learn special terminology and practices for determining the value of APD claims. APD losses can be partial losses or total losses, and claim representatives must consider factors that apply to each. Additionally, claim representatives should consider diminished value losses in some jurisdictions. Partial losses, total losses, and diminished value losses are examined in this section.

Partial Losses

OEM part
A new vehicle part that is made by the vehicle's original equipment manufacturer.

Aftermarket part
A new vehicle part that is made by a manufacturer other than the vehicle manufacturer.

LKQ part
A vehicle part that is taken from a salvage yard and that is of like kind and quality to the original part.

The first type of APD loss is a partial loss. Most APD claims are for partial losses. In a partial loss, the damage can be repaired or the parts replaced without exceeding the auto's value. For example, a front-end collision on a newer car is usually a partial loss. The bumper, the headlight assemblies, the radiator, the fan blades, and the hood might need to be repaired or replaced, but the cost to repair or replace them is less than the auto's value.

When auto parts are damaged and need to be replaced instead of repaired, claim representatives have several options for replacing them. However, they should be aware of the insurer's guidelines and state laws regarding the use of certain types of parts. Claim representatives can use new parts from the original equipment manufacturer (**OEM parts**), new parts from another parts supplier (**aftermarket parts**), used parts of like kind and quality (**LKQ parts**)

EXHIBIT 5-3

ACORD Automobile Loss Notice

ACORD® — AUTOMOBILE LOSS NOTICE

DATE (MM/DD/YYYY)
12/01/20X0

AGENCY	PHONE (A/C, No, Ext): 610-555-1010	COMPANY	NAIC CODE:	MISCELLANEOUS INFO (Site & location code)

Tim Stevens

Danford Insurance

POLICY NUMBER	POLICY TYPE	REFERENCE NUMBER	CAT #

FAX (A/C, No):	E-MAIL ADDRESS:
CODE: 66 729	SUB CODE:
AGENCY CUSTOMER ID:	

EFFECTIVE DATE	EXPIRATION DATE	DATE OF ACCIDENT AND TIME	AM	PREVIOUSLY REPORTED
11-1-X0	5-1-X1	11-15-X0 4	X PM	YES X NO

INSURED   CONTACT   CONTACT INSURED

NAME AND ADDRESS SOC SEC # OR FEIN: 111-11-1111	NAME AND ADDRESS	WHERE TO CONTACT
Larry Michaels 11 Street Anytown, PA 19355	Same	
		WHEN TO CONTACT

RESIDENCE PHONE (A/C, No) 610-555-6161	BUSINESS PHONE (A/C, No, Ext) 555-7777	RESIDENCE PHONE (A/C, No)	BUSINESS PHONE (A/C, No, Ext)

LOSS

LOCATION OF ACCIDENT (Include city & state) 55 Street, Anytown, PA	AUTHORITY CONTACTED:	VIOLATIONS/CITATIONS
	REPORT #:	

DESCRIPTION OF ACCIDENT (Use separate sheet, if necessary)   Lost control on slick pavement and hit a concrete barrier.

POLICY INFORMATION

BODILY INJURY (Per Person)	BODILY INJURY (Per Accident)	PROPERTY DAMAGE	SINGLE LIMIT	MEDICAL PAYMENT	OTC DEDUCTIBLE	OTHER COVERAGE & DEDUCTIBLES (UM, no-fault, towing, etc)
					$250	

LOSS PAYEE none	COLLISION DED $500

UMBRELLA/ EXCESS	UMBRELLA	EXCESS	CARRIER:	LIMITS:	AGGR	PER CLAIM/OCC	SIR/ DED

INSURED VEHICLE

VEH #	YEAR	MAKE: Chevrolet	BODY TYPE: 4 door	PLATE NUMBER	STATE
1	2004	MODEL:	V.I.N.: IVIVIVIVIVIVIVIVIV		PA

OWNER'S NAME & ADDRESS Same	RESIDENCE PHONE (A/C, No): BUSINESS PHONE (A/C, No, Ext):
DRIVER'S NAME & ADDRESS X (Check if same as owner)	RESIDENCE PHONE (A/C, No): BUSINESS PHONE (A/C, No, Ext):

RELATION TO INSURED (Employee, family, etc.) Same	DATE OF BIRTH	DRIVER'S LICENSE NUMBER	STATE	PURPOSE OF USE	USED WITH PERMISSION? YES NO

DESCRIBE DAMAGE Rt front	ESTIMATE AMOUNT	WHERE CAN VEHICLE BE SEEN? with insured	WHEN CAN VEH BE SEEN?	OTHER INSURANCE ON VEHICLE no

PROPERTY DAMAGED   VEHICLE?   [ ] YES   [ ] NO

DESCRIBE PROPERTY (If auto, year, make, model, plate #) none	OTHER VEH/PROP INS? [ ] YES [ ] NO	COMPANY OR AGENCY NAME: POLICY #:
OWNER'S NAME & ADDRESS		RESIDENCE PHONE (A/C, No): BUSINESS PHONE (A/C, No, Ext):
OTHER DRIVER'S NAME & ADDRESS (Check if same as owner)		RESIDENCE PHONE (A/C, No): BUSINESS PHONE (A/C, No, Ext):

DESCRIBE DAMAGE	ESTIMATE AMOUNT	WHERE CAN DAMAGE BE SEEN?

INJURED

NAME & ADDRESS	PHONE (A/C, No)	PED	INS VEH	OTH VEH	AGE	EXTENT OF INJURY
none						

WITNESSES OR PASSENGERS

NAME & ADDRESS	PHONE (A/C, No)	INS VEH	OTH VEH	OTHER (Specify)
none				

REMARKS (Include adjuster assigned)

REPORTED BY Larry Michaels	REPORTED TO Tim Stevens	SIGNATURE OF INSURED	SIGNATURE OF PRODUCER Tim Stevens

ACORD 2 (2004/06)   NOTE: IMPORTANT STATE INFORMATION ON REVERSE SIDE   © ACORD CORPORATION 1988

Reman part
A vehicle part that has been reconditioned or remanufactured.

from a salvage yard, or remanufactured parts (**reman parts**) that have been used and reconditioned. Some state laws require the use of OEM parts on newer autos.

Once the claim representative determines what parts need to be repaired or replaced, the value of the partial loss can be determined in any of the following ways:

- An appraiser can prepare a detailed loss estimate.
- The insured can obtain competitive loss estimates from auto repair facilities.
- The insured can take the auto to preferred repair facilities that are insurer-approved.
- The claim representative can prepare a loss estimate.

One way to determine the value of a partial loss is through appraisal. Appraisers inspect damage to autos and prepare repair estimates. Appraisers might work in a drive-in claim center or travel to the auto's location to prepare the estimate. Also, the appraiser might locate an auto repair facility that is willing to repair the damage for the amount of the appraiser's estimate.

Another way to determine the value of a partial loss is through competitive estimates. An insured might obtain estimates from one or more auto repair facilities and submit those estimates to the claim representative. Some insurers have guidelines stating when competitive estimates can be accepted without an on-site inspection. Claim representatives should check each of the estimates against repair manuals to verify that parts and labor prices have been calculated correctly.

Another way to determine the value of a partial loss is through preferred (or direct) repair facilities. Some insurers have developed relationships with certain auto repair facilities to have auto physical damage losses repaired without requiring a claim representative to inspect the damage. For example, windshield breakage claims might be handled by a national chain of windshield repair facilities, making it easy for the insured to replace a windshield no matter where the accident occurred and without the insurer inspecting the damage. These facilities are sometimes called direct repair facilities when an insurer has given advance approval for them to perform the repair work. This arrangement might involve the repair firm completing the estimate and transmitting it to the insurer, who then pays the repair facility directly. The insured pays the appropriate deductible to the repair facility. This approach contrasts with the traditional claim payment in which the insurer issues a check to the insured, who then pays the repair facility.

A claim representative might negotiate with auto repair facilities about the appropriate repair method or the extent of damage caused by the accident. For example, if an auto has preexisting damage, a repair estimate might include fixing that damage in addition to the newer damage caused from the reported accident. However, claim representatives can ask repair facilities to estimate the cost of repairing only the new damage, so the insurer pays only for damage related to the accident under investigation.

Another way for claim representatives or appraisers to determine the value of a partial APD loss is through automated estimating software and crash manuals. Estimating software simplifies preparation of the estimate. However, the appraiser and the claim representative must still know which parts need to be replaced and which can be repaired.

If estimating software is not available, another way for appraisers or claim representatives to determine the value of a partial APD loss is by preparing an estimate manually using repair manuals, often called crash manuals. A crash manual describes auto parts and their costs, the amount of labor required to repair or replace parts, and the labor costs.

Claim representatives might use a combination of ways to determine the value of a partial loss, documenting the ways used so that a review of the claim file can determine proper claim handling. To clarify and justify the proposed loss settlement for the insured, claim representatives explain the ways used to determine the value. In some cases, the claim representative might discover through the determination of value that the cost to repair or replace the damaged parts exceeds the value of the auto. Such a loss is called a total loss, described next.

Total Losses

The second type of APD loss is a total loss. An accident or other causes of physical damage (such as hail damage) could result in a total loss, which occurs when the cost to repair the damaged vehicle equals or exceeds its value, or they could result in a constructive total loss, which occurs when a damaged vehicle cannot be repaired for less than its actual cash value minus the anticipated salvage value.

A total loss can result from several events, including the following:
- A stolen auto is not recovered.
- The loss estimate equals or exceeds the auto's actual cash value (ACV).
- The loss estimate and loss of use equal or exceed the auto's pre-loss ACV less salvage value. This results in a constructive total loss. For example, if repairs cannot be completed for several weeks and the auto cannot be driven, necessitating use of a rental auto, the claim representative should add the auto rental cost to the pre-loss ACV and deduct the salvage value to determine whether the loss is total.

The claim representative determines the value of a total loss by determining the auto's ACV and subtracting salvage value, as described in the previous chapter.

Diminished Value Losses

Claim representatives should consider claims for diminished value losses in jurisdictions in which they are recognized. When an auto has been repaired following a partial loss, some jurisdictions have held that the value of the repaired auto is diminished. **Diminished value losses** are defined in some policies as the real or perceived loss in market or resale value that results from a direct and accidental loss.

Diminished value loss
The real or perceived loss in market or resale value that results from a direct and accidental loss.

Some policies contain endorsements specifically stating that the insurer will not pay for any loss resulting from diminished value, following a direct and accidental loss. However, many courts have heard cases regarding claims for diminished value, but no consensus has been reached. Among states, courts have differed regarding whether diminished value should be paid as part of a loss. Decisions about diminished value are complicated, and even repair firms often cannot agree whether a repaired vehicle has lost some of its value after a good-quality repair has been made. Because diminished value on first-party claims is a contested topic, claim representatives should consult legal counsel for the status on diminished value losses in the jurisdictions where they handle them.

In summary, claim representatives evaluate the extent of the damages and other factors to determine whether an auto loss is partial or total and whether diminished value should be considered. The next section examines forms of dispute resolution that are common for APD claims.

COMMON FORMS OF DISPUTE RESOLUTION FOR AUTOMOBILE PHYSICAL DAMAGE CLAIMS

Claim representatives who handle APD claims should be aware of the common forms of dispute resolution. Insurers prefer certain forms of dispute resolution for different types of claims. They favor negotiation as the primary tool for all types of claims, but when insurers and insureds cannot agree on a settlement value on APD claims, appraisal or forms of alternative dispute resolution (ADR) are sometimes required to avoid litigation.

When negotiation fails in APD claims, a claim representative or an insured might request an appraisal, as provided in the auto policy appraisal provision, to resolve differences. In an appraisal, each party selects a competent appraiser, and the appraisers select a third appraiser to serve as umpire. The two appraisers compare their estimates and, if they cannot agree on the loss amount, they consult the umpire for a third appraisal. If two of the three appraisers agree on an amount, the decision is binding.

In some cases, arbitration or mediation may be used as other alternatives; for example, when the appraisers cannot agree on the loss amount. Similarly, the claim may result in litigation; however, litigation is rarely required to settle first-party auto physical damage claims.

In summary, the previous chapter provided an extensive explanation of APD claim investigation, and this chapter discusses the coverages that a claim representative must investigate for a first-party auto claim. Exhibit 5-4 presents a case that illustrates these concepts through a claim representative's handling an automobile first-party physical damage claim. This exhibit encapsulates topics presented in both this and the previous chapter.

EXHIBIT 5-4

Automobile First-Party Physical Damage Claim

Larry Michaels was driving down a highway when he lost control of his auto on the slippery road surface. He hit a concrete divider, damaging the left front fender, headlight, turn signal, and front bumper and cracking the windshield. Larry's auto could still be driven, so he drove home and called his insurance agent, Tim Stevens. Tim noted that Larry's personal auto policy with Danford Insurance had collision and OTC coverage, so Tim completed an electronic automobile loss notice and transmitted it to Danford.

Danford acknowledged the new claim in its computer system, which set an average reserve for the collision loss. A supervisor assigned the claim to Sophie Matthews and sent the claim file to her. Sophie checked Larry's policy in Danford's policy administration system to ensure that the policy was in force and that it covered the auto shown on the loss notice. Sophie noted that Larry had a $500 collision deductible and a $250 OTC deductible. Because the glass damage was caused by a collision, it can be paid under the collision coverage, so Larry will not have to pay two separate deductibles. Danford Insurance does not have a drive-in claim center, so Sophie called Larry to verify the details of the accident and to arrange a time to inspect the auto. Sophie documented her conversation in the claim file activity log.

When Sophie inspected the damaged auto, she checked the VIN to ensure that it matched the VIN of the insured auto. She inspected the auto and noted its overall condition, and then she photographed the damaged and undamaged areas. Next, Sophie prepared an estimate using estimating software on her laptop computer. Larry wanted to have an auto repair facility inspect the damage before he accepted any settlement. Sophie uploaded her estimate from her laptop to the electronic claim file, documented her investigation in the activity log, and modified the system-generated diary entry to alert her in one week if Larry had not contacted her. If Larry contacted her within that week, Sophie would delete the diary entry.

Larry drove his auto to the repair facility and obtained a damage estimate. Larry sent the estimate to Sophie, who compared the two estimates. Sophie called the repair facility to resolve some minor differences in the estimates. Sophie then called Larry to explain how the differences had been resolved. Larry was pleased and agreed to the settlement amount. Sophie subtracted the $500 collision deductible and issued a check to Larry for the settlement amount. After completing her notes in the activity log, Sophie closed the claim file.

SUMMARY

Auto insurance protects policyholders from the financial losses that they might suffer as the result of covered auto accidents. Auto insurance typically includes auto physical damage (APD) coverage, auto liability coverage, and coverage for other financial losses (such as limited medical, funeral, and rehabilitation costs and lost income).

Auto insurance policies identify insureds, the coverage provided, exclusions, and the conditions that the insured and insurer must satisfy for auto first-party coverage to apply. APD coverage often includes collision, other than collision coverage (also called comprehensive) or specified causes of loss coverage, transportation coverage, and towing and labor coverage. Some policies include medical payments coverage as another first-party coverage.

Endorsements can add to, delete, replace, or otherwise modify coverages that exist in a policy. Common endorsements that provide additional auto first-party coverage include Personal Injury Protection (PIP), uninsured motorists (UM) and underinsured motorists (UIM), customizing equipment, and electronic equipment.

Claim representatives can encounter special issues regarding auto first-party claims, including auto coverage issues and APD loss issues. They must also be aware of the common forms of dispute resolution for APD claims. Claim representatives must verify that the driver and other first-party claimants are insured under the policy, that the auto is covered by the policy, and that coverage exists for the loss. Auto physical damage losses can be partial or total, and certain considerations apply to each. Additionally, diminished value losses should be considered in jurisdictions in which they are recognized. Claim representatives and insureds typically resolve first-party APD claim disputes through negotiation. If negotiation fails, claim representatives and insureds might request appraisals to resolve disputes. Parties might also use arbitration, mediation, and litigation as other, less common options for dispute resolution.

This chapter helps claim personnel understand the policy provisions and coverages that affect auto first-party losses and explains the types of APD losses and the dispute resolution methods commonly used for APD claims. The next chapter examines first-party property claims. It describes the coverages and provisions of property policies, first-party property claim issues, catastrophe claim-handling issues, and specialty property claims. Knowledge of these topics assists claim representatives in investigating and determining property coverages and in settling first-party property claims.

Chapter 6

Direct Your Learning

First-Party Property Claims

After learning the content of this chapter and completing the corresponding course guide assignment, you should be able to:

■ List the various persons or organizations and interests that might be insured under a property policy.

■ Describe what is covered, what is not covered, and what limitations apply under the following property coverages:
  - Buildings and other structures or premises
  - Personal property
  - Loss of use and business income coverages

■ Distinguish between the coverage provided by:
  - Special form coverage and specified perils coverage in homeowners insurance
  - Basic, broad, and special causes of loss forms

■ Identify four reasons why exclusions are included in first-party property coverages, and illustrate such exclusions.

■ Explain why a claim representative must understand the conditions and optional coverages in property insurance policies.

■ Summarize the coverage provided by property insurance endorsements that claim representatives frequently encounter.

■ Describe the first-party property claim considerations involved in the loss amount and the statement of loss.

■ Explain what common forms of dispute resolution are used for first-party property claims and when they are used.

■ Describe catastrophe claim-handling issues.

■ Summarize the coverage and claim considerations for the following areas in which claim representatives can specialize: crop insurance, inland marine insurance, ocean marine insurance, and crime insurance.

■ Define or describe each of the Key Words and Phrases for this chapter.

Develop Your Perspective

What are the main topics covered in the chapter?

This chapter describes the coverage relating to homeowners and commercial property first-party losses. It also describes first-party property claim-handling issues such as how to determine the loss amount and how to prepare a statement of loss. The chapter examines issues involved with handling catastrophe claims and ends with an overview of selected specialty property coverages in which claim representatives might want to specialize.

Review a homeowners or a commercial policy.

- Who is insured under the policy?
- What first-party causes of loss are covered under this policy? Where did you find this information?

Why is it important to learn about these topics?

To effectively handle property claims, claim representatives must understand the various sections of property policies and the way coverage is provided or excluded. They must also understand the effect of any additional or optional coverages, conditions, or endorsements. Claim representatives must examine all of the facts when determining loss amounts and must be able to complete a statement of loss. They should understand how catastrophe claim handling differs from typical claim handling and be aware of specialty claim areas that present alternate career paths.

Examine a property policy that your organization uses.

- What types of first-party property damage losses would your organization decline to cover based on the policy provisions?
- Which policy provisions would support the decision to decline those losses?

How can you use what you will learn?

Analyze a property damage claim.

- What coverage issues are documented in the claim file?
- Did valued policy laws or debris removal and other additional coverages affect the loss determination? If so, in what ways?

Chapter 6

First-Party Property Claims

Property owners suffer many types of damages attributable to house fires, burglaries, hurricanes or tornados, and other causes of loss. Property owners will often protect themselves from the financial loss associated with these types of damage by purchasing property insurance. Those who have purchased appropriate property insurance coverages can recoup their losses and then repair or rebuild their property after a loss.

This chapter begins by describing first-party homeowners and commercial policy provisions that relate to buildings and personal property and explains the claim-handling implications of these provisions. Property claim representatives must understand the various coverage provisions in order to handle claims properly. The coverage discussion is broadly based on general homeowners and business property policies because different insurers may use different wording in their policies. The chapter continues with a description of first-party property claim considerations. A case study demonstrates how a claim representative would handle a first-party property claim. Next, the chapter describes catastrophe claim handling, and it ends with a description of specialty property coverages.

Property insurance policies distinguish between **real property** and **personal property** because they are usually valued differently in the policy. Generally, land and anything attached to land or embedded in it are considered real property. All other tangible and intangible property is personal property. Personal property, or contents, includes furniture, most machinery, merchandise, and personal effects. Although the land itself is not insurable, buildings and all of the construction materials and elements incorporated into and attached to them are, as is personal property contained in or near buildings.

Most real and personal property losses are **direct losses**, meaning that a reduction in value of the property is the direct consequence of an insured cause of loss, such as fire, lightning, or hail. The same causes of loss can produce indirect losses. An **indirect loss** is a loss arising out of an insured's inability to use property that was damaged by another peril. For example, when a fire severely damages a home, the family might incur rental housing or hotel expenses until their home has been repaired. Loss of use of the home is an indirect loss. A business might suffer an indirect loss when it incurs extra expenses to temporarily relocate or when it loses income while damage is repaired. In some cases, an indirect loss can exceed the value of the direct loss.

Real property
Land, buildings, and other structures attached to the land or embedded in it.

Personal property
All tangible or intangible property that is not real property.

Direct loss
A reduction in the value of property that results directly, and often immediately, from damage to that property.

Indirect loss
A loss arising out of an insured's inability to use property that was damaged by another peril.

Insurance policies that contain first-party property coverages promise to pay (1) direct losses, including the costs to repair or replace buildings and personal property identified in the policy, and (2) indirect losses, including extra expenses that insureds incur because their property was damaged by an insured cause of loss. Policies that provide coverage for first-party property losses include the following:

- Homeowners policies
- Watercraft policies
- Inland marine policies
- Boiler and machinery policies
- Commercial property package policies
- Aircraft policies
- Ocean marine policies
- Builders' risk policies

Some policies are called package policies, meaning that they contain several coverages. Homeowners policies are package policies because they provide property and liability coverages. Insurers provide commercial package policies that include both property and liability insurance in the policy, as well as stand-alone property policies. Commercial property policies and commercial package policies can include a variety of coverages, and specific conditions and provisions can apply to each coverage. This chapter focuses on the real and personal property coverage sections of homeowners policies and commercial property policies, and it includes sections that apply to both types of policies. The liability coverage in the homeowners policy and in the commercial general liability policy is discussed in the next chapter.

COVERAGE PROVIDED FOR FIRST-PARTY PROPERTY LOSSES

To determine whether coverage applies to a loss, claim representatives must understand the sections of and attachments to homeowners and commercial property policies. Claim representatives must understand which sections of various policies apply to first-party property claims. Exhibit 6-1 outlines the structure of the property coverage provisions in a homeowners policy.

Homeowners and the various commercial property policies generally include declarations that list the applicable coverage forms. To illustrate the difference in the information contained on the various declarations pages, Exhibit 6-2 shows a homeowners declarations page, and Exhibit 6-3 shows a commercial property declarations page.

One obvious difference is that the homeowners policy shows the insured premises in the mailing address area. The commercial property policy lists the locations that are covered by the policy separately from the mailing address. Another difference is that commercial property policies include specific property coverages and conditions through forms that become part of the policy.

In the homeowners policy, most property coverages and conditions are contained within the policy. For example, in the commercial declarations shown in Exhibit 6-3, form CP 00 10 describes the building and personal property coverages included in the package policy, and form CP 00 90 describes commercial property conditions.

EXHIBIT 6-1

Outline of Common Homeowners Coverages

AGREEMENT (applicable to entire policy)

DEFINITIONS (applicable to entire policy)

SECTION I—PROPERTY COVERAGES

    Coverage A—Dwelling

    Coverage B—Other Structures

    Coverage C—Personal Property

        Special Limits of Liability (applicable to Coverage C)

        Property Not Covered (applicable to Coverage C)

    Coverage D—Loss of Use

    Additional Coverages

SECTION I—PERILS INSURED AGAINST

    Coverage A—Dwelling and Coverage B—Other Structures ("all-risks" coverage except for listed exclusions)

    Coverage C—Personal Property (specified perils)

SECTION I—EXCLUSIONS (applicable to Coverages A, B, C, D, and the Additional Coverages)

SECTION I—CONDITIONS (applicable to Coverages A, B, C, D, and the Additional Coverages)

SECTION II—LIABILITY COVERAGES

    Coverage E—Personal Liability

    Coverage F—Medical Payments to Others

SECTION II—EXCLUSIONS

    Coverages E and F

    Coverage E

    Coverage F

SECTION II—ADDITIONAL COVERAGES

SECTION II—CONDITIONS

Includes copyrighted material of Insurance Services Office, Inc. with its permission. Copyright ISO Properties, Inc., 2000. Homeowners 3—Special Form HO 00 03 05 01.

EXHIBIT 6-2

HO-3 Declarations

Homeowners Policy Declarations

POLICYHOLDER: David M. and Joan G. Smith   **POLICY NUMBER:**   296 H 578661
(Named Insured)   216 Brookside Drive
                          Anytown, USA 40000

POLICY PERIOD: **Inception:**   March 30, 20X0   Policy period begins 12:01 A.M. standard time
                          Expiration: March 30, 20X1   at the residence premises.

FIRST MORTGAGEE AND MAILING ADDRESS:

Federal National Mortgage Assn.
C/O Mortgagee, Inc.
P.O. Box 5000
Businesstown, USA 55000

We will provide the insurance described in this policy in return for the premium and compliance with all applicable policy provisions.

SECTION I COVERAGES	LIMIT	
A—Dwelling	$ 200,000	**SECTION I DEDUCTIBLE:** $ 500
B—Other Structures	$ 20,000	**(In case of loss under Section I, we cover**
C—Personal Property	$ 100,000	**only that part of the loss over the**
D—Loss of Use	$ 40,000	**deductible amount shown above.)**

SECTION II COVERAGES	LIMIT	
E—Personal Liability	$ 500,000	**Each Occurrence**
F—Medical Payments to Others	$ 2,000	**Each Person**

CONSTRUCTION: Masonry Veneer   **NO. FAMILIES:** One   **TYPE ROOF:** Approved

YEAR BUILT: 1990   **PROTECTION CLASS:** 7   **FIRE DISTRICT:** Cook Township

NOT MORE THAN 1000 FEET FROM HYDRANT

NOT MORE THAN 5 MILES FROM FIRE DEPT.

FORMS AND ENDORSEMENTS IN POLICY: HO 00 03, HO 04 61

POLICY PREMIUM: $ 550.00   **COUNTERSIGNATURE DATE:** March 1, 20X0   **AGENT:** A.M. Abel

EXHIBIT 6-3

BPP Declarations

COMMERCIAL PROPERTY
CP DS 00 10 00

COMMERCIAL PROPERTY COVERAGE PART
DECLARATIONS PAGE

POLICY NO. SP 0001   EFFECTIVE DATE 10 / 1 / X0   ☒ "X" If Supplemental
                                                           Declarations Is Attached

NAMED INSURED

    AMR Corporation

DESCRIPTION OF PREMISES

Prem.	Bldg.	Location, Construction And Occupancy
No. 001	No. 001	2000 Industrial Highway, Workingtown, PA 1900
		Joisted Masonry
		Storm Door Manufacturing

COVERAGES PROVIDED   Insurance At The Described Premises Applies Only For Coverages For Which
                          A Limit Of Insurance Is Shown

Prem.	Bldg.	Coverage	Limit Of Insurance	Covered Causes Of Loss	Coinsurance*	Rates
No. 001	No. 001	Building	800,000	Special	80%	See Schedule
		Business Personal Prop.	1,120,000	Special	80%	
		Personal Prop. of Others	50,000	Special	80%	
		Business Income w/o	880,000	Special	80%	
		Extra Expense	*If Extra Expense Coverage, Limits On Loss Payment			

OPTIONAL COVERAGES   Applicable Only When Entries Are Made In The Schedule Below

Prem.	Bldg.	Agreed Value			Replacement Cost (X)		
No.	No.	Expiration Date	Cov.	Amount	Building	Pers. Prop.	Including "Stock"
001	001				X		

Inflation Guard (%)		*Monthly Limit Of	Maximum Period	*Extended Period
Bldg.	Pers. Prop.	Indemnity (Fraction)	Of Indemnity (X)	Of Indemnity (Days)
3%	3%			

*Applies to Business Income Only

MORTGAGEHOLDERS

Prem.	Bldg.	Mortgageholder Name And Mailing Address
No. 001	No. 001	Workingtown Federal Savings and Loan Assn.
		P.O. Box 100
		Workingtown, PA 19000

DEDUCTIBLE

$500. Exceptions:
                $2,000 all coverages

FORMS APPLICABLE

To All Coverages: CP 00 10, CP 00 32, CP 00 90, CP 10 20, CP 10 30 As specified above.
To Specific Premises/Coverages:

Prem. No.	Bldg. No.	Coverages	Form Number

CP DS 00 10 00   Copyright, Insurance Services Office, Inc., 1999   Page 1 of 1   ☐

Claim representatives analyze property policies, including all attached forms, to determine coverage. They apply coverage to a claim by analyzing all of the following:

- Insured and other parties with an insurable interest in the property
- Deductible and applicable policy limits
- Property coverages
- Causes of loss and related exclusions
- Exclusions
- Conditions
- Optional coverages
- Endorsements

To familiarize the claim representative with these property coverage provisions, the following sections describe each of the provisions or attachments as they relate to homeowners and commercial property losses.

Insured Persons and Interests

As part of determining coverage, claim representatives must analyze who the insured persons and interests are. Doing this enables a claim representative to determine who is insured, other than the parties named in the declarations (named insured). As described in the definitions and conditions, other parties are considered insureds based on their relationship to the named insured or their insurable interest in the insured property.

In property policies, the definition of "insured" can seem complex. For example, the HO-3 policy, a widely used ISO homeowners policy that provides broad coverage, defines insured to include the following:[1]

1. The named insured (you)
2. Any residents of your household who are your relatives
3. Any other persons under age twenty-one and in your care or the care of any of your resident relatives
4. Any relative of yours under age twenty-four who is a student enrolled full-time in school and who was a resident of your household before moving out to attend school
5. Any person under age twenty-one who is in your care or the care of your resident relative, who is a student enrolled full-time in school, and who was a resident of your household before moving out to attend school.

The following text box is an example of the various people who can be insured under a homeowners policy.

Example of Insured Persons Under a Homeowners Policy

Paul Holden is the named insured on his homeowners policy. He and his wife, who lives with Paul, would be considered named insureds. Their ten-year-old daughter and their eight-year-old son are also insureds. If the Holdens took in a six-month-old foster child, that child would be an insured. If Paul's mother, Jan, moved in along with her sixteen-year-old foster child, she and her foster child would be insureds as well. If Jan's foster child moved out at age eighteen to attend school full time, that child would still be an insured under the Holdens' homeowners policy.

The declarations page of commercial property policies shows the named insured, who can be an individual or a business entity, and the mailing address of the named insured. Large corporations and sole proprietors are designated as named insureds in the same manner. The insured is the business entity named in the declarations. Relatives and household residents are not considered insureds when the named insured is a business entity. As mentioned, the mailing address does not have to correspond with the insured location, although it often does. If a post office box is shown as the mailing address, the declarations lists the insured location as well. The following text box is an example of who is insured under a commercial property policy.

Example of Insured Persons Under a Commercial Property Policy

Oliver Hoover is a sole proprietor, and the name on the declarations page of his commercial property policy is Oliver Hoover doing business as Oliver's Pet Store. The named insured is Oliver's Pet Store. None of his customers, employees, or family members is an insured.

The same rules apply to partnerships. If Linda Douglas and Jane Manning form a partnership, they could insure their business property under its name, Douglas & Manning Accountants. The partnership is the named insured because that is the business entity. Both Douglas and Manning would have rights under the policy.

Other parties might have an insurable interest in the named insured's property. These parties are insured in property policies to the extent of their financial interest and could be named in the declarations or in an endorsement. The insured's mortgage holder has a financial interest in the insured's home in the amount of the mortgage balance that the insured owes. Therefore, the insured's mortgage holder, called the mortgagee, is typically covered by the property policy as an insured. Also, loss payees that have collateral agreements (agreements that specify their financial interest in named property)—for example, retail stores that finance personal property (such as furniture) for the insured—could also be covered as insureds.

Deductible

To properly apply coverage and handle a claim, claim representatives must consider the deductible. Most property policies specify a deductible in the declarations or in another coverage form or endorsement. Some property policies include a deductible provision to describe the deductible and how to apply it. The deductible is usually subtracted from the loss amount after any coinsurance is applied (coinsurance is described in a subsequent section). Insurers pay the amount of the loss that exceeds the deductible, up to the limits of insurance specified in the policy. (Limits of insurance are also called limits of liability, amount of insurance, policy limit, dollar limit, or limit.)

As a simple example, suppose that the claim representative determines that the property damage to a home was $24,000, a $500 deductible applies, and the coverage amount (limit) for property damage is $180,000. The claim representative subtracts the deductible from the damage amount ($24,000 – $500) and issues a check for $23,500, payable to the insured and the mortgagee. Because the loss is $24,000, exceeding the policy limit is not an issue.

Property Coverage Provisions

Another part of determining coverage is for claim representatives to analyze the property coverages. Claim representatives also examine the property coverages to decide how the loss will be valued and how the claim should be handled. Property policies provide coverage for the following:

- The insured building and other structures or premises
- Personal or business personal property on the building premises
- Loss of use and business income coverages
- Additional coverages, such as coverage for other expenses associated with a property loss
- Coverage extensions

Buildings and Other Structures or Premises

Homeowners policies cover dwellings (the insured's home) under one coverage and other structures (such as detached garages or sheds) under another coverage. Exhibit 6-2 shows a homeowners policy in which the coverages are indicated. The dwelling's location is described in the declarations, and a limit of insurance that applies to the dwelling is specified. The limit of insurance for other structures is usually a percentage of the dwelling limit. Commercial property policies cover the insured building and other buildings or structures. Each commercial building and structure (the term "building" will include structures throughout the remainder of this chapter) is identified separately in the declarations with a specific location and limit of insurance. (Exhibit 6-3 shows a common commercial property declarations page.)

Homeowners dwelling coverage includes structures attached to the dwelling and any materials that the insured intends to use to construct, alter, or repair the dwelling. Similarly, commercial property coverages apply to property related to the described buildings. This property may include completed additions; permanently installed fixtures, machinery, and equipment; outdoor fixtures; personal property used to maintain or service the building or premises; improvements and additions under construction, alteration, or repairs; and materials and supplies that the insured intends to use for those alterations or repairs to the buildings. Insurers sometimes include coverage for maintenance equipment in commercial property policies so that property owners who do not occupy the building can purchase building coverage only. Without this commercial property coverage, insureds would be required to buy personal property coverage just to cover the maintenance equipment and items used to service the building. Some commercial property policies extend limited coverage for newly constructed buildings on the insured premises and newly acquired buildings that are not on the premises. This extension gives insureds temporary coverage until they can acquire appropriate property coverage for the new buildings.

Most insured dwellings are one-family homes. However, a two-family home, such as a duplex, qualifies for homeowners coverage, but only the unit owned and occupied by the insured is covered. Special homeowners policies are available for condominium owners and people who rent apartments, rooms, or a whole house. The following text box provides examples of property insured under homeowners dwelling coverages.

Examples of Property Insured Under Homeowners Dwelling Coverages

- Insured's house
- Lumber, shingles, and drywall stored on the premises for a room addition
- Attached garage
- Screened-in back porch
- Plumbing, heating, and central air conditioning
- Built-in refrigerator

The homeowners policy's other structures coverage is sometimes called appurtenant structures or dwelling extensions. A clear space must separate the other structure from the dwelling. The only connection that can exist between the dwelling and the other structure is a fence, a utility line, or a similar connection. The following text box offers examples of the property insured under the homeowners policy's other structures coverage.

Examples of Property Insured Under Homeowners Other Structures Coverage

- Detached garages
- Gazebos
- Free-standing mailboxes
- Garden fountains
- Tool sheds
- Fences
- Swimming pools
- Patios

Other structures insured under homeowners policies are usually cemented into the ground or anchored to the ground with the intention of leaving them on the premises. Doghouses, play equipment, and similar property that is movable and not permanently affixed to the ground are not considered "other structures." Such items are insured under personal property coverage, described in the next section.

Because each building requires separate coverage under commercial property policies, the coverage distinctions between buildings and other structures just described for homeowners policies are not an issue in commercial property policies.

Personal Property

Homeowners and commercial property policies cover the insured's personal or business personal property and provide some coverage for other people's property in certain circumstances. This section discusses the following topics related to personal property:

- Insured's personal or business personal property
- Personal property of others
- Special limits of liability
- Geographic scope of personal and business personal property coverages

The first two topics describe types of personal property that are covered under property policies. The last two topics include special considerations for personal property coverages.

One type of personal property covered is the homeowner's personal property or the business owner's business personal property. Personal property covered under homeowners policies generally includes property inside the dwelling, such as furniture, clothes, jewelry, rugs, and other property that is not attached to the dwelling. Homeowners policies also cover movable property outside the dwelling, such as property stored in other buildings or left outside in the open. The insured's lawn mower, tools, ladder, and bicycle are examples of such personal property. Some homeowners policies provide worldwide coverage for personal property, so that personal property used while away from home would be covered. The following text box provides examples of the personal property covered under a homeowners policy.

Example of Homeowners Coverage for Personal Property Used by the Insured

If Jim borrows Gail's camcorder to take on his Caribbean vacation, her camcorder, as well as his personal property, are covered against the causes of loss named in his policy. If the camcorder is damaged in a windstorm, Jim's insurance will pay to repair or replace it. Gail does not have to file a claim under her HO-3 policy.

Commercial property policies generally cover the insured's business personal property while it is in the insured building or within a specified distance of the premises (for example, 100 feet from the premises). The kinds of property covered differ considerably from homeowners personal property. Business personal property might include the following:

- Furniture and fixtures

- Machinery and equipment

- Stock such as merchandise, raw materials, and goods still in process or finished

- Labor, materials, or services rendered on personal property of others

- Interest as a tenant in improvements and betterments

- Personal property leased under a contract requiring insurance

Under both the homeowners policy and the commercial property policy, personal property and business personal property are generally **unscheduled property**, meaning that insureds do not list (or schedule) the personal items they want to insure. The limit of insurance shown in the policy's declarations is an aggregate sum for all personal property. Unscheduled coverage gives insureds flexibility. They can buy, replace, or discard property during the policy period without reporting these changes to their insurer. However, insureds can also schedule certain property, which means they can list a specific item and the amount of insurance for that item. Scheduled coverage is usually used to provide broader coverage for specific items of personal property. Scheduled coverage is discussed in the endorsements section of this chapter.

Unscheduled property
Property not specifically listed (scheduled) on a policy but generally covered with a single limit for all items (or each class) of property that are not excluded.

Under homeowners policies, claim representatives must determine whether property is part of the dwelling or is personal property, to decide which coverage applies to a loss. The dwelling and personal property coverages have different causes of loss, and the methods for determining the value of the dwelling and personal property differ. Built-in appliances or cabinets clearly intended to be part of the building structure are covered under dwelling coverage. Appliances that can be removed without leaving a hole or defacing the building are covered under personal property coverage. Such appliances could include free-standing refrigerators or stoves, portable dishwashers, countertop microwave ovens, and washers and dryers connected to the house only by hoses or exhaust vents.

Another type of personal property covered in homeowners and commercial property policies is the personal property of others. Many homeowners policies cover damage to personal property of others when that property is on the insured's premises while the insured is living there. For example, Bob allows his neighbor to temporarily store her golf clubs in his basement. If a fire destroys them, Bob's homeowners policy should generally provide coverage.

Some commercial property policies cover other people's personal property when the property is in the insured's care, custody, or control and is located in or on the building premises described in the declarations. They also cover other people's personal property within a specified distance of the insured's described premises (for example, within 100 feet of the premises). This coverage protects commercial policyholders, such as dry cleaners, shoe repair shops, or clothing consignment stores, who take customers' property for repair, for consignment, or for some other service.

One consideration for personal property coverages is special limits of liability. While the homeowners policy provides actual cash value or replacement cost for most types of personal property, some property is subject to special limits of liability. These special limits are additionally restricted by the limit specified for all personal property in the personal property coverage. These limits and restrictions are placed on these types of property because they can be difficult to value or because they can be insured more fully by endorsement. The following text box provides examples of personal property for which special limits apply.

Examples of Property Covered Under Homeowners Personal Property Coverage for Which Special Limits Apply

- Money, bank notes, stored value cards, and smart cards
- Jewelry, watches, furs, and precious stones
- Securities, accounts, deeds, and passports
- Watercraft and their trailers and equipment
- Other trailers or semitrailers
- Electronic apparatus and accessories (tapes, discs, or other media; antennas; and wires)
- Firearms and related equipment
- Silverware and goldware, including tea sets
- Business use property

Homeowners special limits of liability for some categories of personal property may be subject to specific provisions, as illustrated in the following examples:

- The special limits on jewelry and firearms apply only to theft losses.
- The special limits on business use property depend on the property's location at the time of the loss.
- The special limits on electronic apparatus and accessories apply to their use in or on a motor vehicle, and separate limits apply to such apparatus as specified for personal or business use.

Another consideration for personal property coverage is the geographic scope of the coverage. Homeowners personal property and commercial property coverages differ in their geographic scope. Homeowners personal property coverage protects property that is owned or used by the insured worldwide. The policy describes limitations that apply in specific circumstances. The following examples illustrate two of these limitations. When an insured moves personal property to a new principal residence, personal property coverage is provided for thirty days, after which the insured must purchase insurance coverage on the new residence that includes personal property coverage. When an insured temporarily takes personal property from his or her primary residence to a vacation home, coverage is provided. However, personal property that is part of the contents of the vacation home must be covered by a policy on the vacation home. For example, if the insured takes skis from his or her primary residence to his or her vacation home in Vermont to use while on vacation, the homeowners policy on the primary residence would cover the skis. However, if the vacation home contains furniture that remains there year round, that furniture would not be covered by the policy on the primary residence. Instead, it would be covered by a policy on the vacation home.

In contrast to homeowners policies, business personal property coverage under commercial property policies is limited to property located in or on the described premises or within a specified distance of the premises. Commercial property policies do not cover business personal property while it is being transported; specialized policies provide such coverage.

Property Not Covered

Most homeowners and some commercial property policies specify property that is not covered. Homeowners policies do not cover land, and they do not cover structures that the insured uses for business purposes. For example, the personal property coverage section of the HO-3 excludes ten categories of personal property, as shown in Exhibit 6-4.

Many commercial property policies also specify property that is not covered, including business personal property and property that might be considered a building or structure. For example, Exhibit 6-5 lists seventeen categories of property that are not covered under a commercial Building and Personal Property Coverage Form (BPP).

Loss of Use and Business Income Coverages

Depending on the policy form, homeowners policies might provide coverage for loss of use, and commercial property policies might provide business income coverage. Most homeowners policies include coverage for loss of use of insured property. This coverage includes additional living expenses or fair rental value when insured property is damaged and when civil authority prohibits use of the insured property because of damage to neighboring premises by an insured's cause of loss. **Additional living expense coverage** pays the insureds' increased costs to maintain their normal standard of living while they are living in temporary lodgings. Such expenses include hotel or apartment rental costs and reasonable restaurant bills that exceed the insureds' normal expenditures. Payments continue as long as the home is unfit to live in or the policy limit is reached.

Fair rental value coverage pays insureds for lost rent on the part of their home that they rent to others or hold for rental to others when a loss occurs

Additional living expense coverage
Coverage for expenses that an insured incurs in the attempt to maintain a normal standard of living after a property loss and while the dwelling is uninhabitable.

Fair rental value coverage
Coverage for losses that arise when the insured's rental property, whether rented or not, has been damaged and is no longer available for rental.

EXHIBIT 6-4

Personal Property Not Covered in the HO-3

Type of Property	Reason Property Is Not Covered
Articles separately described and specifically insured in this or other insurance	Reduce the likelihood of coverage duplications.
Birds, fish, or other animals	Eliminate coverages requiring special treatment; specialty insurers are more appropriate.
Motor vehicles or other motorized land conveyances and their equipment, accessories, and electronic apparatus	Eliminate coverages requiring special treatment; motor vehicles should be insured under an auto policy.
Aircraft and parts	Eliminate coverages requiring special treatment; aircraft should be insured under an aircraft policy.
Hovercraft (self-propelled motorized ground effect vehicle) and parts	Eliminate coverages requiring special treatment; specialty insurers are more appropriate.
Property of roomers, boarders, and other tenants	Eliminate coverages requiring special treatment; tenant's property should be insured under a tenant's policy.
Property in an apartment regularly rented or held for rental to others by an insured	Eliminate coverages requiring special treatment; business property should be insured under a business policy.
Property rented or held for rental off the residence premises	Eliminate coverages requiring special treatment; business property should be insured under a business policy.
Business data	Eliminate coverages requiring special treatment; business property should be insured under a business policy.
Credit cards or fund transfer cards	Assist in keeping premiums reasonable; limited coverage is available as an additional coverage.

to that property. Reimbursement applies as long as it takes to repair or to replace the premises, whichever is shorter. If the loss of fair rental value occurs because civil authority prohibits use, the reimbursement period is limited to two weeks or less.

Commercial property policies include a similar coverage to replace business income after a covered loss. When business property is damaged or destroyed, organizations can suffer losses that go beyond property damage. For example, the damage or destruction of property might interfere with an organization's operations. That interference could cause loss of revenue or increased expenses, both of which would harm the organization. Such losses of revenue or increased expenses are called business income losses. A **business income loss** is a financial loss that occurs when tangible commercial property is damaged or destroyed, resulting in a loss of revenue or increased expenses during the time that the property is being replaced or repaired.

Business income loss
A financial loss that occurs when tangible commercial property is damaged or destroyed, resulting in a loss of revenue or increased expenses during the time that the property is being replaced or repaired.

EXHIBIT 6-5

Business Personal Property Not Covered Under a BPP

1. Accounts, bills, currency, food stamps or other evidences of debt, money, notes, or securities

2. Animals, unless the insured boards animals owned by others or the insured's own animals are for sale inside buildings

3. Automobiles held for sale

4. Bridges, roadways, walks, patios, or other paved surfaces

5. Contraband or property in the course of illegal transportation or trade

6. The cost of excavations, grading, backfilling, or filling

7. Foundations of buildings and structures; machinery; or boilers if their foundations are below the lowest basement floor or below the ground surface, if no basement exists

8. Land, water, growing crops, or lawns

9. Personal property while airborne or waterborne

10. Bulkheads, pilings, piers, wharves, or docks

11. Property covered under another similar coverage form or under a policy that specifically describes the property, except on an excess basis

12. Retaining walls that are not part of a building

13. Underground pipes, flues, or drains

14. Electronic data, except as provided under Additional Coverages

15. The cost to replace or restore information in valuable papers and records

16. Vehicles or self-propelled machines, including aircraft or watercraft, when they are licensed for use on public roads and operated principally away from the premises

17. The following property while outside the buildings: grain, hay, straw, or other crops; fences; radio or television antennas and equipment associated with them; detached signs; and trees, shrubs, or plants that are not stock

Includes copyrighted material of Insurance Services Office, Inc. with its permission. Copyright ISO Properties, Inc., 2001. Building and Personal Property Coverage Form CP 00 10 04 02.

Additional Coverages and Coverage Extensions

Personal and commercial property policies often include additional coverages and coverage extensions to help meet the policyholder's insurance needs. Additional coverages and coverage extensions are included as separate sections in the policy because they do not apply strictly to buildings or personal property. Additional coverages and coverage extensions might provide new coverage or restore excluded coverage. Some homeowners policies provide additional coverages in a specific Additional Coverages section. Exhibit 6-6 lists the additional coverages found in that section of a homeowners policy.

EXHIBIT 6-6

Additional Coverages in the Homeowners Policy

HO-3 Additional Coverages

- Debris removal
- Reasonable repairs
- Trees, shrubs, and other plants
- Fire department service charge
- Property removed
- Credit card, electronic fund transfer card, forgery, and counterfeit money

- Loss assessment
- Collapse
- Glass or safety glazing material
- Landlord's furnishings
- Ordinance or law
- Grave markers

Includes copyrighted material of Insurance Services Office, Inc. with its permission. Copyright ISO Properties, Inc., 2000. Homeowners 3—Special Form HO 00 03 05 01.

In commercial property policies, some additional coverages and coverage extensions are described in the policy forms, while others are described in the causes of loss forms (discussed later in this chapter). Exhibit 6-7 lists additional coverages and coverage extensions provided in a BPP and the commercial causes of loss forms.

Some of the common personal and commercial additional coverages or coverage extensions under which claim representatives handle claims are described below.

- *Debris removal.* If repair costs to an insured building reach or exceed the policy limits, a debris removal clause provides limited additional coverage to remove debris; volcanic ash, dust, or particles; or trees knocked down by a covered cause of loss.

- *Reasonable repairs and preservation of property.* Homeowners policies provide reasonable repairs coverage as an additional coverage, which encourages the insured to make temporary repairs to prevent further damage. Commercial property policies encourage the preservation of property from further loss or damage by covering the expense of moving covered property to another location to prevent further damage.

- *Trees, shrubs, and other plants.* In the homeowners policy and BPP coverage form, the trees, shrubs, and other plants clause provides limited coverage for damage caused by specified causes of loss to trees, shrubs, and plants that are part of an insured's landscaping.

- *Fire department service charge.* In both the homeowners policy and the BPP coverage form, the fire department service charge clause provides limited additional coverage for insureds who owe service charges because of contracts with fire departments or because of local ordinances.

EXHIBIT 6-7

Additional Coverages and Coverage Extensions in the BPP and Causes of Loss Forms

Additional Coverages in the BPP and Causes of Loss Forms	Coverage Extensions in the BPP and Causes of Loss Forms
• Debris removal	• Newly acquired or constructed property
• Preservation of property	• Personal effects and property of others
• Fire department service charge	
• Pollutant cleanup and removal	• Valuable papers and records—cost of research
• Electronic data	• Property off premises
• Increased cost of construction to comply with enforcement of an ordinance or a law	• Outdoor property
	• Non-owned detached trailers
• Collapse	• Property in transit
• Limited coverage for damage caused by fungus, wet rot, dry rot, or bacteria	• Water damage; damage from other liquids, powder, or molten material
	• Glass

- *Credit cards and electronic fund transfer cards.* When credit cards and electronic fund transfer cards are lost or stolen, most card providers generally hold the insured responsible for $50 or less per card for unauthorized use before the insured reports the cards missing. Under some homeowners coverages, a credit card and electronic fund transfer card clause provides insureds up to $500 to pay their resulting legal obligations to the card companies. The coverage also limits insureds' losses from forged checks, negotiable instruments, and counterfeit currency. The BPP does not have a corresponding policy provision.

- *Association assessments.* The homeowners loss assessment clause covers members of homeowners' associations when they are assessed their share for repairs to damaged association property, such as a clubhouse, tennis court, or pool. The coverage pays the cost to repair or replace association property that was damaged by a covered cause of loss, up to a specified limit. The BPP does not have a corresponding policy provision.

- *Collapse.* Because damage caused by collapse of buildings and other structures is not covered in most property policies, a collapse clause in the causes of loss form and in the homeowners policy restores coverage for direct physical loss to an insured's property when specifically listed causes of loss or events cause the collapse. Exclusions might apply to collapse of certain kinds of property (such as awnings, fences, patios, and swimming pools, among others).

- *Glass.* The homeowners policy contains a glass breakage clause, which covers the repair of glass or safety glazing material that is part of the insured building or structure, storm door, or storm window, regardless of the cause. It also pays for damage directly and solely caused by splinters or pieces of broken glass or glazing. The glass extension in some commercial property causes of loss forms pays expenses for installing temporary plates or boards over window openings and expenses to remove or replace obstructions when repairing or replacing building glass. Commercial property policies contain a similar coverage provision.

- *Ordinance or law.* The homeowners policy contains an ordinance or law clause, which provides limited coverage for the insured's increased costs to construct, demolish, remodel, or reconstruct a building or structure covered by a property cause of loss when those costs result from an ordinance or a law. This coverage applies to damaged and undamaged portions of the buildings and structures and includes costs to remove associated debris. Most commercial property policies exclude ordinance or law coverage, but it can be purchased by way of endorsement.

- *Pollutant cleanup and removal.* Pollutant cleanup and removal coverage in the BPP coverage form pays a limited amount of the cost to extract any pollutants released into or around the insured's property if a covered cause of loss caused the release of the pollutant. Homeowners policies usually contain an exclusion for pollution.

- *Electronic data.* Electronic data coverage in both the homeowners policy and the commercial property policy provides for replacement of the media on which the electronic data were stored. The coverage varies depending on the causes of loss form that applies, but the covered causes of loss include viruses and other harmful computer code. The coverage limits the amount that the insurer will pay for electronic data claims.

- *Fungus.* The limited fungus coverage in both the homeowners policy and the commercial property policy provides for removal of fungus, wet or dry rot, or bacteria; replacement of the affected part of the building; and testing costs if the loss was caused by a covered cause of loss or by flood (only if the Flood Coverage Endorsement applies). If business income or extra expense coverages apply to the loss that caused the fungus, then a limited extension of those coverages is provided while the fungus damage is repaired.

- *Outdoor property.* The BPP coverage form has an outdoor property extension that restores limited coverage for outdoor property, such as fences and television antennas, when they are damaged by specified causes of loss. The homeowners policy does not have parallel coverage. However, it does have limited coverage for outdoor property if the cause of loss is directly related to collapse of a building or any part of a building.

Limitations on Recovery

Homeowners coverages and commercial property insurance coverages generally specify limits on what the insurer will pay for a claim. These limits are usually expressed as dollar amounts, such as the dollar limits in the declarations. Other limits are described in phrases in the policy provisions. For example, a policy might state that the insurer's liability is the "cost to repair or replace damaged property." Some property policies specify limits both ways. This section examines both policy and form limits and special limits.

The first type of limits used in property policies are policy and form limits. Virtually all property coverages have a policy limit. A policy limit is the maximum amount the insurer will pay on a claim, regardless of the actual value of the damaged property. For example, an insured's home has a policy limit of $150,000 listed in the declarations under dwelling coverage. A fire totally destroys the home. Although the cost to rebuild the home is $255,000, the maximum the insurer will pay under the dwelling coverage is $150,000 (plus any other applicable coverage extensions) because that is the limit of the policy.

Homeowners policies have limits for each different type of coverage. The dwelling limit is based on the cost to rebuild the house. The other coverage limits are percentages of the dwelling limit. For example, the other structures limit might be 10 percent of the dwelling limit, the personal property limit might be 50 percent of the dwelling limit, and the loss of use limit might be 20 percent of the dwelling limit. In Exhibit 6-2, the homeowners declarations page shows the policy limits that apply to each coverage.

In most commercial property policies, the insurer specifies the value of each insured building and the value of personal property. The policy limits for each coverage form are listed separately in the declarations, as shown in Exhibit 6-3.

The other type of limits used in property policies is special limits. Many property policies have dollar limits on specified types of property. Homeowners policies have special limits for additional coverages and for specified categories of personal property. For example, Exhibit 6-8 summarizes the personal property special limits of liability for the HO-3 homeowners policy. The special limits are the amounts of coverage provided for each type of property. Insureds who need higher limits can purchase endorsements to increase their limits. Optionally, insureds can insure the property with a personal articles policy or another scheduled coverage form.

In commercial property policies, special limits for additional coverages, coverage extensions, and special limits of insurance are described in the appropriate sections of the policy or policy forms. Exhibit 6-9 lists some of the special limits in the BPP.

EXHIBIT 6-8

HO-3 Personal Property Special Limits

$200	• Money, bank notes, bullion, gold other than goldware, silver other than silverware, platinum, coins, and medals
$500	• Property away from the residence premises used for business purposes
$1,500	• Securities, accounts, deeds, evidences of debt, letters of credit, notes other than bank notes, manuscripts, personal records, passports, tickets, and stamps
	• Watercraft, including their trailers, furnishings, equipment, and outboard engines or motors
	• Trailers or semi-trailers not used with watercraft
	• Theft of jewelry, watches, furs, and precious and semi-precious stones
	• Electronic apparatus, equipped to be powered by the power system of a motor vehicle or motorized land conveyance, while it is in or upon the vehicle or conveyance
	• Electronic apparatus, equipped to be powered by the power system of a motor vehicle or motorized land conveyance, while it is away from the residence premises, but not in a vehicle, and that is being used for any business purpose
$2,500	• Theft of firearms
	• Theft of silverware, silver-plated ware, goldware, gold-plated ware, platinumware, platinum-plated ware, and pewterware
	• Property on the residence premises used for any business purpose

---

Includes copyrighted material of Insurance Services Office, Inc. with its permission. Copyright ISO Properties, Inc., 2000. Homeowners 3—Special Form HO 00 03 05 01.

Causes of Loss and Related Exclusions

Another part of determining coverage is for claim representatives to analyze the causes of loss and related exclusions. Property policies (both the homeowners and commercial property policy) identify the causes of loss (or perils) that the policy covers. Homeowners policies use the term "perils" to describe perils covered and excluded. Commercial property declarations identify the causes of loss covered by indicating either basic form, broad form, or special form causes of loss for each coverage listed (such as building, business personal property, personal property of others, and business income and extra expense). The following sections describe homeowners perils and commercial property causes of loss.

EXHIBIT 6-9

Special Limits in the BPP Coverage Form

Fire department service charge

$1,000, with no deductible

Pollutant cleanup and removal

$10,000 for each described premises, per twelve-month period

Electronic data

$2,500 for all loss or damage sustained in any one policy year, regardless of the number of loss occurrences or the number of premises, locations, or computer systems

Newly acquired or constructed property

Buildings: $250,000 for each building

Business personal property: $100,000 at each building

Personal effects and property of others

$2,500 at each described premises

Valuable papers and records—cost of research to recreate the data

$2,500 at each described premises unless a higher limit is shown in the declarations

Property off premises

$10,000 in total

Outdoor property

$1,000 per occurrence, but not more than $250 for any one tree, shrub, or plant

Homeowners Perils

People who own their home; have a home mortgage; or rent an apartment, condominium, townhouse, or house can purchase property insurance to protect their financial interests in their residence and other property from loss as a result of perils specified in the policy. Several homeowners policies exist for various types of property, including condominium policies, renters policies, and homeowners policies. Homeowners policies can cover the building and the personal property within it, along with other structures on the premises. The ISO HO-3 Homeowners Special Form policy provides one of the broadest coverages for dwellings and other structures. Additionally, the HO-3 provides specified perils coverage for personal property.

One homeowners peril coverage form is special form coverage, also called "all-risks" or "open-perils" coverage. **Special form coverage** covers every cause of direct physical loss that is not specifically excluded in the policy. Homeowners policies generally provide special form coverage on the dwelling and other structures.

Special form coverage
An insurance coverage form that covers "risks of direct physical loss," subject to the form's exclusions and limitations (traditionally known as "all-risks" coverage).

Specified perils coverage
Insurance that covers losses only if they result directly from a peril or cause of loss listed in the policy.

The other homeowners peril coverage form is specified perils coverage, also called "named perils" coverage. **Specified perils coverage** covers a loss only if it was a direct result of a peril listed in the policy. Under many homeowners policies, personal property is covered for specified perils. Exhibit 6-10 shows the coverages and perils insured against through an HO-3 policy.

EXHIBIT 6-10

Personal Property Perils Insured Against in a Homeowners Policy

- Fire
- Lightning
- Windstorm or hail
- Explosion
- Riot or civil commotion
- Aircraft
- Vehicles
- Smoke
- Vandalism or malicious mischief
- Falling objects

- Accidental discharge or overflow of water or steam
- Volcanic eruption
- Theft
- Weight of ice, snow, or sleet
- Sudden and accidental tearing apart, cracking, burning, or bulging
- Freezing
- Sudden and accidental damage from artificially generated electrical current

---

Includes copyrighted material of Insurance Services Office, Inc. with its permission. Copyright ISO Properties, Inc., 2000. Homeowners 3—Special Form HO 00 03 05 01.

Some of the perils that commonly lead to claims include fire; lightning; windstorm or hail; smoke; vandalism or malicious mischief; theft; and weight of snow, ice, or sleet. A claim representative needs to understand what each of these perils is and how they cause damage in order to correctly apply coverage. A brief description of these common perils follows. However, claim representatives should be aware that court interpretations of these perils differs.

Fire is the rapid oxidation of combustible materials, which releases heat and flame. According to many jurisdictions, without flame, there is no fire. Fire can be distinguished as friendly fire or hostile fire. A friendly fire is deliberately created in a place designed to contain fire, such as an oven or a fireplace. A hostile fire is any other fire.

Lightning losses can include direct hits, near misses, and ground surges (that damage the wiring to a building or an electrical appliance). If fire results from lightning, then the fire damage is usually covered under the fire peril. Various exclusions might apply to lightning damage.

Windstorm damage occurs from wind velocity having sufficient force to cause damage. Windstorm includes tornadoes and many storms of much lesser velocity. Windstorm damage that occurs because of hurricanes in beachfront areas can create difficulties for claim representatives, who must distinguish between wind and flood damage.

Hail is precipitation in the form of hard pellets that can cause damage on impact. Icy snow and sleet are not hail. Large hail and forceful hail of any size can cause considerable damage to structures, especially those made of steel or aluminum. Sometimes, when repairs are not possible, claim representatives settle claims based on loss of value caused by the damaged appearance. This approach is often called an appearance allowance.

Smoke damage must result from a sudden, accidental cause to be covered. The damage cannot result from an accumulation over time. Smoke damage from a friendly fire is covered if it is sudden and accidental, such as the damage that occurs when an insured forgets to open the damper in the fireplace.

Vandalism is the willful or malicious destruction or defacement of public or private property and is sometimes called malicious mischief. For a vandalism claim, the insured must show that the damage was caused willfully or maliciously. This proof can be established by circumstantial evidence such as graffiti on floors or walls, a pattern of broken windows, or similar damage to other property in a neighborhood. Damage caused by animals is not considered vandalism because animals cannot form the intent needed to establish vandalism.

Theft is generally defined as the fraudulent taking of personal property belonging to another without consent and with the intent to deprive the owner of its value. Claim representatives must read the individual policy carefully to determine what thefts are covered. The theft peril is often limited in property policies. For example, Exhibit 6-8 describes limits for thefts of certain types of personal property, such as jewelry, watches, furs, precious stones, firearms, and silverware and goldware.

Most policy forms cover damage caused by the weight of snow, ice, or sleet that accumulates on the roof of a dwelling, an appurtenant structure (such as a garage), or a commercial building. When faced with a roof collapse, the claim representative should consider this peril as a potential cause of loss.

Some peril descriptions contain detailed qualifying language. For example, water damage is usually covered if it is sudden and accidental and if it was the direct result of the breaking apart or cracking of an appliance or a system that contains water or steam. The resulting damage is usually covered, but repair of the system that caused the damage is not. For example, the damage caused when a dishwasher water line burst and flooded a kitchen would be covered, but the cost to repair the water line would not be.

The claim example in the following box illustrates the application of HO-3 special form and specified perils coverages.

An Application of HO-3 Special Form and Specified Perils Coverages

An insured accidentally spills a can of a caustic chemical in his kitchen. The chemical splashes on the linoleum floor, table, chairs, and area rug. Because spills are not excluded under special form coverage on the dwelling, the damage to the linoleum floor is covered. Because spills are not a named peril under specified perils coverage on the contents, the damage to the table, chairs, and area rug is not covered.

Commercial Property Causes of Loss Forms

In commercial property policies, the applicable causes of loss forms are listed with the insured property on the declarations page, as mentioned. The commercial property declarations page in Exhibit 6-3 shows how these forms are listed. Endorsement forms are specified under "Forms Applicable" in the declarations for each cause of loss listed next to a coverage. One of three forms, Causes of Loss—Basic Form, Causes of Loss—Broad Form, or Causes of Loss—Special Form, is attached to the policy to complete the coverage. These forms are described in this section.

One commercial property causes of loss form is the Causes of Loss—Basic Form. Commercial property Causes of Loss—Basic Form is seldom used, but it lays a foundation for describing the broad form causes of loss. Basic form causes of loss lists eleven causes of loss that are similar to the homeowners specified perils. These causes of loss are listed in Exhibit 6-11.

EXHIBIT 6-11

Commercial Property Causes of Loss—Basic Form

1. Fire
2. Lightning
3. Explosion
4. Windstorm or hail
5. Smoke
6. Aircraft or vehicles
7. Riot or civil commotion
8. Vandalism
9. Sprinkler leakage
10. Sinkhole collapse
11. Volcanic action

Commercial property basic form causes of loss lists several exclusions that are similar to the HO-3 policy exclusions, described later in the chapter. Certain additional exclusions apply only to business income coverage. Most of these additionally excluded causes of loss relate to improper maintenance of water pipes or systems that use water, such as sprinkler systems.

A second commercial property causes of loss form is the Causes of Loss—Broad Form. Commercial property Causes of Loss—Broad Form is so named because it provides broader coverage than the basic form. It includes the same coverages listed in Exhibit 6-11 for basic form causes of loss, plus the following three additional causes of loss:

1. Falling objects
2. Weight of snow, ice, or sleet
3. Water damage

The same causes of loss are excluded in the broad form as in the basic form, except that fewer exclusions apply for business income coverage. The broad form also adds additional coverages for collapse and fungus, which are described in the form.

A third commercial property causes of loss form is the Causes of Loss—Special Form. Similar to homeowners special form coverage, commercial property Causes of Loss—Special Form covers all direct physical causes of loss except those that are specifically excluded or limited in the form. Causes of Loss—Special Form provides the broadest commercial property coverage available. Because Causes of Loss—Special Form is a form that covers every cause of loss that is not specifically excluded, it does not list the covered causes of loss. Instead, it includes detail about exclusions and limitations. Among these exclusions are those listed in the basic form, as well as numerous other exclusions. Some of these exclusions are smoke from agricultural smudging or industrial operations; smog; wear and tear; rust or corrosion; mechanical breakdown; explosion of steam boilers; dishonest or criminal acts by the insured; rain, snow, ice, or sleet damage to personal property; collapse; and discharge of pollutants. When determining coverage for a claim, claim representatives must read the coverage form for the details about these exclusions.

Because the coverage provided under the special form is so broad, insurers must restrict the coverage through a variety of limitations. Many of these limitations are similar to those found in the basic form and broad form causes of loss.

Causes of Loss—Special Form also includes the same additional coverages for collapse and fungus found in the broad form, but it adds an additional coverage extension for limited coverage for the insured's personal property while in transit; water damage and damage from other liquids, powder, or molten material; and glass.

In summary, the complexities of these perils or causes of loss and their exclusions reinforce the need for claim representatives to read the policy carefully when determining coverage for property losses.

Exclusions

Another part of the policy that claim representatives check is the exclusions. Exclusions are meant to eliminate or limit coverage. Many property insurance policies contain similar exclusions. Exhibit 6-12 lists the exclusions contained in the homeowners policy.

Exclusions are included in property policies for many reasons. One reason is that insurance is not intended to cover property that wears out. For example, roof shingles might be worn out rather than damaged by hail. Another reason for exclusions is that the insured should control some causes of loss rather than insure them. For example, insureds should attempt to prevent water damage from frozen pipes by maintaining heat in the building. Insureds should not neglect their property and then expect to collect for damage. Two other reasons for exclusions are that property is uninsurable or should be covered by specialized policies. For example, settling of pavement is uninsurable, while discharge of pollutants is best covered by specialized policies.

EXHIBIT 6-12

Homeowners Policy Exclusions

- Ordinance or law
- Earth movement
- Water damage
- Power failure
- Neglect

- War
- Nuclear hazard
- Intentional loss
- Governmental action

Includes copyrighted material of Insurance Services Office, Inc. with its permission. Copyright ISO Properties, Inc., 2000. Homeowners 3—Special Form HO 00 03 05 01.

Concurrent causation
A loss involving two or more perils occurring either simultaneously or sequentially.

Although losses involving concurrent causation are not listed as a separate exclusion, property policies include language that is meant to exclude them. This language is usually found in the introductory portion of the exclusions section of a policy. **Concurrent causation** is a single loss that was caused by two or more causes of loss, occurring simultaneously or sequentially. An example is a house that is damaged by an earthquake and a fire that results from the earthquake. Concurrent causation becomes an issue when one of the causes of loss is covered and the other is not. Generally, insurers take the position that a loss is not covered if caused by an excluded cause, whether or not that excluded cause is the predominant cause. However, courts sometimes take a different position. Claim representatives should be aware of the concurrent causation position that courts have taken in the jurisdictions where they handle claims.

Conditions

Another part of the policy that claim representatives must be aware of are the conditions. Because the homeowners and commercial property policies are package policies, claim representatives must be aware of the conditions for each applicable coverage in the package. For example, as illustrated in Exhibit 6-1, the homeowners policy has general conditions that apply to all the coverages, other conditions that apply to both the property and liability coverages, and other conditions that apply to each section of the policy. Exhibit 6-13 lists the property-related conditions from the homeowners policy. They describe the insured's and the insurer's obligations and specify restrictions and limitations on how much the insurer will pay.

Several sets of conditions apply to a commercial property policy. Conditions apply to the policy in general, to the specific coverage type (such as property or liability), and to each coverage form included in the package (such as the BPP coverage form). The following descriptions apply to a commercial package policy with a BPP coverage form attached.

EXHIBIT 6-13

Property-Related Homeowners Policy Conditions

- Insurable interest and limit of liability
- Duties after loss
- Loss settlement
- Loss to a pair or set
- Appraisal
- Other insurance and service agreement
- Suit against us
- Our option
- Loss payment
- Abandonment of property
- Mortgage clause
- No benefit to bailee
- Nuclear hazard clause

- Recovered property
- Volcanic eruption period
- Policy period
- Concealment or fraud
- Loss payable clause
- Liberalization clause *
- Waiver or change of policy provisions *
- Cancellation *
- Nonrenewal *
- Assignment *
- Subrogation *
- Death *

* Applies to both the property and liability sections of the policy

Includes copyrighted material of Insurance Services Office, Inc. with its permission. Copyright ISO Properties, Inc., 2000. Homeowners 3—Special Form HO 00 03 05 01.

The first set of conditions that apply to a commercial property package policy with a BPP Coverage Form attached is the Common Policy Conditions (ISO form IL 00 17). This form is listed on the policy declarations page and is attached to all commercial package policies. As shown in Exhibit 6-14, the Common Policy Conditions form lists six conditions that describe the policy mechanics.

EXHIBIT 6-14

Common Policy Conditions

- Cancellation
- Changes
- Examination of your books and records

- Inspections and surveys
- Premiums
- Transfer of rights and duties

Includes copyrighted material of Insurance Services Office, Inc. with its permission. Copyright ISO Properties, Inc., 1998. Common Policy Conditions IL 00 17 11 98.

The second set of conditions that apply to a commercial property policy with a BPP coverage form attached is the Commercial Property Conditions (ISO Form CP 00 90). The Commercial Property Conditions form describes eight conditions that relate to all of the coverages in the commercial property portion of the policy. Exhibit 6-15 lists the Commercial Property Conditions.

EXHIBIT 6-15

Commercial Property Conditions

- Concealment, misrepresentation, or fraud
- Control of property
- Insurance under two or more coverages
- Legal action against us
- Liberalization

- No benefit to bailee
- Other insurance
- Policy period, coverage territory
- Transfer of rights of recovery

Includes copyrighted material of Insurance Services Office, Inc. with its permission. Copyright ISO Properties, Inc., 1983, 1987. Commercial Property Conditions CP 00 90 07 88.

The third set of conditions that apply to a commercial property policy with a BPP coverage form attached is the Additional Conditions section of the BPP coverage form. The two additional conditions are coinsurance and mortgageholders.

The remainder of this section of the chapter describes several conditions that are common to homeowners policies and commercial property policies. These conditions are as follows:

- Duties after a loss
- Loss settlement
- Other insurance
- Suit or legal action against us
- Our option
- Mortgagee or mortgageholders
- Concealment, misrepresentation, or fraud
- Liberalization
- Cancellation
- Examination and inspection and survey
- Insurance under two or more coverages
- Coinsurance

These conditions have been selected for discussion because they are the conditions that routinely affect claim handling.

Duties After a Loss Condition

The duties after a loss condition explains that insureds must promptly notify their insurer or producer of a loss. When an insured waits several weeks to report a loss, the evidence related to the loss diminishes. A late report of a loss could be an indicator that the insured may be committing fraud. Insureds must notify the police when a loss is a theft, and, if the loss falls under credit card coverage, they must notify the credit card or electronic fund transfer company.

Delay or failure to report a loss to the police or credit card company are also potential fraud indicators. After insureds have notified the insurer or producer of a loss, the policy requires that they do the following:

- Protect the property from further damage
- Prepare an inventory of the damaged personal property that shows the quantity, description, and value of each item claimed
- Show the insurer the damaged property, provide related records and documents, and submit to an examination under oath
- Submit a signed statement (called a sworn proof of loss) to the insurer within sixty days after the insurer requests one

A **proof of loss** is a document that describes the details of the loss, property values, and insurable interest(s) in the property. The proof of loss commits the insured, under oath, to a specific set of facts. The insured's signed proof of loss contains facts such as the following:

Proof of loss
A document that describes the details of the loss, property values, and insurable interest(s) in the property.

- Time and cause of the loss
- Insured's and others' insurable interest in the property
- Existence of other insurance that might cover the loss
- Changes in the property's title or occupancy during the policy period
- Extent of damage, as shown by repair estimates, personal property inventory, and receipts for loss of use expenses
- Evidence or affidavit supporting a claim under credit card, electronic fund transfer card, or access device coverage or under forgery and counterfeit money coverage stating the amount and cause of loss

Insureds must fulfill their duties under the policy conditions before the insurer is obligated to pay for the loss. Insureds rarely know what their duties are, so claim representatives must contact them promptly and explain them. For example, insureds are usually eager to repair the damage, but claim representatives often need to inspect the damage to establish the cause of loss and verify coverage. Claim representatives should remind insureds to preserve the property for inspection and protect it from further damage.

Loss Settlement Condition

The loss settlement condition specifies whether claim payments will be calculated on an actual cash value (ACV) or a replacement cost basis (both of which were described in a previous chapter). Claims for various types of property, such as personal property and structures that are not considered buildings in a homeowners policy, are settled on an ACV basis. If the amount of insurance is adequate, claims for losses to buildings are often settled on a replacement cost basis. For large claims, the insured can immediately collect the ACV and start repairs. After the damage has been repaired, the insured can submit the final bills and receive a payment for replacement cost.

Other Insurance Condition

The other insurance condition describes the calculation that claim representatives will use when more than one insurance policy covers a loss and coverages overlap that apply to all or part of a claim. This situation could occur if an insured forgot to cancel one policy when acquiring a new policy or when a mortgage company and a property owner each insures the property with separate policies.

Suit or Legal Action Against Us Condition

The suit or legal action against us condition requires full compliance by the insured or other interested party with the coverage terms and with a time limit during which the insured or other interested party must initiate a lawsuit under the policy. Claim representatives must check this condition for the applicable time limit to ensure that a lawsuit has been filed within that time limit.

Our Option Condition

Under an "our option" condition, insurers can repair or replace the damaged property rather than pay insureds for their losses. This condition protects the insurer against unreasonable cash claims. For example, an insured's stolen silverware might be appraised at a high value and be costly to replace from a fine department store. However, replacement services might be able to replace the silverware with the same pattern at a much lower price.

Mortgagee or Mortgageholders Condition

Mortgagees (or mortgageholders, as they are called in some policies) named in the declarations have rights and obligations under property policy conditions. Some of the mortgagees' rights are as follows:

- To receive payment for property damage up to their insurable interest
- To file a separate claim on their own behalf if the insurer denies the insured's claim
- To receive a separate written notice when the insurer cancels or does not renew the policy

Mortgagees are obligated to notify the insurer about changes in ownership, occupancy, or loss exposures; pay premiums if the insured fails to do so; and submit a signed, sworn statement of loss if the insured does not. If the insurer denies the insured's claim but pays the mortgagee, the mortgagee must surrender any claim it has against the insured to the extent of the payment it received. If the insurer chooses to pay the mortgage balance in full, the mortgagee then assigns and transfers the entire mortgage and any collateral to the insurer.

Concealment, Misrepresentation, or Fraud Condition

Anytime an insured commits fraud related to the coverage or intentionally conceals or misrepresents material facts, the insurer can void the policy.

Concealment or misrepresentation could occur when the insured completes the application for insurance. If a claim representative discovers concealment or misrepresentation on the part of the insured, the claim representative must determine whether the facts the insured misrepresented or concealed were material to the underwriting process. In other words, to deny the claim, the claim representative must determine whether the underwriter would have rejected the risk or would have written the policy with significantly different terms had the truth been known.

If a mortgagee is listed in the policy, the mortgagee is not usually penalized for the insured's concealment, misrepresentation, or fraud as long as the mortgagee is unaware of the insured's actions when they occurred.

As mentioned in previous sections, when the claim representative suspects that the insured committed fraud or concealed or misrepresented material facts, the claim representative should follow the insurer's claim guidelines on future handling of the claim, which may necessitate referring the claim to the insurer's special investigation unit (SIU) for investigation.

Liberalization Condition

Under the liberalization condition, any policy revision that broadens the coverage (without charging additional premium) applies to the policy, as long as the revision occurs forty-five days or fewer before the policy's inception or during the policy's term. For example, if a policy revision increases the special limit of liability for cash from $500 to $1,000, the insured would receive the benefit of this increase in the event of a claim.

Cancellation Condition

A cancellation condition describes the parties who can cancel the policy. It also explains the mechanics of the cancellation process. This information can be important to a claim representative in the event that a dispute arises as to whether a policy is in force or not.

Examination and Inspection and Survey Conditions

The examination and the inspection and survey conditions explain the insurer's rights to examine and audit the insured's books and records and to make inspections and surveys of the property, respectively. The inspection condition also explains that the insurer is not obligated to inspect the property and that the insurer does not warrant the condition of the property (except boilers, pressure vessels, or elevators when required by state or municipal laws). The inspection condition preserves the insurer's right to hire other organizations to complete the inspections and surveys.

Insurance Under Two or More Coverages Condition

The insurance under two or more coverages condition protects the insurer from paying more than the actual damages, even when more than one coverage part applies to the property damaged. This condition provides that if an item of property, such as a small refrigerator, might be covered as part of the building or as part of the contents, the insured can have it covered only under one coverage part of a single policy. (This condition is different from the other insurance condition, which deals with property that is insured under two different policies.)

Coinsurance Condition

Through coinsurance provisions, insurers encourage business insureds to purchase adequate insurance for their property based on its value. For example, if the declarations page specifies a coinsurance of 80 percent for the building, the amount of insurance purchased on the building must equal 80 percent of the building's value at the time of the loss for the loss to be paid in full. When included, a coinsurance condition describes the steps used to calculate the coinsurance amount and provides examples that apply the coinsurance amounts.

Optional Coverages

Another part of the policy that claim representatives must be aware of are the optional coverages, because insureds may choose to purchase any of several optional coverages that add coverage to the policy. This section describes four optional coverages that are available: agreed value, inflation guard, replacement cost, and extension of replacement cost to personal property of others. These coverages apply to a policy only if they are listed in the commercial property coverage part declarations page. These four optional coverages are seen most frequently in property claims.

The first optional coverage is agreed value. For the agreed value coverage to apply, the declarations must state the agreed value and an expiration date for that optional coverage. When this coverage is included, the insurer pays for losses to the specified property based on the agreed amount during the policy period, unless the expiration date for that optional coverage has passed. This optional coverage eliminates the use of coinsurance in calculating the loss amount.

A second optional coverage is inflation guard. This coverage provides automatic increases in the insurance coverage to protect the insured against inflation.

A third optional coverage is replacement cost coverage. When replacement cost coverage is listed in the declarations, it pays losses in the same manner as replacement cost does for homeowners policies. The replacement cost coverage excludes personal property of others (except tenants' improvements and betterments to the property), contents of a residence, works of art and other collectibles, and stock (with a stock option exception). As with homeowners policies, the insurer does not pay the replacement cost value until the damaged property has been repaired or replaced—as soon as is reasonably possible.

A fourth optional coverage is the extension of replacement cost to personal property of others. This coverage is used with the replacement cost coverage to restore the excluded replacement cost coverage for the personal property of others. This coverage limits the insurer's liability to the insured's liability under a written contract between the insured and a third party, if a contract exists.

Endorsements

Another part of the policy that claim representatives must be aware of are the endorsements, because insureds can purchase endorsements to their property policies to add or remove coverage or to modify coverage terms. Homeowners endorsements that affect the amount of a property loss settlement include scheduled coverage and replacement cost provisions. Insureds might purchase commercial property endorsements to modify coverage in their commercial property policy. The following endorsements are those that claim representatives encounter frequently:

- Scheduled coverage
- Replacement cost provisions
- Ordinance or law
- Business income loss
- Flood
- Earthquake and volcanic eruption

Scheduled Coverage Endorsement

Personal property coverage in homeowners and commercial property policies is limited by the causes of loss covered and their dollar limits. **Scheduled coverage** allows insureds to buy insurance for property specifically listed (scheduled) on a policy, with a specific limit for each item. Insureds can buy scheduled coverage for certain classes of personal property. To purchase this coverage, insureds list the property to be insured, a description of each article, and the value of each article. For some property, such as fine jewelry, insurers require the insured to provide an appraisal. Restrictions and limitations still apply, but the coverage is much broader than the basic personal property coverage.

Scheduled coverage
Insurance for property specifically listed (scheduled) on a policy, with a limit of liability for each item.

Scheduled coverage does not guarantee that insureds will receive the full amount stated in the schedule when the property is destroyed or lost. Insureds often believe they will receive the full amount stated on the schedule when, in fact, the principle of indemnity applies, and insureds will receive the lesser of the scheduled amount or the ACV.

Replacement Cost Provisions Endorsement

Some replacement cost provisions are built into policies, but they might also be added by endorsement. For example, the HO-3 provides replacement cost coverage on the dwelling and other structures if the dwelling is insured for 80 percent of its replacement cost.

Insureds can endorse their property policies and pay an extra premium to receive replacement cost coverage for personal property up to the specified limit. Endorsements list types of property that are not eligible for replacement cost coverage, such as antiques, souvenirs, and obsolete items. Replacement cost coverage is not appropriate for these types of property because of the difficulty in replacing them with items of like kind and quality.

Ordinance or Law Endorsement

Insureds may purchase an ordinance or law endorsement for a property policy. Ordinance or law endorsements include three different coverages, labeled Coverage A, B, and C.

Coverage A covers the reduction in value of the undamaged portion of a building that must be demolished to comply with an ordinance or a law. Coverage can be on either an ACV or a replacement cost basis as indicated in the endorsement. No separate amount of insurance must be shown for Coverage A.

Coverage B covers the cost to demolish the undamaged portion of the structure and remove its debris. A separate amount of insurance must be shown for this coverage, and the coinsurance provision applies.

Coverage C covers the increased cost to repair, reconstruct, or remodel undamaged portions of the property to conform to the minimum requirements of an ordinance or a law. Insureds must combine this option with replacement cost coverage. A separate limit of insurance must be indicated on the declarations page, and coinsurance applies. Coverage C describes specific types of repair or reconstruction that are covered.

None of these coverages applies to losses that require a response to, or an assessment of, the effects of pollutants. Also, the coverages do not pay for losses that occur when the insured failed to comply with an ordinance or a law if compliance was required before the loss occurred.

Business Income Loss Endorsement

Insureds can purchase a business income coverage form to add business income losses coverage to a commercial property policy that does not provide the coverage. Business income loss coverage was described earlier in this chapter, and it may be included in commercial property coverage as an additional coverage.

Flood Endorsement

Some property insurers add flood coverage to commercial property policies by endorsement. Insureds may purchase flood coverage as a covered cause of loss for damage to the building and contents, for business income losses, and for ordinance or law coverage. Usually the flood endorsement has a limit of insurance that is lower than the regular policy limit.

An alternative means for insureds to obtain flood coverage is through the National Flood Insurance Program (NFIP), a government program that provides this insurance to properties in flood plains. The NFIP may provide more coverage for flood damage than an endorsement offered by an insurer.

Earthquake and Volcanic Eruption Endorsement

Most insureds do not need earthquake and volcanic eruption coverage because their properties do not lie along fault lines or near active volcanoes. However, for commercial properties that do, insureds can purchase one of two endorsements provided by ISO that add earthquake and volcanic eruption as covered causes of loss. These endorsements differ in that one endorsement includes a coinsurance clause and the other does not.

These endorsements do not define "earthquake" but do indicate that all earthquakes and shocks occurring within a 168-hour period are considered a single quake. The same time period applies to volcanic eruption, which is defined in the endorsements as the eruption, explosion, or effusion of a volcano. Were it not for this wording, every quake or aftershock might be interpreted as a separate event, leading to the application of multiple deductibles and policy limits.

In summary, property insurance policies consist of many parts. The complexities of the policies stem from the many detailed provisions included in the various sections of property policies and any attached endorsements. Policy definitions, additional and optional coverages, special limitations, causes of loss forms, coverage and policy exclusions, and conditions can add and exclude coverage, supplement the limits of underlying coverage, or reinstate coverage that had been excluded. Therefore, claim representatives should systematically analyze policies to check all the important provisions before determining coverage. The next section describes how claim representatives apply first-party coverages when they handle first-party property claims.

FIRST-PARTY PROPERTY CLAIM CONSIDERATIONS

For all property claims, claim representatives perform the activities in the claim-handling process that are outlined in the previous chapters. As with all claims, the loss notice is the starting point for a claim representative's property loss investigation. Exhibit 6-16 shows an ACORD Property Loss Notice.

The following two considerations are particularly important for claim representatives when they handle first-party property claims:

1. Loss amount
2. Statement of loss

EXHIBIT 6-16

ACORD Property Loss Notice

ACORD®

PROPERTY LOSS NOTICE

		DATE (MM/DD/YYYY)

| AGENCY | PHONE (A/C, No, Ext): 610-555-1111 | | MISCELLANEOUS INFO (Site & location code) | | DATE OF LOSS AND TIME 8-24-X0 2 | AM X PM | PREVIOUSLY REPORTED YES X NO |

Small Agency
Malvern, PA

POLICY TYPE	COMPANY AND POLICY NUMBER	NAIC CODE	POLICY DATES
PROP/ HOME	CO: Atwell Insurance Co.		EFF: 1-1-X0
	POL: 99-23456		EXP:

FAX (A/C, No):	E-MAIL ADDRESS:	FLOOD	CO:		EFF:
CODE: 555	SUB CODE:		POL:		EXP:
AGENCY CUSTOMER ID		WIND	CO:		EFF:
			POL:		EXP:

INSURED

| | CONTACT | CONTACT INSURED |

NAME AND ADDRESS OF INSURED	DATE OF BIRTH	NAME AND ADDRESS OF INSURED
Kids Science Kits, Inc. 111 Street Malvern, PA	SOC SEC # OR FEIN:	Susan Reed

| RESIDENCE PHONE (A/C, No) | BUSINESS PHONE (A/C, No, Ext) | | |

| NAME AND ADDRESS OF SPOUSE (IF APPLICABLE) | DATE OF BIRTH | RESIDENCE PHONE (A/C, No) 610-555-4444 | BUSINESS PHONE (A/C, No, Ext) 610-555-6666 |
| | SOC SEC # OR FEIN: | WHERE TO CONTACT | WHEN TO CONTACT |

LOSS

LOCATION OF LOSS	Same	POLICE OR FIRE DEPT TO WHICH REPORTED Local

| KIND OF LOSS | X FIRE | LIGHTNING | FLOOD | OTHER (explain) | PROBABLE AMOUNT ENTIRE LOSS $15,000 |
| | THEFT | HAIL | WIND | | |

DESCRIPTION OF LOSS & DAMAGE (Use separate sheet, if necessary)

Fire started in kitchen and spread to another room. Science kits damaged.

POLICY INFORMATION

MORTGAGEE

X   NO MORTGAGEE

HOMEOWNER POLICIES SECTION 1 ONLY (Complete for coverages A, B, C, D & additional coverages. For Homeowners Section II Liability Losses, use ACORD 3.)

A. DWELLING	B. OTHER STRUCTURES	C. PERSONAL PROPERTY	D. LOSS OF USE	DEDUCTIBLES	DESCRIBE ADDITIONAL COVERAGES PROVIDED
					ON

COVERAGE A. EXCLUDES WIND

SUBJECT TO FORMS (Insert form numbers and edition dates, special deductibles)

FIRE, ALLIED LINES & MULTI-PERIL POLICIES (Complete only those items involved in loss)

ITEM	SUBJECT OF INSURANCE	AMOUNT	% COINS	DEDUCTIBLE	COVERAGE AND/OR DESCRIPTION OF PROPERTY INSURED
	X BLDG CNTS	175,000	80	250	2 story office bldg
	BLDG X CNTS	40,000		250	science kits
	BLDG CNTS				

SUBJECT TO FORMS (Insert form numbers and edition dates, special deductibles)

FLOOD POLICY	BUILDING:	DEDUCTIBLE:		ZONE	PRE FIRM	DIFF IN ELEV	FORM TYPE	GENERAL	CONDO
	CONTENTS:	DEDUCTIBLE:			POST FIRM			DWELLING	
WIND POLICY	BUILDING	DEDUCTIBLE	CONTENTS	ZONE	FORM TYPE	GENERAL	CONDO		
						DWELLING			

REMARKS/OTHER INSURANCE (List companies, policy numbers, coverages & policy amounts)/NY ONLY: PREVIOUS ADDRESS OF INSURED & WIFE'S MAIDEN NAME

CAT #	FICO #	ADJUSTER ASSIGNED		ADJUSTER #	DATE ASSIGNED

REPORTED BY Susan Reed	REPORTED TO agent	SIGNATURE OF INSURED	SIGNATURE OF PRODUCER

ACORD 1 (2004/06)   NOTE: IMPORTANT STATE INFORMATION ON REVERSE SIDE   © ACORD CORPORATION 1988

Loss Amount

Determining the loss amount in first-party property claims involves some special considerations. These considerations include coinsurance conditions, valued policy laws, and debris removal coverage and other additional coverages that may apply to the claim. When determining the loss amount, claim representatives must calculate the claim based on ACV, replacement cost value, or a stated value as specified in the policy and described in the coverage sections. These valuations are affected by valued policy laws and, in some cases, debris removal coverage or other additional coverages.

Valued Policy Laws

In states with **valued policy laws**, insureds may recover the policy limit for certain losses regardless of the actual value of the property. States enacted these laws to protect insureds after a loss by prohibiting insurers from offering less than the policy limit for total losses. Because the insurer collected a premium based on the insurance amount that the insured purchased, proponents of the law believed that the insurer should pay the entire face amount to the insured for a total loss. Generally, valued policy laws have the following characteristics:

Valued policy law
A law that specifies that insureds may recover the policy limit for certain losses regardless of the actual value of the property.

- They do not apply to partial losses.
- They apply only to buildings and structures.
- They apply only to certain causes of loss, such as fire or lightning.

When insureds inflate the value of their property, valued policy laws violate the principle of indemnity and increase moral hazard. Claim representatives who suspect that a policyholder deliberately insured property at an inflated value should alert the underwriter.

Debris Removal Coverage and Other Additional Coverages

Claim representatives must consider the provisions of debris removal coverage and other additional coverages when determining the value of a loss. For example, when the damage to a building exceeds a certain percentage of its value, some city ordinances do not allow the insured to repair the building. The insured must demolish the building and build a new one. Also, ordinances might specify that the city be included as a payee on the loss payment to ensure that debris is cleared.

Property debris can be expensive to remove. Debris removal costs, when combined with the cost of rebuilding, might exceed the insured's total policy limit. Homeowners and commercial property policies provide limited coverage above the total limit of liability to pay the debris removal costs. Claim representatives add the debris removal costs (up to the coverage limit) to the final settlement amount.

In addition to having debris removal coverage, some property policies include additional limits for such costs as pollution cleanup or fire department service charges. When these additional coverages apply, claim representatives must add costs under these coverages to the final claim payment.

Statement of Loss

Statement of loss
A summary of a property claim that shows the property claimed, the property's value, the property loss amount, and the amount claimed under the policy.

A claim representative prepares a statement of loss upon closing the claim. The **statement of loss** is a summary of the claim settlement. Generally, this statement is a four-column list showing the property claimed, the property's value, the property loss amount, and the amount claimed under the policy. In the statement of loss, the claim representative indicates the recommended claim amount and the reasons that the amount is appropriate. Claim representatives outline their proposed claim adjustment in the statement and attach supporting documents so that examiners or auditors can see the source of their figures. Often, the claim will be settled based on this figure. If the insured disputes the claim settlement, the parties may choose to use one of the methods of dispute resolution discussed next.

COMMON FORMS OF DISPUTE RESOLUTION FOR FIRST-PARTY PROPERTY CLAIMS

Most property claim disputes are resolved through negotiation and appraisal. If, after negotiation and appraisal, the parties have failed to resolve their dispute, or if the dispute involves coverage questions, the parties may try alternative dispute resolution (ADR) methods, such as arbitration and mediation, to settle the dispute. If these methods fail, litigation is the final recourse for resolving property claim disputes.

Common Forms of Dispute Resolution for First-Party Property Claims	
• Negotiation	• Mediation
• Appraisal	• Litigation
• Arbitration	

Appraisal
A procedure, prescribed by a provision in a property insurance policy, for the insured and the insurer to settle disputes regarding the value of a covered loss.

Negotiation may fail to resolve a dispute about the value of a claim. In such a case, property policies include an appraisal provision that enables either party to a claim to demand an appraisal to determine the value of the claim. An **appraisal** is a procedure, prescribed by a provision in a property insurance policy, for the insured and the insurer to settle disputes regarding the value of a covered loss. Neither party can refuse this demand without violating the policy conditions; if the insured refuses appraisal, the insurer could deny the insured's claim based on the violation of the appraisal condition. Appraisal is a prerequisite to legal action. Appraisal enables parties to resolve disputes about the value of a property loss without litigation. Appraisal cannot be used to resolve coverage issues or policy language interpretation. Claim representatives must be thoroughly familiar with the appraisal procedure at the onset and must ensure that the appraisal conforms to the policy language and the insurance laws of the state where it is conducted.

The appraisal provisions in a property policy state that each party will choose a competent, disinterested appraiser within a specific time frame. The two selected appraisers then choose an umpire. Each appraiser separately establishes the loss amount based on the appraiser's own review of the loss site, the damage, suggested repair techniques, and costs. After their reviews, the two appraisers generally work together to determine the loss amount. If the appraisers do not agree on a loss amount, they involve an umpire. Some policies require the appraisers to submit to the umpire only the loss amounts on which they differ. Others require that the appraisers submit all of their loss amounts to the umpire for consideration. Any agreement between two of the three parties sets the loss amount, and it is binding on all parties. Parties can challenge the decision, but usually only fraud, collusion, or mistake of law are valid grounds for a challenge.

Because appraisal can resolve only disputes concerning the value of a claim, other methods are used to resolve coverage disputes or challenge the results of the appraisal process. If all parties agree, mediation or arbitration, as described in previous chapters, can be used to try to resolve a dispute. If these methods are unsuccessful, litigation is the final method that can be used to resolve the dispute.

Property claim disputes occasionally result in litigation, but, generally, negotiation, appraisal, or ADR can be used to settle them. Exhibit 6-17 presents a case study that illustrates a claim representative handling a first-party property claim that is resolved by negotiation.

CATASTROPHE CLAIM-HANDLING ISSUES

Catastrophes are single events that cause widespread losses. Property Claim Services (PCS) of American Insurance Services Group/ISO officially recognizes and assigns a catastrophe serial number, or cat number, to any single event that causes more than $5 million in insured damage. The most frequent causes of catastrophes are wind, hail, tornadoes, hurricanes, floods, and earthquakes.

Catastrophe
A single event that causes widespread losses.

Catastrophes strain insurance claim-handling resources because claim representatives must be sent to the area of the catastrophe to handle large numbers of claims, while at the same time they must still be available to handle the regular volume of claims. When handling catastrophe claims, claim representatives adjust several aspects of claim handling, including their response to claims and reserving methods, communication with insureds, settlement costs, claim-handling

EXHIBIT 6-17

First-Party Property Claim

Susan Reed, owner of Kids' Science Kits, Inc., owned a small, two-story office building. Her business office was on the upper level, and she hoped to rent out the office space on the street level. At the time of her loss, she had no tenants. She arrived at her office at 2:00 PM and found fire engines in front of the building.

A fire had started in a small kitchen on the second floor. The firefighters extinguished it quickly, but the fire had spread to an adjacent room, where some of her science kits were stored. Susan reported the claim to her producer immediately. The customer service representative at her producer's office recorded the loss information over the phone, entered it into Atwell Insurance Company's computerized claim entry system, and uploaded it to the insurer. At Atwell, a claim supervisor reviewed the report, verified that Susan was an insured, and assigned the claim to claim representative Bob Smith.

Bob called Susan to get more information about the loss. Susan suggested that a bagel in her toaster oven may have started the fire after she had left for an emergency business meeting. Bob made an appointment to meet Susan at the loss site the next day to inspect the damage.

Meanwhile, Bob reviewed Susan's BPP coverage. She had special form replacement cost coverage on her building and broad form coverage on her business personal property. Bob's preliminary conclusion was that Susan's fire loss should be covered, because fire is a covered cause of loss under both the special form and the broad form.

At the loss site the next day, Bob inspected the damage, starting with the building. A five-foot by five-foot area in the roof required repair. The drywall and three support studs on the wall behind the toaster oven needed to be replaced. Fire and smoke damage had occurred, and water used to extinguish the fire had caused damage, including seepage into the ceiling of the room below the kitchen. Approximately half of Susan's supply of 200 science kits in the office were burned entirely or were melted.

After Bob inspected the building damage and prepared a scope of the loss, Bob and Susan developed a list of the damaged business personal property. Susan was upset that half of the kits were damaged but explained that they were samples that she gives to customers at presentations and expositions. The kits that Susan sells were stored at the manufacturing plant, so she would be able to continue filling orders. Bob noticed that Susan did not have business income coverage. Therefore, he suggested that she discuss this coverage gap with her producer to protect her in the event of future losses.

After observing that the building looked well-maintained and that Susan's business had been thriving, Bob did not suspect arson. Bob provided Susan with sources to help her locate a suitable contractor to repair the damage, and he left a blank inventory sheet with Susan in case she remembered other personal property.

Back at his office, Bob completed the estimate on a computer estimating system. After Bob calculated the structural repairs, cleaning, painting, and carpet removal and replacement, his estimate showed that the damage to the building totaled $8,500. The business personal property loss, including the value of the damaged science kits, which were insured as stock, totaled $2,100. The policy limits for the building and the business personal property were $175,000 and $40,000, respectively. Both coverages were written with 80 percent coinsurance limits, and a $250 deductible applied to the building and business personal property. The building and business personal property were insured for more than 80 percent of the value of the property, so Susan did not have to share in the loss through coinsurance. After the deductible was applied, the final payment came to $10,350.

The fire department confirmed that the toaster oven was the source of the fire, but no defect could be confirmed because the toaster oven was destroyed in the fire. Bob discussed with his supervisor a subrogation possibility against the toaster oven manufacturer, on the grounds that the toaster oven might have been defective. However, because the toaster oven was destroyed and because the manufacturer had no history of producing defective toaster ovens, Bob and his supervisor agreed that Atwell did not have sufficient grounds to pursue subrogation.

Two days later, Susan called Bob to tell him that the contractor estimated $9,000 to repair the building. Bob asked Susan to fax him the itemized estimate because the contractor's estimate was $500 more than his. Bob discovered that the contractor's estimate included replacement of the entire floor covering in the storage room, while only one-third of the floor covering was damaged. The existing carpet was only one year old, and identical industrial carpeting was available. Because Susan maintained her property well, the replacement section of carpet should blend neatly with the older carpeting.

Bob called Susan to explain the difference between the contractor's estimate and his own and explained the reason that he believed his offer was fair. Susan was skeptical that the "patch job" would look acceptable and explained that she would call the contractor to discuss it. The contractor told Susan that the partial repair would probably be acceptable and said that the carpet company would warrant its work. Susan called Bob to accept his settlement offer, and they agreed to make the draft payable to her and the contractor.

Later, Bob met Susan in her temporary office on the lower level of her building. Susan completed and signed the proof of loss, Bob gave her the check, and they agreed that the claim was closed.

standards, and need for stress management so they can better meet the needs of their clients. These aspects of claim handling that claim representatives adjust are described in the following sections.

Insurer Response and Reserving Methods

One aspect of claim handling that claim representatives adjust for catastrophes is insurer response and reserving methods. Most insurers have a predetermined catastrophe response plan, but plans vary. Commonly, claim staff members are preassigned to catastrophe duties and teams (cat teams). Claim representatives from other areas, volunteers from the claim staff, or independent adjusters are also assigned duties.

As part of the response plan, insurers typically send an initial survey team to the catastrophe area as soon as possible to determine the geographic scope and degree of damage. PCS provides an estimate of the total insured losses. Insurers use the PCS cat number and estimate to activate their reinsurance agreements, estimate their bulk reserves (the gross estimates of their loss), and determine staffing needs.

The response plan may also involve arrangements with restoration services to assist in the mitigation of losses after a catastrophe by drying, dehumidifying, decontaminating, cleaning, removing soot from, inventorying, and packing property. Salvage companies save and recover as much value from damaged property as possible.

Communication With Insureds

Another aspect of claim handling that claim representatives adjust for catastrophes is communication with insureds. The need for effective communication with insureds is heightened because of the magnitude of loss, but catastrophes create obstacles that hinder good communication. Telephone services could be overloaded or inoperable, local claim offices and producers' offices might be damaged, and insureds who have evacuated the area are hard to locate. Additionally, insureds may be in shock and unable to deal with their loss. To reach insureds, claim representatives can use cell phones (when insureds' cell phone numbers are available), and telephone companies usually reroute lines quickly. Insurers can also use billboards, radio and television messages, and other creative methods to get information to their insureds.

Settlement Costs

Another aspect of claim handling that claim representatives adjust for catastrophes is settlement costs. Building supplies and contractor prices increase after a catastrophe because demand increases. Claim representatives should not insist that normal prices can be obtained and, therefore, refuse to settle claims for a higher amount. Normal prices are unlikely to return until most damaged properties have been repaired, and insureds should not wait long to repair their property. Delays might increase the damage to the property, increase loss of use or business income claims, or alienate insureds.

Even in a catastrophe environment, claim representatives evaluate losses and strive to pay amounts that indemnify, but do not enrich, the insured. They must carefully review estimates from contractors. Claim representatives must be alert to insureds who attempt to take advantage of the catastrophe by submitting inflated claims or by claiming damage that was not caused by the catastrophe. For example, after a hail storm, a homeowner might claim that pre-existing scratches, chips, and dents in his aluminum siding were caused by the hail storm.

Claim-Handling Standards

Another aspect of claim handling that claim representatives adjust for catastrophes is claim-handling standards. In a catastrophe, rapid, efficient work is essential. Claim representatives are likely to be less thorough in their claim-handling procedures and more flexible about settlement costs. For example, claim representatives might not require sworn proofs of loss if they have realistic estimates to document the loss and settlement amount. Insureds have a duty to protect their property from further damage, but claim representatives must be aware that fulfilling this duty might not be feasible in a catastrophe situation. For example, repair materials, generators, and pumps might not be available shortly after a catastrophe, so insureds may not be able to comply with the duty to protect their property from further damage.

Need for Stress Management

Another aspect of claim handling that claim representatives adjust for catastrophes is the claim representative's need for stress management. Handling catastrophe claims is stressful for cat teams and the office claim staff who process the high volume of catastrophe claims and routine claims while other claim representatives are dealing with the catastrophe. The cat team is under pressure to handle losses as quickly as possible. The team must find office space, such as its local claim office, a producer's office, a block of motel rooms, or an empty building, such as a school during summer break. To set up the office, the team must locate or transport office furniture and install computers, copiers, fax machines, and communications systems. The pressure to get the office set up quickly can be very stressful for all involved. Insurers can help manage this stress by planning as much of the setup as possible.

Claim representatives also experience stress as they work with insureds who are upset about their loss. Many catastrophes result in deaths and serious injuries. Although property claim representatives do not handle bodily injury losses, they might be working with insureds who have been severely injured or who have lost family members. Catastrophe claim representatives must also deal with public authorities, contractors, and other claim representatives who are under a great deal of stress. These claim representatives must be empathetic while maintaining professionalism.

In a catastrophe, claim representatives are working in uncomfortable conditions, using unfamiliar equipment, dealing with people under great stress, and working long hours separated from their families. Such circumstances are both physically and emotionally taxing, adding to the claim representative's stress. Claim representatives must effectively manage the claim-handling issues while recognizing the need to manage their own stress level.

SPECIALTY PROPERTY CLAIMS

In addition to catastrophe claims, the property claim field provides numerous opportunities for claim representatives who want to specialize in a particular type of claim. Claim representatives can gain experience and knowledge in a property insurance area, such as those in the list that follows, and then specialize in handling related claims. The following sections introduce these specialty claim areas:

- Crop insurance
- Inland marine insurance
- Ocean marine insurance
- Crime insurance

Crop Insurance Claims

Crop insurance covers damage to crops from insects, disease, and poor weather conditions, such as drought, hail, and floods. However, policies do not cover damage to the plants that produce the crops. For example, damage to oranges is covered, but damage to orange trees is not. Neglect, poor farming practices, and theft are generally excluded. Claim representatives who handle crop insurance claims must be familiar with expected crop yields and the effects of insects, disease, and adverse weather conditions on crop yields.

Inland Marine Insurance Claims

Inland marine insurance provides coverage to many types of property that are mobile or are related to transportation. The types of property covered include imports, exports, domestic shipments, bridges and instrumentalities of transportation or communication (such as telephone, television, and radio equipment towers and antennas), bailees–bailors, installment sales, contractors' equipment, and builders' risk. Inland marine insurance also involves floater policies (such as for furs, jewelry, fine arts, surgical instruments, patterns and dies, and exhibitions), dealers' policies, and miscellaneous policies (such as for valuable papers and electronic data processing equipment).

Inland marine property can be insured for specified perils or on a special form coverage basis. Inland marine insurance claims can present special loss issues, such as the custody or the use of property by someone other than the owner. Because of the varied property and issues, claim representatives face many challenges in handling inland marine claims.

Ocean Marine Insurance Claims

Ocean marine insurance covers damage to ships and barges and their cargoes. These policies provide "all-risks" coverage to ship and cargo owners. This coverage includes loss from a ship colliding with another object, weather-related damage, pirating, dishonesty of crew members, and even disposal of goods into the sea when necessary to save the voyage, among many other causes of loss. Claim representatives who gain extensive knowledge of ocean shipping, cargo, and voyage perils; laws governing liability for damages; and accounting and documentation associated with ocean shipping are well-equipped to handle ocean marine claims.

Crime Insurance Claims

Crime insurance covers causes of loss that are not covered by commercial property insurance, such as losses from employee dishonesty, forgery, burglary, robbery, and extortion. In addition, crime insurance covers money and securities that are not covered by commercial property insurance. Insurers provide many different crime coverage forms and endorsements. Claim representatives who specialize in crime claims should be familiar with all of the forms and endorsements and the specific definitions used in each so that they can handle these claims properly.

SUMMARY

Homeowners and organizations often insure their property under homeowners policies and commercial property coverage forms, respectively. Claim personnel check the named insureds listed in the declarations or in other forms to determine who is insured and to identify parties with an insurable interest in the property. Most property policies specify a deductible in the declarations.

Some homeowners policies provide property coverage for insured buildings and other structures, as well as personal property coverage. Under commercial property coverages, each commercial building and structure is identified in the declarations with a specific address and limit of insurance. Some commercial property policies provide coverage for the insured's business personal property up to a limit specified in the declarations.

Many property policies specify property that is not covered. Loss of use coverage in homeowners policies pays additional living expenses or fair rental value when insured property is damaged, while business income coverages in commercial property package policies replace business income following a loss.

Property policies provide numerous additional coverages and coverage extensions, and property coverages generally specify limits in the declarations or in other forms that describe the policy provisions. Homeowners policies provide special form coverage for the dwelling and other structures and specified perils coverage (named perils) for personal property. Commercial property policies give insureds their choice of causes of loss forms for each property listed in the declarations, including basic form, broad form, or special form coverage.

Property policies contain numerous exclusions and sometimes multiple conditions sections that affect coverage and explain how the policies operate and how claims will be settled. Commercial policies can contain optional coverages that further affect the coverage and loss settlements.

Insureds can purchase endorsements to their property policies to add or remove coverage or to modify coverage terms.

Claim representatives perform the activities in the claim-handling process for all property claims. They should read policies systematically and check all the important provisions before deciding whether a claim is covered. When determining the loss amount, claim representatives calculate the claim based on ACV, replacement cost value, or a stated value as specified in the policy and described in the coverage sections. These valuations are affected by valued policy laws and, in some cases, debris removal coverage or other additional coverages. To conclude a property claim, a claim representative prepares a statement of loss to document the amount of the loss and provide a basis for settlement discussion.

Most property claims are settled through negotiation; however, either party can demand an appraisal to resolve a dispute about the claim value. Arbitration, mediation, and, as a final recourse, lawsuits can determine the final settlement amount and resolve coverage disputes.

When handling catastrophe claims, claim representatives adjust their response to claims and reserving methods, communication with insureds, settlement costs, claim-handling standards, and need for stress management.

Property claim representatives can specialize in insurance claim areas such as crop insurance, inland marine insurance, ocean marine insurance, and crime insurance. These claim representatives should gain experience and knowledge in the desired areas to apply in handling claims.

The next chapter examines liability claims, and it describes legal liability concepts, coverage provided for liability losses, liability claim considerations, and special liability claims. These topics assist claim representatives in investigating and determining liability and liability coverage, and in handling liability claims.

CHAPTER NOTE

1. Adapted from Insurance Services Office, Inc., Homeowners 3—Special Form (ISO Properties, Inc., 2000), pp. 1–2.

Chapter 7

Direct Your Learning

Liability Claims

After learning the content of this chapter and completing the corresponding course guide assignment, you should be able to:

■ Describe the three sources of legal liability.

■ Describe the elements of negligence and the legal principles affecting liability.

■ Describe the following liability insurance policy provisions:

- Covered losses under liability coverages

- Insured persons

- Limits of liability

- Exclusions

- Conditions

- Supplementary payments

■ Describe liability claim considerations.

■ Explain why parties might use arbitration or mediation for liability claim disputes.

■ Describe the following types of special liability claims:

- Environmental liability

- Professional liability

■ Define or describe each of the Key Words and Phrases for this chapter.

Develop Your Perspective

What are the main topics covered in this chapter?

This chapter describes the coverage considerations related to liability claims, including the sources of liability, the elements of negligence, the legal principles that affect negligence, and liability coverage provisions that affect liability losses. The chapter also describes liability claim considerations and common methods of alternative dispute resolution. Two special liability coverages under which claim representatives might handle losses and in which they might choose to specialize are environmental liability and professional liability.

Review a liability policy or a liability coverage section of a policy.

- What types of liability losses are covered under this policy? Where did you find this information?
- What is the insurer's duty to defend the insured for liability claims?

Why is it important to learn about these topics?

Every third-party liability loss has the potential to become a lawsuit. Claim personnel must understand the bases for legal liability, read liability policies carefully to determine whether coverage exists, and learn to respond appropriately when handling liability claims. Doing so enables them to avoid litigation, when possible, and to prepare liability claim files for litigation in the event a lawsuit ensues.

Examine a closed liability claim.

- Was coverage provided for the claim?
- What investigation was performed?
- Was the liability determination well documented?

How can you use what you will learn?

Analyze the same closed claim.

- What actions, if any, did the claim representative take to avoid or to prepare for potential litigation of the claim?
- What evidence did the claim representative use to support his or her position regarding the claim?
- What, if anything, might you have done differently if you were handling the claim?

Chapter 7
Liability Claims

Previous chapters describe first-party claims that insureds file against the insurer to recover damages for losses that they personally have suffered. Liability claims are filed against the insured by a third party who claims to have suffered a loss caused by the insured and for which the insured could be held legally liable. This chapter discusses coverage provisions for such claims. It also discusses the sources of liability, the elements of negligence, and the legal principles that affect negligence. Finally, the chapter describes liability claim considerations, common methods of dispute resolution, and the specialized claim areas of environmental and professional liability.

LEGAL LIABILITY

People face many liability loss exposures every day in their private and their professional lives. Liability exists when a person or an organization is responsible, or liable, for injury or damage suffered by another person or organization. For example, driving an automobile presents several loss exposures. If a driver causes an automobile accident, that driver could be held liable for any injuries suffered by the other autos' occupants or by any pedestrians, and for any damage to other autos involved in the accident or any real or personal property. In another example, business owners or homeowners might be held liable for injuries to customers or visitors caused by accidents that occur on their property. Business owners can be held liable for injuries to third parties that result from their business operations or from the use of the products they make or sell. In addition, certain professionals, such as engineers, healthcare professionals, lawyers, and architects, face liability loss exposures from losses that result from practicing their professions.

Liability arises when one person violates a duty or responsibility owed to another person. For every right that a person enjoys, other people have a related duty to respect that right. For example, every person has a right to personal safety. Therefore, others have a duty to behave in a manner that does not jeopardize the safety of others.

One source of liability is **torts**, which are any civil wrongs other than a breach of contract. Torts are committed by one party against another. Torts are based in common law, which developed over time from court decisions. A second source of liability is statutes (enacted laws), and a third is contracts. Workers' compensation liability is one example of liability created by statute. This chapter focuses on liability based on torts.

Tort
Any civil wrong other than a breach of contract.

Exhibit 7-1 illustrates the sources of legal liability.

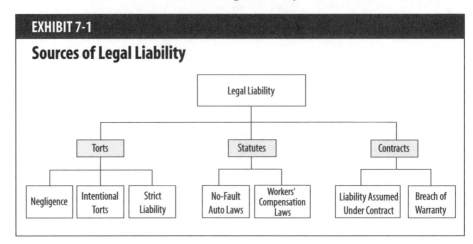

EXHIBIT 7-1

Sources of Legal Liability

An individual or organization can face a claim for legal liability in tort because of the following:

- Negligence
- Intentional torts
- Strict liability

Exhibit 7-2 illustrates the laws that establish legal liability.

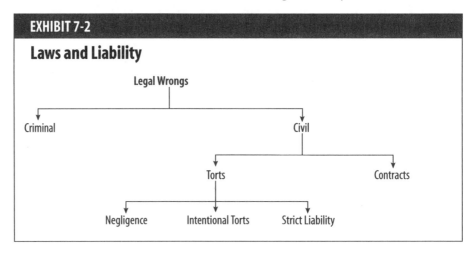

EXHIBIT 7-2

Laws and Liability

Negligence

Negligence

The failure to exercise the care of a reasonable person under the circumstances, so as not to cause harm.

Legal liability in tort can be based on negligence. **Negligence** is the failure to exercise the care of a reasonable person under the circumstances, so as not to cause harm. Liability based on negligence concerns those rights that are protected by common law.

Negligence is the most common cause of liability. Liability can exist without negligence, but if negligence leads to a loss, then the negligent person is usually liable for the damages (unless a legal document disclaims such liability). Claim representatives handle claims that result from torts caused by negligent acts.

Elements of Negligence

Liability based on negligence requires four elements to exist, as shown in the following box. All four elements must exist for a claim to be brought on the basis of negligence.

Elements of Negligence

A plaintiff in a negligence claim must establish each of the following four elements of negligence:

1. The defendant owed a legal duty of care to the plaintiff.

2. The defendant breached the duty of care owed to the plaintiff.

3. The defendant's breach of duty was the proximate cause of the plaintiff's injury or damage.

4. The plaintiff suffered actual injury or damage.

The first requirement to establish liability based on negligence is that a legal duty of care must be owed to the plaintiff. A legal duty owed is a legal obligation of persons or organizations to be careful in their activities so that they do not harm others. The relationship between the parties involved is crucial, because the relationship creates the duty. If no relationship exists, no duty exists. For example, Jim, an automobile owner, must maintain his auto so that it does not present a hazard to others. Jim knows that his brakes are not working well. However, before he has them repaired, his auto is stolen, and the thief is injured in an accident caused by the faulty brakes. Jim and the thief have no relationship, so Jim does not owe any duty to the thief. Therefore, Jim was not negligent and is not liable for the thief's injuries. However, suppose Jim had driven his car knowing that the brakes were faulty. Also suppose that Jim injured another person in an accident due to his car's faulty brakes. Jim would be liable because he owed the other person the duty to drive safely. In this case, Jim had a relationship with his fellow drivers, in the sense required to prove negligence.

The second requirement to establish liability based on negligence is a breach of (failure to meet) the duty of care owed to the plaintiff. When a duty of care is owed, the person owing the duty must exercise reasonable care in performing that duty. Because it would be impossible to define the level of care owed for every conceivable situation, courts have developed the reasonable person standard to determine the degree of care that should be exercised. The reasonable person standard means that a person's conduct is judged by comparing it with the conduct of a reasonable person under similar circumstances. The following examples help explain how this concept works. George adjusts his radio while driving around a sharp curve in the road. His auto drops off the edge of the pavement, and he loses control and strikes a wooden fence post, damaging the post and the attached fencing material. A reasonable person would not adjust the radio while driving around a sharp curve. In this case, George failed to meet the duty of care owed to others and could be held liable for the damage to the fence post. In another example, a homeowner must dig a hole in the sidewalk where he knows people will be walking. Homeowners have a duty to protect others from harm when they use sidewalks on the homeowner's property. A reasonable homeowner would place barriers to mark the hole and would cover the hole with a large sheet of heavy plywood to make it safe for others. Failure to do so would be a failure to meet the duty of care owed. If the homeowner failed to take such precautions and a neighbor's child fell into the hole and was injured, the homeowner would be liable for the resulting injuries.

The third requirement to establish liability based on negligence is that the defendant's breach of duty was the proximate cause of the injury or damage. **Proximate cause** is an event that sets in motion an uninterrupted chain of events contributing to a loss. The breach of the duty of care owed must be the accident's proximate cause, which means that the breach must directly cause the accident. For example, after Wayne drove his auto through a red light, Tami, the driver in the auto behind him, followed him through the red light. A third driver, Mark, attempted to cross the intersection legally through the green light from the adjacent street. Tami's auto struck and damaged Mark's auto. Even though Wayne had a duty to stop for the red light and did not, he is not liable for Mark's damages. Tami made an error that was the direct cause of the accident, so Tami is liable. (However, if the incident were visually recorded, Wayne and Tami would probably both be fined for their traffic violations.)

Proximate cause
An event that sets in motion an uninterrupted chain of events contributing to a loss.

The fourth requirement to establish liability based on negligence is that the plaintiff must suffer actual injury or damage. Injury or damage can include bodily injury, property damage, or damage arising out of personal injury or advertising injury. For example, Pam drives her auto into the rear of another auto, but the other auto's bumper absorbs the shock so that the other auto is not damaged and the driver is not injured. Because there are no damages, Pam is not liable due to negligence.

After determining the insured's liability for a loss based on negligence, the claim representative must consider a number of legal principles that affect liability to properly handle the claim. The next section examines those legal principles.

Legal Principles Affecting Liability

The following legal principles affect the determination of liability based on negligence by clarifying when legal liability applies or by providing a defense against liability:

- Vicarious liability
- Contributory and comparative negligence
- Assumption of risk

Vicarious liability
The legal responsibility that occurs when one party is held liable for another party's actions.

One legal principle that affects the determination of liability is vicarious liability. **Vicarious liability** holds persons or organizations responsible for losses that are caused by the actions of other parties. The responsibility for damages is transferred to the persons or organizations because some relationship exists between them and the parties who are actually negligent. The relationship found most commonly in liability claims is that between an employer and an employee. The employer is held vicariously liable for damages that result from the negligent acts of employees when the employees are acting within the scope of their employment. For example, suppose that in the course of his employment with Southland Enterprises, Dustin negligently forgets to reset a valve on a boiler. The boiler explodes and injures Boyd, a visitor who is touring the facility. Southland Enterprises is vicariously liable for Boyd's injuries, even though Dustin was negligent, because Dustin's act occurred in the course of his employment.

Two other legal principles that affect the determination of liability are contributory and comparative negligence. Sometimes, injured parties are partly responsible for their own losses. In such cases, contributory negligence or comparative negligence might apply and could provide a good defense for the party accused of causing the accident. Contributory and comparative negligence are similar in that they modify liability. Therefore, they are described together in this section.

Under **contributory negligence**, if the injured party is found to be at fault in any way for an accident, the injured party cannot collect any damages from the other party. An example follows that shows how an injured party could be at fault in some way.

Contributory negligence
A common law principle that prevents people from recovering damages if they contribute in any way to their own bodily injury or property damage.

Contributory Negligence Example

In a state that allows contributory negligence, Merriman's manufactured a circular saw and placed warning labels on the saw and in the owner's manual. The labels stated that the saw should not be used to cut synthetic concrete and that doing so could cause the saw to overheat and cause injuries. Calvin disregarded the warnings and used the saw to cut through synthetic concrete. When the saw began to overheat, a defect in a pin securing a safety shield caused the shield to malfunction, and Calvin was injured. Merriman's was not previously aware that the pin was defective. The defective pin was determined to be the proximate cause of Calvin's injuries, but Calvin contributed by using the saw improperly. Merriman's could base a defense against Calvin's claim on Calvin's contributory negligence.

Many people consider contributory negligence excessively harsh and unfair. Therefore, most states have replaced contributory negligence with comparative negligence.

Under **comparative negligence**, a partially at-fault injured party can recover from another negligent party. However, the injured party can recover only to the degree to which the other party contributed to the loss. For example, if the injured party is 20 percent at fault for the accident and the other party is 80 percent at fault, the injured party can collect 80 percent of the damages from the other party. Comparative negligence rules vary by state. Some states require the injured party to be less than 50 percent at fault to recover damages. In some other states, the injured party can be 50 percent at fault and still recover the other 50 percent of the damages. A few states require that the

Comparative negligence
A common law principle that requires both parties to a loss to share the financial burden of the bodily injury or property damage according to their respective degrees of fault.

party's negligence must be "slight" for that party to be able to recover damages. The following example demonstrates how a court might assign fault in a case.

> ### Comparative Negligence Example
>
> Continuing with the defective-saw example described previously, but assuming the state allows comparative negligence, Merriman's liability insurer or a trial court would determine a percentage of fault for Merriman's because of the defective pin and a percentage of fault for Calvin for using the saw in an inappropriate manner (to cut synthetic concrete despite warnings against such use). Suppose that the insurer or the trial court assigned 65 percent of the fault to Merriman's and 45 percent of the fault to Calvin. Also suppose that state comparative negligence laws required that the injured party be less than 50 percent at fault. Because he was less than 50 percent at fault, Calvin would likely receive a reduced damage award.

Assumption of risk

An acceptance of the chance of bodily injury or property damage by a person who is aware that a threat exists, understands the threat, and chooses to accept the threatening situation.

Another legal principle that affects the determination of liability is assumption of risk. Sometimes a person knows about a risk for a certain activity but chooses to engage in the activity anyway. This choice is called an **assumption of risk**. If injury or damage occurs after the risk has been knowingly assumed, the injured person cannot recover, even if another person caused the injury or damage. For example, spectators at baseball games assume the risk of being hit by a ball batted into the stands during the game. Even though being hit by a baseball would be the proximate cause of a spectator's injury, injured spectators cannot recover damages because they assumed the risk by attending the baseball game.

Intentional Torts and Strict Liability

In addition to negligence, legal liability can also result from intentional torts and strict liability in tort. Persons or organizations commit **intentional torts** when they purposefully injure another party or cause damage to another party's property. Liability policies generally do not cover intentional torts. For example, Brandon insults Dan. Dan responds by declaring, "Brandon, I'm going to bust your ugly nose," and then Dan punches Brandon and breaks his nose. Because Dan intended to injure Brandon, his action is an intentional tort.

Intentional tort

A deliberate act (other than a breach of contract) that causes harm to another person.

Strict liability

Liability that results from an act that causes harm to another person; liability is imposed even though the defendant acted neither negligently nor with intent to cause harm.

Strict liability is liability that results from an act that causes harm to another person and for which liability is imposed even though the defendant acted neither negligently nor with intent to cause harm. Strict liability in tort is caused by ultra-hazardous activities or dangerously defective products, abnormally dangerous instrumentalities, owning or leasing aircraft, and owning or keeping wild animals. Common law and statutes provide the legal basis for strict liability in tort. Claim representatives should examine policy provisions carefully because many ultra-hazardous activities are excluded from coverage on standard homeowners and commercial liability policies. However, when people or organizations purchase appropriate liability coverages for such activities and are held strictly liable for damages, liability insurers pay for those damages.

Courts hold people and organizations strictly liable for injury and damage caused by ultra-hazardous activities such as blasting, erecting or maintaining dams, drilling oil wells, and certain mining operations. For example, suppose that a company uses explosives to demolish a building and accidentally causes damage to surrounding buildings. The company is responsible for the damages caused by the explosives, regardless of any precautions it takes. Strict liability asserts that such ultra-hazardous activities place the community at an unusual risk of harm. Therefore, parties that engage in such activities should be held responsible.

Courts have held manufacturers (and even distributors and retail operators) strictly liable for injuries caused by defective products. The manufacturer can argue that the product was not defective or that it was misused. However, if the evidence proves that the product was defective and was used properly, then the manufacturer's degree of care and reasonableness has no effect on its liability.

Courts hold people or organizations strictly liable when they use, store, or transport dangerous instrumentalities, such as nitroglycerin, flammable gas, explosives, or crop-dusting chemicals. For example, nitroglycerin is highly susceptible to explosions. Consequently, parties who use, store, or transport nitroglycerin must use every precaution to avoid an explosion that might injure others or damage the property of others.

Courts in a number of states hold people or organizations that own or lease aircraft strictly liable for any injury or damage that results from any accident involving the aircraft. In some states, strict liability for aircraft is not needed because courts already require a greater degree of responsibility for aircraft than for ordinary vehicles in those states.

Courts hold people or organizations that own or keep wild animals or abnormally dangerous pets or livestock strictly liable for any injury or damage that those animals cause. Additionally, some states have statutes that require owners to keep their pets leashed or fenced in. An owner who allows a pet to roam freely might be strictly liable for injury or damage caused by the pet.

In summary, legal liability in tort can occur because of negligence, intentional torts, and strict liability. Except for intentional torts that cause injury or damage, insurers pay damages for which their insureds are held legally liable, provided the insureds have purchased the appropriate liability coverages. Claim representatives must determine whether the appropriate liability coverage exists when they handle liability claims. The next section describes the liability insurance that covers liability losses.

LIABILITY INSURANCE

To determine whether an insured has the appropriate coverage for a liability loss, the claim representative must examine the various provisions of the liability insurance policy. Insurers offer liability policies that cover the common liability loss exposures of most individuals and organizations.

Liability loss exposure
A condition or situation that presents the possibility of a claim or lawsuit alleging legal responsibility of a person or business for injury or damage suffered by another party.

Liability loss exposures are conditions or situations that present the possibility of a claim or lawsuit alleging legal responsibility of a person or business for injury or damage suffered by another party. Common insurance policies that provide liability coverage include the following, with the first three also providing property coverage:

• Personal Auto Policy
• Business Auto Coverage Form
• Homeowners policies
• Commercial General Liability Coverage Form

Liability losses involve the cost of damages owed to others for the harm done, the cost to settle and defend liability claims, and certain other (supplementary) costs, explained in this section. Insureds with atypical liability loss exposures can buy additional coverage through endorsements or policies that specifically address their needs.

The following section describes, in general, the provisions of liability policies shown in the box below.

Liability Policy Provisions

• Liability coverages
• Covered losses
• Insured persons
• Limits of liability

• Exclusions
• Conditions
• Supplementary payments

Liability Coverages

Various personal and commercial insurance policies include coverage for the following types of liability:

• Auto liability
• Premises and operations liability
• Products liability
• Professional liability
• Completed operations liability

Covered Losses

The insuring agreement under auto liability coverages specifies that the insurer will pay for losses due to bodily injury and property damage. These losses include any pretrial interest for which the insured is responsible because of an accident. Additionally, the coverage specifies that the insurer will settle or defend any claims or lawsuits, as the insurer considers appropriate. These claims or lawsuits must arise from acts that cause bodily injury or property damage covered by the policy. The insuring agreement also specifies that the insurer will pay the defense costs in addition to the limit of liability, until that limit has been reached as a result of a judgment or a voluntary settlement. Additionally, the liability coverage under the business auto coverage form will pay covered pollution costs or expenses under certain conditions. For example, if a truck hauling chemicals were damaged in an accident for which an insured driver was legally responsible, the insurer would pay the expenses of cleaning up any chemicals that spilled during the accident.

Premises liability coverage is included in most package policies. This liability coverage covers losses for bodily injury or property damage caused by accidents resulting from the condition or maintenance of the owner's property. For example, if a visitor slips on an icy front step, the homeowner or business owner might be liable for losses attributable to any resulting injury.

Operations liability coverage pays for bodily injury or property damage losses caused by accidents that occur away from the premises and in the course of a business's ongoing operations. For example, if a building and its contents were damaged by water when a plumbing contractor working in the building negligently disconnected the valve on a water supply line, the contractor's operations liability coverage might pay for the loss.

Products liability coverage pays for bodily injury or property damage losses due to accidents caused by the insured's products. For example, a child's injury caused by a defective toy might be covered by the toy manufacturer's products liability coverage.

Professional liability coverage pays for bodily injury or property damage losses due to accidents that are caused by certain professionals. Architects, doctors and other healthcare professionals, and engineers are among those who purchase professional liability insurance.

Completed operations liability coverage pays for bodily injury or property damage losses due to accidents that are caused by completed work that the insured has performed away from its premises. For example, a person is injured when a defectively installed retaining wall collapses. The completed operations liability coverage of the contractor who built the wall might cover the injured person's medical expenses.

Insured Persons

Liability policy provisions also identify the insured persons. Every insurance policy states the named insured (or policyholder) on its declarations page. Other parties might also be insured under that policy, but they must have a relationship with the named insured, as defined by the policy. The insurance policy generally describes all insured parties under the policy either in a specific "insured" section or in the policy definitions.

Limits of Liability

Liability coverages include provisions for limiting the insurer's liability for any claim to the limits of coverage shown in the declarations.

Liability limits are expressed in the following different ways:

- Each person limit
- Each occurrence limit
- Aggregate limit
- Split limits
- Single limits

Each person limit
The maximum amount an insurer will pay for bodily injury or property damage to any one person for a covered loss.

Each occurrence limit
The maximum amount an insurer will pay for all covered losses from a single occurrence, regardless of the number of persons incurring bodily injury or the number of parties incurring property damage.

Aggregate limit
The maximum amount an insurer will pay for all covered losses during the covered policy period.

Split limits
Separate limits of insurance that an insurer will pay a claimant for bodily injury and for property damage.

Single limit
A single limit of liability for the combined total of bodily injury and property damage from any one accident or occurrence.

An **each person limit** is a specific limit on the amount the insurer will pay any one person for bodily injury or property damage for a covered loss. If several persons are injured in a given occurrence, this limit applies separately to each person. Many commercial liability coverages establish an each person limit.

An **each occurrence limit** is a specific limit on the amount an insurer will pay for all covered losses from a single occurrence, regardless of the number of persons injured or the number of parties claiming property damage. Several different covered occurrences might take place during one policy period.

An **aggregate limit** is the maximum amount an insurer will pay for *all* covered losses during the covered policy period. Personal umbrella policies and commercial policies generally establish an aggregate limit on liability losses that the insurer will pay during a policy period.

Separate limits for bodily injury and property damage liability coverage are called **split limits**. Insurers can split limits in many ways. For example, an auto liability policy might provide split limits of $300,000/$500,000/$100,000. These limits would provide a maximum of $300,000 bodily injury coverage for each person, $500,000 of bodily injury coverage per accident, and $100,000 of property damage coverage per accident.

A **single limit** applies to any combination of bodily injury and property damage liability claims arising from the same occurrence. For example a $300,000 single limit covers a bodily injury loss up to $300,000, a property damage liability loss up to $300,000, or any combination of bodily injury and property damage arising from a single occurrence up to $300,000.

Exclusions

Insurance policies define certain situations in which the insurer will not provide coverage. Liability policies often exclude coverage for damages that result from intentional losses; some types of contractual liability; damage to property in the insured's care, custody, or control; and injuries to employees. An insured can pay an extra premium for endorsements that eliminate certain exclusions.

Conditions

Liability policy conditions specify the insured's required duties, such as ensuring the accuracy of the statements in the application and declarations, providing information about a claim, forwarding information about lawsuits, and attending hearings and trials related to a claim. The insured must not admit to negligence or fault for the accident. The insured must keep the insurer informed of any developments relating to the accident and must cooperate with the insurer's efforts to investigate and settle a loss.

The insurer also has duties. For example, if the insured becomes bankrupt, the insurer's responsibility for its insurance policy obligations continues. Some of the insurer's duties are described in separate provisions. One particularly important duty is the insurer's duty to defend.

The insurer has a duty to defend its insured when another party files a liability lawsuit against the insured, if one or more of the allegations appear to be covered under the policy. For example, suppose that Jill is legally responsible for an auto accident in which Harold is injured. Harold sues Jill for damages, and Callaway Insurance, Jill's automobile insurer, defends her in the lawsuit.

The duty to defend generally continues until the policy limits have been paid, a court enters a judgment in the insured's favor, or the insurer determines that the policy's coverage does not apply. Generally, defense expenses are unlimited and are not included in the policy limits. However, this varies by policy.

Supplementary Payments

In liability policies, the insurer often agrees to make certain payments beyond those directly related to claim settlement. These **supplementary payments** do not reduce the policy limits but cover reasonable expenses incurred by the insured at the insurer's request. For example, the commercial general liability policy states that the insurer agrees to pay any expenses it incurs in defending a claim and reasonable expenses incurred by the insured at the insurer's request in defense of a claim, including the insured's lost wages. Therefore, if insureds lose wages because they must attend trials, the insurer would pay for those lost wages, often subject to a limit.

Supplementary payment
The amount in a liability policy that the insurer agrees to pay in addition to the liability limits for reasonable expenses incurred by the insured at the insurer's request.

When handling liability claims, claim representatives must examine all liability coverages and other provisions to determine whether coverage exists for the loss and to determine the insurer's responsibilities in settling the claim and defending the insured. The next section reviews liability claim considerations in this regard.

LIABILITY CLAIM CONSIDERATIONS

Although different insurers have different procedures for and philosophies about how to handle liability claims, claim representatives follow the claim-handling activities outlined in previous chapters for all liability claims.

This section discusses some additional considerations that claim representatives should review or act on when handling liability claims.

Once the claim representative has been notified of an occurrence or a claim, he or she must consider certain issues specifically related to liability claims, including the following:

- The type of liability loss
- Whether coverage is provided or whether the insurer has a duty to defend the insured
- Whether the claimant has engaged legal counsel
- The quality of each piece of evidence
- The classification of liability into clear liability, probable liability, doubtful or no liability, or questionable liability
- The completion of any reports required for the specific type of liability claim

The claim representative must first consider the type of liability loss that is alleged. The loss may be bodily injury, property damage, or personal or advertising injury, or a combination of these. Exhibit 7-3 shows a standard loss notice for a general liability claim, which illustrates the information insurers require insureds to provide so they can properly investigate claims.

Claim representatives must read the policy and consider whether coverage is provided or whether the insurer has a duty to defend the insured. As with the insured, claim representatives should contact the claimant early in the investigation. This contact helps claim representatives establish rapport with claimants, which could facilitate the investigation and a timely settlement. The claim representative must consider whether the claimant has engaged legal counsel, and, if so, the claim representative must conduct all communications with the claimant's lawyer rather than with the claimant.

When investigating liability for a claim, claim representatives should consider the quality of each piece of evidence as if the claim were going to result in litigation, including witnesses' reliability and potential conflicts of interest, timeliness of photos, evidence collection and storage, and admissibility of the evidence in court. Claim representatives should consider that a claim supported with reliable, admissible evidence in the early stages creates a sound claim file for a good faith investigation and helps ensure the insurer's success in the event the claim is litigated.

As a result of their investigations, claim representatives classify liability into one of the following four categories:

1. Clear liability
2. Probable liability
3. Doubtful or no liability
4. Questionable liability

EXHIBIT 7-3

General Liability Notice of Occurrence/Claim

ACORD

GENERAL LIABILITY NOTICE OF OCCURRENCE/CLAIM

DATE (MM/DD/YYYY)
8/24/X0

AGENCY	PHONE (A/C, No, Ext): 610-555-1111

Small Agency
Malvern, PA 19355

NOTICE OF OCCURRENCE	DATE OF OCCURRENCE AND TIME	X AM	DATE OF CLAIM	PREVIOUSLY REPORTED
X NOTICE OF CLAIM	8/24/X0	PM		YES X NO

EFFECTIVE DATE	EXPIRATION DATE	POLICY TYPE	RETROACTIVE DATE
1-1-X0	1-1-X1	X OCCURRENCE CLAIMS MADE	

COMPANY	NAIC CODE:	MISCELLANEOUS INFO (Site & location code)
Blithe Insurance Co.		

FAX (A/C, No):	E-MAIL ADDRESS:

CODE: 555	SUB CODE:

POLICY NUMBER 99-012345	REFERENCE NUMBER

AGENCY CUSTOMER ID:		

INSURED   **CONTACT**   CONTACT INSURED

NAME AND ADDRESS	SOC SEC # OR FEIN: 111-11-1111	NAME AND ADDRESS	WHERE TO CONTACT
Mike Belden Malvern, PA 19335			WHEN TO CONTACT

RESIDENCE PHONE (A/C, No) 610-555-2222	BUSINESS PHONE (A/C, No, Ext) 610-555-3333	RESIDENCE PHONE (A/C, No)	BUSINESS PHONE (A/C, No, Ext)

OCCURRENCE

LOCATION OF OCCURRENCE (Include city & state)	A public park near Mike's home in Malvern, PA	AUTHORITY CONTACTED

DESCRIPTION OF OCCURRENCE (Use separate sheet, if necessary)	Mike's daughter, Allison, was walking the family dog, Shiloh, when Shiloh bit a woman.

POLICY INFORMATION

COVERAGE PART OR FORMS (Insert form #s and edition dates)	HO-3

GENERAL AGGREGATE	PROD/COMP OP AGG	PERS & ADV INJ	EACH OCCURRENCE	FIRE DAMAGE	MEDICAL EXPENSE	DEDUCTIBLE	PD
			300,000				BI

UMBRELLA/EXCESS	UMBRELLA	EXCESS	CARRIER:	LIMITS:	AGGR	PER CLAIM/OCC	SIR/DED

TYPE OF LIABILITY

PREMISES: INSURED IS	X OWNER	TENANT	OTHER:	TYPE OF PREMISES

OWNER'S NAME & ADDRESS (If not insured)   OWNERS PHONE (A/C, No, Ext):

PRODUCTS: INSURED IS	MANUFACTURER	VENDOR	OTHER:	TYPE OF PRODUCT

MANUFACTURER'S NAME & ADDRESS (If not insured)   MANUFACT PHONE (A/C, No, Ext):

WHERE CAN PRODUCT BE SEEN?

OTHER LIABILITY INCLUDING COMPLETED OPERATIONS (Explain)

INJURED/PROPERTY DAMAGED

NAME & ADDRESS (Injured/Owner)	Unknown at this time—Insured is gathering information.	PHONE (A/C, No, Ext)

AGE	SEX F	OCCUPATION	EMPLOYER'S NAME & ADDRESS	PHONE (A/C, No, Ext)

DESCRIBE INJURY FATALITY	dog bite	WHERE TAKEN	WHAT WAS INJURED DOING?

DESCRIBE PROPERTY (Type, model, etc)	ESTIMATE AMOUNT	WHERE CAN PROPERTY BE SEEN?	WHEN CAN PROPERTY BE SEEN?

WITNESSES

NAME & ADDRESS	BUSINESS PHONE (A/C, No, Ext)	RESIDENCE PHONE (A/C, No)

REMARKS

REPORTED BY Mike Belden	REPORTED TO agent	SIGNATURE OF INSURED	SIGNATURE OF PRODUCER

ACORD 3 (2004/06)	NOTE: IMPORTANT STATE INFORMATION ON REVERSE SIDE	© ACORD CORPORATION 1986

Claim representatives determine clear liability when the insured was entirely at fault for the injury or damage. Claim representatives determine probable liability when the insured's liability is not clear-cut. The insured was probably at fault and probably would not win if the case were presented to a judge or jury in a trial. Claim representatives determine doubtful or no liability when the insured was probably not liable for the injury or damage. They determine questionable liability when it is unclear which party is primarily responsible for the injury or damage. In some cases, multiple parties might be liable, and questions about how the accident occurred might never be resolved. To make this liability determination, claim representatives must thoroughly investigate and consider the circumstances of each claim.

Once liability has been determined and classified, the claim representative can document the claim file. In addition to the usual claim reports a claim representative must complete, insurers might require claim representatives to report certain types of liability claims to supervisors. Such claims could include those involving back, brain, or spinal cord injuries. Therefore, claim representatives must consider any special reports required for liability claims. Because third-party liability claims often take longer to settle than first-party property claims, such reports are very important. More people are likely to review a liability claim file, and they must be able to determine from the file and reports what actions were taken and what determinations were made during the claim process. Once the claim representative has determined the cause of loss, including the liability; has determined a loss amount; and has documented the claim, he or she concludes the claim through negotiation or dispute resolution.

LIABILITY DISPUTE RESOLUTION

Many liability claims are resolved through negotiation. However, some third-party claimants might dispute the settlement amount and might make demands because of outside influences, such as opinions from their friends about the value of their claims or law-firm advertising. If the parties fail to resolve the dispute through negotiation, common alternative dispute resolution (ADR) methods, such as arbitration and mediation, can be used. As with all claims, litigation is a final recourse for resolving liability claim disputes.

ADR includes arbitration and mediation, described previously in the text. In arbitrating liability claims, the parties are usually the claimant and the insurer representing the insured. Parties might prefer arbitration over litigation for the following two reasons:

1. Parties generally require less time to reach a decision in arbitrated cases than in litigated cases.

2. Arbitration is generally less expensive for both parties than litigation.

Parties use mediation more frequently for liability claims than for property claims because liability claim issues are more complex. Mediation helps the parties analyze their dispute, consider possible solutions, and perhaps devise a compromise.

Every liability claim can result in litigation. When the claim representative and the claimant cannot agree on liability issues or the loss amount, the claimant might choose to file a lawsuit and let a judge or jury decide. Parties can continue negotiation after a lawsuit is filed. In fact, disputing parties settle most claims before trial.

An earlier chapter provides an extensive examination of the property damage and bodily injury claim investigations that claim representatives use to determine the value of a liability claim. In summary, this chapter provides information on establishing legal liability and on determining liability coverage. Exhibit 7-4 presents a case study that illustrates a claim representative handling a liability claim from loss reporting to conclusion.

SPECIAL LIABILITY CLAIMS

Claim representatives can improve their job skills and employment opportunities by gaining experience and knowledge in special types of liability claims. The following are some liability areas that offer broad opportunities for claim specialization and are described next:

- Environmental liability
- Professional liability

Environmental Liability Claims

Since the early 1970s, awareness of environmental issues has grown, and numerous federal and state laws have been enacted to help curb pollution. Such laws create environmental liability. Environmental liability is financial responsibility for damages resulting from pollutants being released into the environment.

Often, pollution is discovered that resulted from activities that occurred years earlier. Environmental liability laws hold current landowners responsible for pollution that occurred years ago on their property, as well as any previous landowners who, at the time they owned the property, were aware that the pollution existed. For example, a homeowner decides to convert from an oil-fired furnace to gas heat. When removing the underground oil tank, a contractor discovers that the tank had leaked oil into the soil for many years. Current laws would require the homeowner to pay to remove the contaminated soil.

EXHIBIT 7-4

Bodily Injury Liability Claim

Mike Belden had a homeowners policy with Blithe Insurance Company. Mike's fifteen-year-old daughter, Allison, owned a border collie named Shiloh. On Monday morning, Allison walked Shiloh in a public park near the Beldens' home. There, Shiloh bit a woman who was playing with her children.

On Monday afternoon, Mike called his insurance producer to report the incident. Mike's producer entered the claim information that Mike provided and transmitted it to the Blithe Insurance claim department. Mike did not have any other details about the accident but promised to get them as soon as possible.

A claim manager at Blithe assigned the loss to a claim representative, Peggy Johnson, who began her investigation early Tuesday morning.

The claim file included a work phone number and home phone number for Mike. Peggy called Mike at work to ask him a few questions. Mike told her that Shiloh had never bitten anyone before, although he had snapped at neighbors' children occasionally. When he was not on a leash, Shiloh was kept in a pen.

Mike also told Peggy that he just received a call from Mrs. Voelker, the woman who was bitten. He gave Mrs. Voelker's phone number to Peggy and gave Peggy permission to interview Allison about the incident.

Peggy called Allison and, with her permission, tape-recorded their conversation. Allison explained that while she was walking Shiloh, a mother and her three children approached her. The mother asked Allison whether the children could pet Shiloh. Allison suggested that it might be better if they did not, but the mother reached out to pet Shiloh anyway, just as one of the children accidentally stepped on his tail. Shiloh growled and snapped at the woman's hand. The bite did not appear serious to Allison, although she said it did break the skin. Allison said she apologized for the incident and gave the woman her name and phone number before the woman hurried off to seek medical treatment.

After finishing her talk with Allison, Peggy wrote up her notes from their conversation and then called Mrs. Voelker. Peggy tape-recorded the conversation with Mrs. Voelker's permission. Mrs. Voelker's story differed from Allison's. She said that Allison had had no objection to her family's petting Shiloh. Mrs. Voelker said she did not see any of the kids step on Shiloh's tail but admitted that it could have happened. She told Peggy that she spent three hours in the emergency room waiting to have her hand treated and that the doctor said the cut might leave a scar. She mentioned that the bill from the emergency room totaled $350.

Peggy summarized the conversation in the file activity log. Peggy knew that different states have different laws about dogs and liability for dog bites. The common law in her state allowed a "first bite" before establishing a standard of absolute liability. Although Shiloh had never bitten anyone previously, he did have a history of snapping at children, which was not in the Beldens' favor.

The city had a statute that requires dogs to be on a leash at all times. Allison complied with that statute by keeping Shiloh on his leash, which was a factor in the Beldens' favor. Peggy also thought that Mrs. Voelker might have watched her children more closely as they approached the dog. Peggy reviewed her notes and wrote in the activity log that "Coverage is provided under the terms of the homeowners policy. However, liability appears to be questionable. Although Shiloh bit Mrs. Voelker, Allison alleged that Shiloh was provoked."

Peggy called Mrs. Voelker back and explained why she did not believe the Beldens were liable for the dog bite. Peggy added that if Mrs. Voelker would send her a copy of the hospital bill, she could reimburse her under the policy's medical payments provision, which allowed for limited medical payments without regard to liability. After some discussion, Mrs. Voelker agreed to the offer and promised to mail the bill.

Two weeks later, Peggy received Mrs. Voelker's medical bill and, in turn, sent her a check for $350. Peggy closed her file on the claim and completed the activity log.

Before 1986, most commercial liability insurance policies provided coverage for pollution on an occurrence basis, without aggregate limits, if the polluting event was "sudden and accidental." Homeowners policies and other personal insurance policies had no pollution exclusion. Therefore, if a claim occurred during the policy period of any previous policy, even if the claim was just discovered, coverage would generally apply under the old policy. Contemporary commercial general liability policies specifically exclude pollution or provide a specific limit for pollution liability losses.

Some insurers offer environmental liability policies. The policies they offer are expensive and are underwritten based on restrictive guidelines. Claim representatives who handle serious commercial liability claims are likely to encounter claims for environmental liability, even if the policies do not provide coverage. Because of the complex issues related to the previous owner's responsibility for pollution, environmental liability claims can be complicated and can require claim representatives to perform extensive investigations to locate all parties who are liable for the damage.

Professional Liability Claims

Many professionals develop considerable knowledge and experience in their field. The public trusts these professionals to apply that knowledge and experience when providing professional services. When a professional fails to properly practice the profession (called malpractice), he or she could incur professional liability. Professional liability insurance has evolved to meet the specialized needs of professionals including physicians, lawyers, clergy, registered or licensed practical nurses, dentists, certified public accountants, registered architects, professional engineers, and pharmacists, among others.

Professional liability is not always clear. In malpractice claims, the insured's professional reputation can be adversely affected. This adverse effect can be magnified when claims are paid, so most professional liability policies include consent to settle clauses. Such a clause requires the insured's written consent to settle.

Like environmental liability claims, professional liability claims offers areas in which claim representatives can specialize and develop skills. The following types of professional liability insurance are described next:

- Directors and officers
- Professional liability insurance for medical services providers
- Professional liability insurance for legal services providers

Directors and Officers

One type of professional liability insurance is directors and officers. Persons responsible for the success of various businesses and other organizations, including those who serve on the board of directors or who are trustees of organizations, face liability loss exposures. When decisions or actions of directors and officers result in a loss of value of the organizations they lead, stockholders or others affected by the loss can make legal liability claims against the directors and officers. In these cases, claimants must prove that the directors and officers performed their duties improperly, which resulted in damages. Claim representatives who handle directors and officers claims benefit from knowledge of publicly held corporations, stockholders' rights, and the responsibilities of directors and officers in these corporations.

Professional Liability Insurance for Medical Services Providers

Another type of professional liability insurance is that intended for medical services providers. Laws require that medical professionals exercise proper standards of care. Common professional liability allegations against medical services providers include the following:

- Surgical error
- Improper diagnosis
- Improper tests performed
- Failure to disclose risks of a procedure or treatment
- Failure to properly administer and use anesthetics or drugs

When patients or their families perceive that a physician has failed to meet his or her duty of care, injured parties can file liability claims.

Insurers have developed physicians professional liability insurance policies to address the professional liability of physicians. Physicians are also held liable for the negligence of their employees and of other physicians with whom they have entered into partnerships or professional corporations to practice medicine. Physicians professional liability insurance is one type of professional liability insurance for medical services providers that addresses these types of liability.

Various types of professional liability insurance for medical services providers apply for dentists, nurses, therapists, optometrists, emergency medical technicians, veterinarians, and others, and for hospitals, clinics, nursing homes, and other medical care facilities. Claim representatives handling liability claims for medical services providers benefit from knowledge of the medical profession, including medical terminology and procedures, and from knowledge of medical organizations.

Professional Liability Insurance for Legal Services Providers

Another type of professional liability insurance is that intended for legal services providers. Persons and organizations depend on their lawyers to represent them properly in all legal matters. Proper representation can include filing a complaint within the specified time, completing other paperwork within the specified time, and properly advising clients on legal matters. When a lawyer provides services that fall below the standard of care required of other lawyers in similar situations, the client can suffer financial losses. Clients who believe their former lawyers have provided inferior services can file lawsuits against those lawyers. Some insurers have responded to these loss exposures and developed policies for legal services providers.

In summary, environmental and professional liability claims offer claim representatives challenges and provide chances for them to specialize in a liability claim area. Claim representatives who develop knowledge and experience in these fields can advance into these specialized careers. Claim representatives handling liability claims for legal services providers benefit from extensive knowledge of the legal profession, legal procedures, and court systems.

SUMMARY

Liability claims are filed against the insured by third parties who have suffered losses that they claim the insured caused. An individual or organization can face a claim for legal liability in tort based on negligence, intentional acts, and strict liability. Legal liability of one party for the damages suffered by another can also be based on statutes and contracts.

A plaintiff in a negligence claim must establish each of the following four elements of negligence: (1) The defendant owed a legal duty of care to the plaintiff, (2) The defendant breached the duty of care owed to the plaintiff, (3) The defendant's breach of duty was the proximate cause of the plaintiff's injury or damage, and (4) The plaintiff suffered actual injury or damage.

Vicarious liability, contributory and comparative negligence, and assumption of risk are legal principles that affect the determination of liability based on negligence. Vicarious liability and contributory and comparative negligence clarify how liability laws apply to claims. Insurers assert assumption of risk as a defense when an injured person knew that an activity involved risk but engaged in the activity anyway.

Legal liability can also result from intentional torts and strict liability in tort. Insurance does not usually cover intentional torts. Strict liability in tort is the basis for claims for injuries caused by dangerously defective products, abnormally dangerous instrumentalities, owning or leasing aircraft, or owning or keeping wild animals.

Common insurance policies that provide liability coverage include the Personal Auto Policy, the Business Auto Coverage Form, homeowners policies, and the Commercial General Liability Coverage Form. Liability policies identify or describe liability coverages, covered losses, insured persons, limits of liability, exclusions, conditions (including the insurer's duty to defend), and supplementary payments. These policies include coverage for auto liability, premises and operations liability, products liability, professional liability, and completed operations liability.

Claim representatives follow the claim-handling activities described in previous chapters for all liability claims. Claim representatives must consider certain issues specifically related to liability claims. They must first determine the type of loss that is alleged and then read the policy to determine whether coverage is provided or whether the insurer has a duty to defend the insured.

Claim representatives should contact the claimant early in the investigation and should establish whether the claimant has engaged legal counsel. If so, further communication should be with counsel rather than with the claimant. Furthermore, the claim representative should determine the quality of each piece of evidence as if the claim were going to result in litigation. Evidence can help classify liability into one of four categories: clear, probable, doubtful or no liability, or questionable. Claim representatives must also complete any special reports that relate to certain types of liability claims.

When claim representatives and claimants cannot agree on a negotiated settlement, the parties can use alternative dispute resolution (ADR) methods such as arbitration or mediation. If these methods fail, the claimant might initiate litigation.

Environmental liability insurance and professional liability insurance offer opportunities for claim specialization. Environmental liability laws hold current landowners responsible for pre-existing and current pollution. Environmental liability coverages meet the needs of homeowners and business owners. When professionals fail to practice their professions properly, their occupations present professional liability loss exposures. Professional liability coverages meet the specialized needs of directors and officers, medical services providers, legal services providers, and many other professionals. These coverages offer challenges and provide career opportunities for claim representatives who develop specialized knowledge and experience.

The next chapter examines another challenging area for claim representatives that often requires specialized knowledge and skills: workers' compensation claims. It introduces concepts specific to workers' compensation claims, workers' compensation coverage sources, workers' compensation and employers' liability policy provisions, and unique considerations for handling workers' compensation claims.

Chapter 8

Direct Your Learning

Workers' Compensation Claims

After learning the content of this chapter and completing the corresponding course guide assignment, you should be able to:

■ Describe the benefits of the workers' compensation system for employers and employees and the three statutory requirements for an injury to be compensable.

■ Describe workers' compensation coverage sources that employers can use to guarantee that they will provide benefits for injured employees.

■ Describe the coverages and provisions of a workers' compensation and employers' liability insurance policy.

■ Explain how a claim representative identifies workers' compensation coverage and addresses coverage questions.

■ Describe how to investigate a workers' compensation claim, including:

• Post-accident activity investigation

• Recovery from second injury funds

• Special external workers' compensation reports that must be completed

■ Explain how to determine workers' compensation compensability (the cause of loss) and benefits (the loss amount).

■ Describe the different workers' compensation benefits:

• Medical benefits

• Disability benefits

• Rehabilitation benefits

• Death benefits

■ Explain how workers' compensation claims can be concluded.

■ Define or describe each of the Key Words and Phrases for this chapter.

Develop Your Perspective

What are the main topics covered in this chapter?

This chapter describes the coverage and claim-handling practices related to workers' compensation claims. First, the chapter describes workers' compensation statutory requirements and coverage sources and then the coverage provided in the workers' compensation and employers' liability (WC&EL) insurance policy. Next, the chapter describes claim-handling activities that differ from the claim-handling activities for other types of claims, including the benefits that might be paid under workers' compensation coverages.

Review the workers' compensation and employers' liability (WC&EL) insurance policy.

- What types of coverages are provided under this policy?
- How is this policy similar to a commercial liability policy?
- How does this policy differ from other types of policies described in this course?

Why is it important to learn about these topics?

Workers' compensation is heavily regulated, and claim handling must conform to state and federal laws. While laws regulate workers' compensation, claim personnel must understand the concept of compensability and its application to claim handling as well as the benefits that might be provided by state laws. Claim personnel must also understand the application of employers' liability coverages in workers' compensation claims so that they can properly handle claims that fall under employers' liability coverages.

Examine the workers' compensation benefits for your state.

- What types of workers' compensation benefits would your organization provide based on your state's laws?
- What limitations apply to workers' compensation benefits under your state's laws?

How can you use what you will learn?

Analyze a workers' compensation claim.

- What types of benefits were paid under the claim?
- What is the expected duration of any disability payments made under the claim?
- What other laws or regulations might apply to the facts of the claim?

Chapter 8
Workers' Compensation Claims

News accounts of work-related injuries or deaths, such as the following, are frequent:

Laborer killed in fall from scaffolding	Worker burned in elevator explosion	Worker loses finger in a punch press accident

These losses and many others like them may be paid under workers' compensation statutes (laws that require employers to pay medical expenses and disability to injured workers). The chapter explains the types of policies that protect employers and employees in the event of a work-related injury. It begins by describing workers' compensation statutory requirements and sources for paying worker's compensation losses. It describes the coverage provided under workers' compensation and employers' liability insurance policies, and it describes workers' compensation claim issues.

Workers' Compensation Law Variations

Workers' compensation laws vary widely by state. Claim representatives should be familiar with the laws in each state for which they handle claims. The United States Chamber of Commerce publication *Analysis of Workers' Compensation Laws* is a useful reference tool that is updated annually.

WORKERS' COMPENSATION STATUTORY REQUIREMENTS

Workers' compensation is a system that pays disability benefits (lost wages) and provides medical and vocational rehabilitation benefits to injured workers following employment-related injuries and diseases. This system also pays death benefits to workers' dependents following employment-related fatalities. Workers' compensation laws are designed to benefit the employer *and* the worker. Employers benefit because they avoid costly lawsuits brought by workers injured during employment. Workers benefit through payments for medical expenses and disability without the need to prove the employer was

Workers' compensation
A system that pays lost wages, medical and vocational rehabilitation expenses, and death benefits to injured workers or their dependents for employment-related injuries and diseases.

in any way responsible (at fault) for the injury. These laws create a system whereby workers relinquish the right to sue for certain damages in return for their employers' strict liability for work-related injuries and diseases. These laws make workers' compensation the injured worker's exclusive remedy for injury or disease, except in rare circumstances. (Throughout the remainder of the chapter, the term "injury" will include injury and disease unless otherwise stated.)

State statutes determine workers' compensation benefits. Although liability insurance is based on statutory language regarding negligence, in contrast, fault is generally not a factor in paying workers' compensation benefits.

State statutes also determine the compensability of work-related injuries. **Compensability** is the qualification of a benefit for payment under workers' compensation statutes. Automobile, property, and liability claim professionals determine coverage for losses, while workers' compensation professionals determine whether injuries are compensable to determine whether benefits should be paid. The three statutory requirements for an injury to be compensable under workers' compensation are as follows:

1. An employment relationship must exist.
2. The injury must be covered (it must be an injury described by state laws).
3. The injury must arise out of and in the course of employment.

Claim representatives must evaluate these requirements in sequence. The first requirement must be met before evaluating the second requirement. And then the second requirement must be met before evaluating the third requirement. If an injured worker does not meet the three sequential requirements, then that worker is not entitled to benefits provided under workers' compensation statutes.

Employment Relationship

The first requirement for an injury to be compensable under workers' compensation is for an employment relationship to exist. The injured worker must be an employee rather than an independent contractor (a person who contracts with another to perform a task). An employee is an individual who has consented to work for the employer in exchange for consideration. This consent implies that the worker agrees to be under the employer's authoritative direction and control.

The following three elements are required in an employment relationship:

1. Control
2. Consent
3. Consideration

Control

The first element required in an employment relationship is control. Control includes the employer's right to give orders, direct the manner in which the

Compensability
The qualification of a benefit for payment under workers' compensation statutes.

work is done, and hire and discharge workers. Control is absent for independent contractors. Independent contractors determine the means and methods of accomplishing their work.

Consent

The second element required in an employment relationship is consent. An employer must freely offer employment to the worker, who must freely accept the terms of the employment. This consent is required for workers' compensation coverage to apply. For example, consent exists when Sheer Windows Company offers a job to Darrin after interviewing several applicants. Darrin agrees to accept the job at the wage offered by Sheer Windows, as opposed to a job offer he received from Duncan Steel. This consent would exist even if Darrin were the only job applicant at Sheer Windows and if its offer were Darrin's only job offer. In contrast, consent does not exist when prison inmates work as part of their sentences because they have no choice about whether to work or at what types of jobs, and because the prison does not select its workers. In summary, for consent to exist, the worker must freely accept the employment terms and must be competent to make an employment agreement. Questions of consent have led some states to expressly exclude employment of the employer's spouse or child from workers' compensation coverage.

Consideration

The third element required in an employment relationship is consideration. The employer must give something of value to the worker in exchange for services. This consideration can be money or other tangible or intangible objects. For example, room and board and memberships in health clubs could constitute consideration. Workers performing gratuitous services (provided at no charge) are not covered under workers' compensation. For example, as a gesture of friendship, a neighbor mows Joe's lawn while Joe is on vacation. Joe's neighbor would not be Joe's employee in this case because no consideration was provided.

Excluded Employments

Some employments are excluded from workers' compensation coverage by state law, even though an employment relationship exists. Excluded employments vary by state and could include the following:

- Domestic workers
- Agricultural employments
- Real estate salespeople and brokers
- Newspaper carriers
- Intrafamily employments
- Athletes, officials, and taxicab drivers
- Public and federal employments

- Employers having fewer than a minimum number of employees
- Religious, charitable, and nonprofit employments
- Employment in illegal trades
- Casual workers (for example, part-time babysitters)

Some states do not exclude any of these employments, while other states exclude only a few. Claim representatives must know the law in every state for which they handle workers' compensation claims.

In summary, if any the elements of control, consent, and consideration are present and the employment is not excluded, then the employment relationship requirement has been met.

Covered Injury

Assuming an employment relationship exists, the second requirement that must be met for an injury to be compensable under workers' compensation is for it to be a "covered" injury. State and federal laws consider an injury to be covered if it is an **occupational injury**, which is an injury that arises from the worker's employment.

Occupational injury
An injury that arises from a worker's employment.

Workers' compensation laws might not cover all work-related injuries. To be covered, occupational injuries must meet the criteria set in the workers' compensation laws of the state where the injury occurred. Generally, covered injuries fall within the following categories:

- Accidental injury
- Occupational disease
- Mental injury

Accidental Injury

The first category of covered injuries is accidental injury. Some states require that an injury be accidental to be covered. By definition, this requirement excludes workers who intentionally injure themselves. Some laws further restrict the definition by excluding injuries arising from causes such as intoxication or illegal drug use, willful failure to use a safety device or to observe safety regulations, or failure to perform a duty required by law.

Usually, the following two requirements must be met for an injury to be considered accidental and therefore to be compensable:

1. Unexpected
2. Definite time and place

In the past, the "unexpected" requirement was applied to the cause of an accident. Thus, claims for injury caused by normal and usual strains on the job were declined. Today, only the resulting injury, and not the cause of it, must be unexpected to warrant coverage under workers' compensation law.

Some states previously held that the cause of an injury must be traceable to a definite time and place. However, this created problems in awarding compensation for nonspecific injuries from nonspecific causes. For example, lower back pain that resulted from long-term exposure to heavy lifting and bending would not have been compensable. Today, most states recognize the no-fault, strict liability assumed by employers in workers' compensation law.

A hernia is an injury that occurs frequently in the workplace, but because hernias can be congenital and can be caused by normal life experiences or trauma, hernias must meet specific requirements to be covered under workers' compensation laws. Most states require that both the cause of the hernia and the resulting hernia be definite in time and place. Thus, a worker must be performing a work-related activity when the hernia occurs. For coverage to apply, states also could require that the worker had no preexisting hernia, that the employer was notified promptly about the injury, that the worker sought prompt medical attention, or that any combination of these requirements exists.

Occupational Disease

The second category of covered injuries is occupational disease. An **occupational disease** is a disease that is caused by and is peculiar to an industrial setting. Most state workers' compensation laws distinguish between occupational disease (covered) and ordinary disease (not covered). Because states vary in how they define occupational disease, claim representatives should be familiar with the laws of the states within their territories. Occupational disease can include hearing loss caused by industrial noise; allergic reactions to hazardous materials in the workplace; accidental infectious disease; cumulative trauma, such as carpal tunnel syndrome; and progressive trauma, such as pulmonary disease caused by an employee's breathing foreign particles on a job site.

Occupational disease
A disease that is caused by and is peculiar to an industrial setting.

For an occupational disease to qualify for compensation, the following tests must usually be met:

- State law must specify that the disease normally results from the nature of the employment.
- The exposure to the disease must arise from employment.

A worker may not know the date when a disease was contracted; in such instances, to assign a loss date, states apply one of the following guidelines, or triggers:

- The date of last injurious exposure to the harmful stimuli on the job (often the last day of employment)
- The date on which the disease or generalized condition becomes disabling
- The date on which the disease first manifests itself
- The date on which a doctor declares that a worker is suffering from a work-related disease

Mental Injury

The third category of covered injuries is mental injury. Definitions and court interpretations of mental, or psychological, injuries present special challenges for workers' compensation claim representatives. Coverage for mental injuries depends on how "injury" is defined and how courts interpret that definition. States fall roughly into the following four categories regarding their definitions of mental injury and interpretations of mental injury coverage:

1. States that do not cover mental injury unless it results from a compensable physical injury (called physical-mental injury)
2. States that require an unusual, work-related cause for the mental injury
3. States that require the cause of the mental injury to be predominantly work-related
4. States that do not specifically address mental injury damages in their laws and decide case by case

Examples of mental injuries that a worker may suffer include the following:

*   Fear about using a machine that amputated another worker's finger
*   Refusal to be seen in public after being severely burned and scarred in a work-related accident
*   Nervousness and crying spells related to an intimidating supervisor
*   Insomnia and anxiety because of a greatly increased workload

By reviewing state legislation and court decisions, claim representatives can determine the extent of mental injury coverage in the states in which they handle claims.

Arising Out of and in the Course of Employment

Assuming an employment relationship exists and the injury is covered, the third requirement for an injury to be compensable under workers' compensation is for the injury to have arisen out of and in the course of employment. The injury must occur while the employee is working and as a result of some condition that is reasonably incidental to that employment. This requirement usually includes two separate tests, "arising out of" and "in the course of." Most states require that both tests be met for an injury to be compensable. However, some states apply these rules separately and require only one test to be met.

"Arising Out of"

The "arising out of" test of compensability determines whether the cause of an injury was work related. Not all injuries that occur during employment are considered to be work related. For example, if an employee is injured during a brawl in the company parking lot with a personal acquaintance who has no relationship to the employer, that injury did not arise out of the employment. An injury is considered to have arisen out of the employment if it was caused by some circumstance of the employment.

Some conditions that cause injury affect the general public to the same extent that they affect workers. In such cases, the "arising out of" employment test is met when the worker is exposed to a greater degree of risk than the public at large. At times, the nature of the employment leads to greater risk of injury. For example, compared with the general public, police officers are exposed to increased risk of injury from gunfire because of their work.

"In the Course of"

The "in the course of" test examines the time and place that the injury occurred and the worker's activities at that time. If the worker was engaged in work-related activities or activities incidental to the work at the time and place required by the employment, then the test is met. Activities incidental to the work could include cleaning up, setting up, or moving to a different work area.

For example, a stockroom attendant who strains his back while lifting heavy boxes sustains injuries arising out of and in the course of employment. A manager who is attacked in his home by an angry former employee whom he has terminated sustains injuries arising out of employment, but not in the course of employment. In the latter example, the second test is not met and, therefore, workers' compensation benefits might not apply.

Many types of employment are not restricted to set times and locations. Injuries sustained outside a fixed schedule or work area present a greater challenge in determining whether they occurred in the course of employment. For example, claims involving workers injured while working from their homes can require more investigation to determine whether the injury occurred in the course of employment.

Satisfying the Tests

Although most courts hold that the two tests are satisfied separately, courts can weigh each test's results unequally. Courts look for a sufficient relationship between the injury and the employment, regardless of whether the "arising out of" and "in the course of" tests are both met. If one test shows a strong relationship, the other test might not be strictly enforced. Unless an employer or its insurer can prove that an injury is not work related, compensation is usually provided.

Claim representatives must investigate a given injury carefully to determine whether it is compensable under workers' compensation statutes. The injury must be compensable for workers' compensation insurance to pay a claim. Whether or not insurance applies to the loss, when all of the tests under each of these sequential requirements are met, the injury is compensable. The next step is to determine the sources of workers' compensation coverage that are available to pay the injured worker's medical expenses and disability.

WORKERS' COMPENSATION COVERAGE SOURCES

Compensable injuries can be covered under a variety of workers' compensation sources. To satisfy state workers' compensation laws, employers must prove that they have financial resources available to pay workers' compensation benefits to injured workers. In many states, employers are not required to carry workers' compensation insurance; insurance is only one option to prove their ability to pay. Sources for securing payment required by workers' compensation laws are often dictated by the law in a particular state. The most common sources are listed in the following box and are described in the sections that follow.

Workers' Compensation Coverage Sources

- Voluntary private insurance
- Assigned risk plans
- State funds
- Qualified self-insurance plans

Voluntary Private Insurance

One source that employers use for workers' compensation coverage is voluntary private insurance. In many states, private workers' compensation insurance is available from insurers that voluntarily provide the coverage.

Private insurers must be authorized by the state to provide workers' compensation coverage and are heavily governed by state workers' compensation law. States that allow private insurance specify the provisions that can be included in the workers' compensation policy.

Private insurers compete for the business of employers that meet their guidelines within their underwriting territories. Private insurers also compete with competitive state funds, described in the following section.

Assigned Risk Plans

Assigned risk plan
A program that makes insurance available to those who cannot obtain coverage because private insurers will not voluntarily provide it.

Another source that employers use for workers' compensation coverage is an assigned risk plan. In general, an **assigned risk plan** is a program that makes insurance available to those who cannot obtain coverage because private insurers will not voluntarily provide it. In the framework of workers' compensation, an assigned risk plan is a state-organized pool of workers' compensation insurers who are required to accept employers that are unable to obtain insurance from voluntary private insurers. For example, some employers cannot obtain private insurance because of excessive losses or hazardous employments that prevent them from meeting insurers' underwriting criteria. Because states require employers to provide workers' compensation coverage, the penalties imposed for not providing coverage could force these employers out of business. An employer that was rejected by private insurers can apply to the assigned risk plan in the appropriate state to obtain coverage.

Assigned risk plans allocate losses fairly among the participating insurers. Regulators require these insurers to meet rigid rules for providing and pricing the workers' compensation insurance.

State Funds

Another source that employers use for workers' compensation coverage in states that sponsor them is state funds. State funds can be private or competitive.

A few states require that employers contribute to a monopolistic state fund by paying premiums into the fund. A **monopolistic state fund** is a state fund that is the only licensed source of workers' compensation coverage. In a monopolistic state fund, the premiums collected serve as security for payment of all workers' compensation claims. When a claim is submitted, injured workers are paid from the state fund. This approach eliminates the need for and existence of private workers' compensation insurance and assigned risk plans.

Monopolistic state fund
A state fund that is the only licensed source of workers' compensation coverage.

A few states offer public workers' compensation insurance through a **competitive state fund**, which competes for business with voluntary private insurers. Applicants can apply to the state fund or to private insurers. As with monopolistic state funds, the premiums collected by the competitive state fund serve as security for payment of workers' compensation claims.

Competitive state fund
A state fund that sells workers' compensation insurance in competition with private insurers.

Qualified Self-Insurance Plans

A final source that employers use for workers' compensation coverage is qualified self-insurance plans. Large, financially stable employers might opt to self-insure their workers' compensation losses. Most states allow an employer to qualify as self-insured when they meet the state's financial criteria. When employers self-insure their workers' compensation, they are agreeing to pay workers' compensation benefits from their own funds. States differ in the requirements that employers must meet to prove they have financial security to pay benefits. Some states require a financial statement indicating ability to pay. Others require a security deposit or other collateral.

Because total self-insurance is not financially possible for most employers, some states permit an employer to self-insure only a portion of the workers' compensation loss exposure, and then require that the employer purchase excess insurance to cover losses above a set amount or provide some other form of security to satisfy the states' requirements. These employers might use insurance to control costs and limit their loss exposure to losses above a set amount.

In most states, businesses in related industries or municipalities can form pools to mutually insure their workers' compensation losses. These pools provide a broader form of self-insurance.

In summary, employers choose one or more coverage sources to meet their state's workers' compensation coverage requirements. The employer's size and financial resources, combined with the state's provisions for workers' compensation coverage, drive the choice for each employer.

WORKERS' COMPENSATION AND EMPLOYERS' LIABILITY INSURANCE POLICY

Many private workers' compensation insurers offer a policy that provides two separate coverages: workers' compensation, which pays benefits prescribed by state law, and employers' liability, which protects employers from suits initiated by injured workers attempting to recover monetary damages beyond the workers' compensation benefits. This section describes these two coverages as provided by the National Council on Compensation Insurance (NCCI) workers' compensation and employers' liability (WC&EL) insurance policy that is used or adapted by most private insurers, and it describes other provisions of the WC&EL policy.

Workers' Compensation Insurance

The workers' compensation insurance policy provides that the insurer will make payments for all benefits that are payable to workers as required by the applicable state's workers' compensation law. The policy describes the states in which the employer has business locations and is licensed. The laws of each state determine the coverage and benefits for a given injury. Generally, workers' compensation benefits include the following:

- Medical benefits
- Disability benefits
- Rehabilitation benefits
- Funeral expense benefits
- Survivors' benefits

The insurer assumes the insured's entire liability for occupational injury as prescribed by workers' compensation laws, except for any punitive damages or damages assessed to deter other employers from similar behavior. State law sets limits for the kind and extent of benefits payable for a given injury, so the policy specifies no limits for workers' compensation benefit payments.

The following sections describe the workers' compensation policy provisions listed in the box below.

Workers' Compensation Policy Provisions

• Policy period	• Other insurance	• Rights of recovery
• Defense	• Reimbursements	• Statutory provisions
• Costs paid		

Policy Period

Under the workers' compensation policy, coverage applies when a work-related injury occurs in the specified state during the policy period. As mentioned earlier, it can be difficult to establish the loss date for occupational disease and cumulative trauma. However, under the WC&EL insurance policy, if the last day of the last exposure that causes or aggravates the disease or trauma occurs during the policy period, then coverage applies.

Defense

The insurer investigates, settles, and defends any claims, proceedings, or suits brought against the insured for benefits that could be payable under the workers' compensation policy. The insurer pays defense costs when the policy covers the basis for the suit—for example, when the claimant files a lawsuit alleging permanent disability.

Costs Paid

In addition to paying statutory benefits, the insurer pays other costs that are incidental to the claim, such as bond premiums, expert witness fees, and interest accrued on judgments.

Other Insurance

If other insurance or self-insurance applies, the loss is split equally among all the insurers and the self-insurance plan. If limits of any insurance or self-insurance are exhausted, all remaining insurers contribute equally until the loss is paid.

Reimbursements

The employer is required to pay the claimant any court-awarded judgments that exceed the benefits specified by workers' compensation law. Those judgments might be assessed against an employer for any of the following:

- Serious or willful misconduct
- Illegal employment of a worker
- Failure to comply with health or safety regulations
- Illegal discharge of or discrimination against a worker

If the insurer pays any of those judgments along with the benefit payments, the employer is required to reimburse the insurer for those excess payments. This provision ensures that insurers pay only those benefits that are required by the policy.

Rights of Recovery

Workers' compensation laws provide that if a compensable workers' compensation injury was caused by a third party's negligence, the insurer (or the self-insured employer) can seek reimbursement from that party. The employer or its insurer pays workers' compensation benefits. However, the subrogation provision grants the right of recovery of those payments from negligent third parties. For example, if a worker is injured by a defective product, the employer or its insurer can subrogate against the product manufacturer for the medical and disability benefits paid to the injured worker. Additionally, the injured worker can then pursue recovery against the product manufacturer for any damages owed to the injured worker that are not covered by workers' compensation, such as pain and suffering. The policy reinforces the insurer's right to recover the amount of its payments from a negligent third party. The insured must protect that right and assist the insurer in exercising it.

Statutory Provisions

The statutory provisions of the policy specify that certain conditions apply when those conditions are required by law. These provisions are as follows:

* *First notice of loss.* If an employer has notice of an injury, the insurer is also deemed to have notice of the injury.

* *Insurer duties when an employer becomes bankrupt or insolvent.* An insurer is not relieved of its duties under workers' compensation laws because of bankruptcy or insolvency of the insured employer. Therefore, even if the employer is bankrupt, the insurer must still pay workers' compensation benefits.

* *Insurer contractual liability.* The insurer is contractually liable for any benefits to which an injured worker is entitled, and the insurer's duties under the policy can be enforced against the insurer, the employer, or both.

* *Jurisdiction and decisions against the employer.* For the states specified in the policy, the insurer is subject to any workers' compensation jurisdiction that governs the employer and must comply with any decisions made against the employer that conform to the state workers' compensation law and that meet the policy provisions.

* *Policy conformity with state workers' compensation law.* The policy will conform with the state workers' compensation law that prescribes benefits payable and any special taxes, security payments, or assessments that must be paid.

* *Insurance terms that conflict with workers' compensation law.* This provision changes any policy terms that conflict with the state workers' compensation law so that they conform to that law in any way required.

All of the preceding policy provisions are described in the workers' compensation insurance section of the WC&EL policy. Together they describe how the policy applies and pays benefits to injured workers according to state workers' compensation statutes.

Employers' Liability Insurance

Although workers' compensation benefits are intended to be the exclusive remedy of workers for covered injuries and diseases, workers or their families can make claims and bring tort suits for damages outside of workers' compensation laws. The following examples describe circumstances that are not covered by workers' compensation statutes, but for which employers' liability would provide coverage:

• Loss of consortium is claimed by the spouse or other family members of an injured worker.

• An employee of a subsidiary might sue a parent company.

• Injured workers can sometimes reject workers' compensation benefits under elective laws and sue their employers.

• Workers who are excluded from workers' compensation coverage or who have injuries or diseases that are not covered can sue their employers.

Under employers' liability coverage, the insurer promises to pay all amounts that the employer is legally required to pay to a worker for injuries as defined in the policy, such as those listed in the preceding examples. The employers' liability policy also contains exclusions, such as payment for punitive damages, illegal employment, intentional injury, and workers' compensation losses.

Employers' liability coverage contains specified limits for two types of injury: bodily injury by accident and bodily injury by disease. Each limit is specified in the policy declarations. The policy further specifies that those limits are the maximum amounts the insurer will pay for covered damages. After the applicable limit of liability has been met, the insurer has no further obligation to pay claims for damages.

Other States Insurance

The information page of the policy allows employers to list other states where they have operations and where workers' compensation loss exposures could arise. Exhibit 8-1 shows a workers' compensation declarations page with other states listed. Using the exhibit information in an example, David, an AMR Corporation computer system designer who travels to clients' work sites, falls and breaks his leg while visiting a client in Alabama. The workers' compensation laws for the state of Alabama determine the benefits available to David, and, because Alabama is listed on the declarations page under "Other States Insurance," the Other States Insurance coverage described in Part Three of the policy will apply to his injury.

Other Provisions

The remainder of the policy specifies major policy provisions such as the insured's duties should an injury occur, how premium is determined, and policy conditions.

EXHIBIT 8-1

Sample Workers' Compensation Declarations

WORKERS COMPENSATION AND EMPLOYERS LIABILITY INSURANCE POLICY

INFORMATION PAGE

Insurer:

```
P O L I C Y   N O .
| | | | | | | | | | | | | | | | | | | | | | | | | |
```

1. **The Insured:** AMR Corporation   ___ Individual   ___ Partnership
    Mailing address: 2000 Industrial Highway   X Corporation or _____
                          Workingtown, NE 68000

    Other workplaces not shown above:

2. **The policy period is from**   10/1/20X0   **to**   10/1/20X1   **at the insured's mailing address.**

3. A. **Workers Compensation Insurance:** Part One of the policy applies to the Workers Compensation Law of the states listed here: NE

    B. **Employers Liability Insurance:** Part Two of the policy applies to work in each state listed in Item 3.A. The limits of our liability under Part Two are:

Bodily Injury by Accident	$ 100,000	each accident
Bodily Injury by Disease	$ 500,000	policy limit
Bodily Injury by Disease	$ 100,000	each employee

    C. **Other States Insurance:** Part Three of the policy applies to the states, if any, listed here:

    All except those listed in Item 3A and ME, MN, ND, OH, WA, WV, WY and OR

    D. **This policy includes these endorsements and schedules:**

    See Schedule

4. **The premium for this policy will be determined by our Manuals of Rules, Classifications, Rates and Rating Plans. All information required below is subject to verification and change by audit.**

Classifications	Code No.	Premium Basis Total Estimated Annual Remuneration	Rate Per $100 of Remuneration	Estimated Annual Premium
Computer system designers or programmers— exclusively office	8810	400,000	0.44	1,760
Computer system designers or programmers—traveling	8803	200,000	0.15	300
		Experience Modification of 1.382 Applied		787
		Estimated Premium Discount		0
		Total Estimated Annual Premium $		2,847

Minimum Premium $ 500   **Expense Constant $**   XXX

Countersigned by _____ A. M. Abel _____
                              (authorized representative)

WC 00 00 01 A
© 1987 National Council on Compensation Insurance.

Duties

The policy describes several duties of the insured when an injury occurs. The first and most important duty is to inform the insurer promptly, if not immediately, if an injury occurs that might be covered by the policy. Other duties include the following:

- Providing medical attention to the injured worker
- Providing names and addresses of injured workers and witnesses
- Presenting any notices, demands, or legal papers
- Cooperating with and assisting in investigating and settling claims or lawsuits
- Protecting the insurer's right of recovery
- Avoiding acceptance of responsibility for the accident and avoiding making any payments, except at the insured's own cost

Premium

The policy describes how the premium is determined. It also explains that the insurer is entitled to examine and audit any of the insured's records that relate to the policy anytime within three years after the policy expiration because workers' compensation premiums can be adjusted based on the insured employer's loss experience.

Conditions

Conditions affect the duties and obligations of the insured and insurer. The most significant condition involves inspecting the premises and operations covered by the policy. The insurer uses inspections to obtain underwriting information, to evaluate loss control activities, and to determine the premium. Conditions further stress that the inspections are not safety inspections, that the insurer has no obligation to provide for the health and safety of the workers or the public, and that the insurer does not warrant the workplace to be safe or in compliance with safety laws. Other conditions address the policy term, transfer of the insured's rights and duties, cancellation, and the role of the first named insured as the only representative for the policy.

WORKERS' COMPENSATION CLAIM CONSIDERATIONS

When a worker is injured or contracts an occupational disease in the course of employment, the worker gives notice to the employer, who files a workers' compensation claim with the insurer. The following sections describe the claim-handling activities for workers' compensation claims that differ from those for other types of claims.

The injured worker usually provides the first report of an injury (loss) to the employer. Most states require that the worker report the injury to the employer within thirty days of its occurrence. However, it is very difficult for an insurer to deny a claim based on late notification.

Employers (insureds) are then required to notify their insurer promptly of any potential claim by this worker. The employer/insured should report all injuries and should not attempt to judge whether the injury qualifies for workers' compensation coverage. The insurer will determine whether the injury is compensable.

Many states require that the employer/insured also report the loss to the Workers' Compensation Commission. This report is filed on a First Report of Injury or Illness form (available from ACORD) or a similar form, and the information might be entered into the insurer's claim information system and then submitted to the insurer electronically. If the employer/insured fails to file the form within the specified number of days, the state could impose fines or other penalties. Some insurers file these forms for their insureds, but the employer/insured remains responsible for prompt filing. Filing the form is not an acknowledgment that the claim meets the requirements of a workers' compensation claim. Exhibit 8-2 shows an ACORD First Report of Injury or Illness form.

Identifying Workers' Compensation Coverage

Most occupational injuries are covered under workers' compensation; therefore, identifying whether coverage exists is generally straightforward. However, coverage questions can arise. Employments or situations that could raise questions about coverage include the following:

- Illegal employment of minors
- Out-of-state workers
- Failure of the insured to cooperate in investigation or defense
- Collusion between the employer and claimant
- Material misrepresentation of the loss exposure, such as an auto repair shop that reports it does no painting, when in fact it does
- Independent contractor status of the injured worker

Coverage questions can be addressed in several ways. First, the claim representative should send a reservation of rights letter to the employer or obtain a signed nonwaiver agreement from the employer; either can be used to preserve the insurer's coverage defenses. The claim representative may then retain legal counsel to help interpret the laws of the state concerning coverage or to pursue a declaratory judgment from a court to interpret the coverage questions.

As part of the policy identification, claim representatives must establish preliminary reserves for the claim. Claim representatives establish reserves in the following three areas for workers' compensation claims:

1. Medical
2. Disability
3. Expense

EXHIBIT 8-2

ACORD Workers Compensation—First Report of Injury or Illness

ACORD® WORKERS COMPENSATION - FIRST REPORT OF INJURY OR ILLNESS

EMPLOYER (NAME & ADDRESS INCL ZIP)	CARRIER/ADMINISTRATOR CLAIM NUMBER *	REPORT PURPOSE CODE *
XYZ Insurance Company 111 Street Anytown, PA 19355	JURISDICTION * JURISDICTION CLAIM NUMBER *	
	INSURED REPORT NUMBER	
	EMPLOYER'S LOCATION ADDRESS (IF DIFFERENT)	LOCATION #:
SIC CODE EMPLOYER FEIN		PHONE #

CARRIER/CLAIMS ADMINISTRATOR

CARRIER (NAME, ADDRESS & PHONE NO)	POLICY PERIOD	CLAIMS ADMINISTRATOR (NAME, ADDRESS & PHONE NO)
Stateside Compensation Carrier, Inc. 123 Main Street Anytown, PA 19355	7/1/20X0 7/1/20X1 TO	
	CHECK IF APPROPRIATE SELF INSURANCE	

CARRIER FEIN *	POLICY/SELF-INSURED NUMBER 98-7744321	ADMINISTRATOR FEIN *
AGENT NAME & CODE NUMBER	Wilson Insurance Agency	

EMPLOYEE/WAGE

NAME (LAST, FIRST, MIDDLE) Simmons, Darrell	DATE OF BIRTH	SOCIAL SECURITY NUMBER	DATE HIRED 7/1/XX	STATE OF HIRE

ADDRESS (INCL ZIP) 999 Road Anytown, PA 19355	SEX 　MALE 　FEMALE 　UNKNOWN	MARITAL STATUS X UNMARRIED SINGLE/DIVORCED 　MARRIED 　SEPARATED	OCCUPATION/JOB TITLE Roofer
			EMPLOYMENT STATUS Full time
PHONE 555-7777	# OF DEPENDENTS	UNKNOWN	NCCI CLASS CODE *

RATE $769.23	PER: X WEEK	DAY MONTH OTHER:	AVERAGE WEEKLY WAGES	# DAYS WORKED/WEEK 5	FULL PAY FOR DAY OF INJURY? X YES NO DID SALARY CONTINUE? YES NO

OCCURRENCE/TREATMENT

TIME EMPLOYEE BEGAN WORK 8 X AM 　PM	DATE OF INJURY/ILLNESS 8-1-20X0	TIME OF OCCURRENCE 3	AM X PM	LAST WORK DATE 8-1-20X0	DATE EMPLOYER NOTIFIED 8-1-20X0	DATE DISABILITY BEGAN 8-1-20X0

CONTACT NAME/PHONE NUMBER	TYPE OF INJURY/ILLNESS herniated disk, fractured femur	PART OF BODY AFFECTED back
DID INJURY/ILLNESS EXPOSURE OCCUR ON EMPLOYER'S PREMISES? 　YES 　NO	TYPE OF INJURY/ILLNESS CODE *	PART OF BODY AFFECTED CODE *

DEPARTMENT OR LOCATION WHERE ACCIDENT OR ILLNESS EXPOSURE OCCURRED Sam Smith's house (insured by XYZ)	ALL EQUIPMENT, MATERIALS, OR CHEMICALS EMPLOYEE WAS USING WHEN ACCIDENT OR ILLNESS EXPOSURE OCCURRED ladder, crowbar, hammer
SPECIFIC ACTIVITY THE EMPLOYEE WAS ENGAGED IN WHEN THE ACCIDENT OR ILLNESS EXPOSURE OCCURRED Replacing old shingles	WORK PROCESS THE EMPLOYEE WAS ENGAGED IN WHEN ACCIDENT OR ILLNESS EXPOSURE OCCURRED Shingling roof

HOW INJURY OR ILLNESS/ABNORMAL HEALTH CONDITION OCCURRED. DESCRIBE THE SEQUENCE OF EVENTS AND INCLUDE ANY OBJECTS OR SUBSTANCES THAT DIRECTLY INJURED THE EMPLOYEE OR MADE THE EMPLOYEE ILL Lost balance while removing a shingle that stuck down	CAUSE OF INJURY CODE *

DATE RETURN(ED) TO WORK Not yet	IF FATAL, GIVE DATE OF DEATH	WERE SAFEGUARDS OR SAFETY EQUIPMENT PROVIDED?　YES　NO WERE THEY USED?　YES　NO

PHYSICIAN/HEALTH CARE PROVIDER (NAME & ADDRESS) Dr. McCoy Anytown, PA	HOSPITAL (NAME & ADDRESS) Anytown General Hospital Anytown, PA 19355	INITIAL TREATMENT 　NO MEDICAL TREATMENT 　MINOR: BY EMPLOYER 　MINOR CLINIC/HOSP 　EMERGENCY CARE
WITNESSES (NAME & PHONE #) Sam Smith 555-8787		X HOSPITALIZED > 24 HRS 　FUTURE MAJOR MEDICAL/ LOST TIME ANTICIPATED

DATE ADMINISTRATOR NOTIFIED	DATE PREPARED 8/2/20X0	PREPARER'S NAME & TITLE Sue Jones, WC Coordinator	PHONE NUMBER 555-6666

ACORD 4 (2004/06)   **SEE BACK FOR IMPORTANT STATE INFORMATION/SIGNATURE**
REPRINTED WITH PERMISSION OF IAIABC   © ACORD CORPORATION 1993

Medical reserves cover medical costs. Disability reserves cover lost wages for disabled workers or their survivors. Expense reserves cover costs associated with independent medical exams, private surveillance, medical records, and legal and court reporter fees. Rehabilitation costs might be included in either the medical reserve or the expense reserve.

Many other factors affect the reserve, including the following:

- Type of injury
- Severity of the injury
- Claimant's average weekly wage
- Lawyer involvement
- Jurisdiction
- Claimant's claim history
- Claimant's age
- Union status
- Claimant's occupation
- Availability of light or limited duty employment
- How employable or trainable the claimant seems to be

Factors affecting reserves for fatalities include the claimant's marital status, surviving dependents and their ages, and the surviving spouse's life expectancy.

Investigating and Documenting the Workers' Compensation Claim

A workers' compensation investigation can take many different forms, and all aspects of the investigation must be documented to avoid duplicate work and to create a complete claim file.

A previous section of this chapter described the insured's duties. The insured's failure to perform any duties could affect coverage for an injury. Nonetheless, claim representatives face challenges in asserting applicable defenses against the insured when the investigation reveals that the insured failed to perform its duties. For example, workers' compensation policy provisions require the insured/employer to provide prompt, if not immediate, notice of injury to the insurer. Courts determine the meaning of "prompt" reporting. Usually, to deny coverage because of late notice, the insurer must establish strong evidence that its ability to investigate or defend the workers' compensation claim was prejudiced by the late reporting. Furthermore, late notification is tolerated for certain "excusable" reasons, such as the following:

- The injured worker was not initially aware of the injury's severity, extent, or prognosis.
- The symptoms of the occupational disease did not manifest themselves until some time after the exposure had occurred.

Additionally, the severity of the workers' compensation injury determines the extent of investigation necessary. Reporting-only claims occur when an accident occurs and the claim representative does not expect to pay any benefits. Reporting-only claims require no investigation. Medical-only claims can be paid and closed with minimal investigation, such as verification that the accident occurred in the workplace and determination of the extent of injury.

In contrast, an investigation of the insured or the claimant could include signed or recorded statements from co-workers who witnessed the accident; a statement from the immediate supervisor about job duties, length of employment, and opinions about the claim; and a copy of the claimant's personnel file. The claim representative might inspect the location where the injury occurred, obtain information to support subrogation, and determine whether modified work is available for the injured worker. The claim representative completes investigations that are appropriate for the nature of the injury. In addition to performing the claimant investigations, insured/ witness investigations, medical investigations, and prior claim investigations described earlier in this text, claim representatives might perform a post-accident activity investigation for a workers' compensation claim. This investigation is described next.

Post-Accident Activity Investigation

A post-accident activity investigation could defeat a workers' compensation claim by proving that the claimant is not disabled. Activity checks and surveillance might be used to show that the claimant is physically able to work. Activity checks are conducted by questioning neighbors about the claimant's activity level. This could reveal a discrepancy between the alleged injury and the types of activity in which the claimant engages. For example, the claimant might have been mowing the lawn or doing strenuous lifting after an alleged back injury on the job.

Claim representatives might conduct surveillance or activity checks if the claimant's alleged disability is in doubt. Often, photos or visual recordings are used to capture the claimant engaging in activities that invalidate the claim. In some cases, insurers hire experts to perform this surveillance.

Recovery From Second Injury Funds

Some employers are reluctant to hire disabled workers because of concern that a new injury could worsen a preexisting disability. For example, a worker with sight in only one eye could be permanently disabled from an injury to the functioning eye. The effect of a second injury is worse because of the preexisting disability. To attempt to address that concern, states include provisions for second injury funds in their workers' compensation laws. A **second injury fund** is a state-controlled fund that contributes compensation for workers who have preexisting conditions and who suffer work-related "second" injuries.

Second injury fund
A state-controlled fund that contributes compensation for workers who have preexisting conditions and who suffer work-related "second" injuries.

Although second injury fund provisions vary by state, most funds limit the employer's liability when a claimant suffers a combined disability that is greater than what would have existed from the second injury alone. The insurer can recover from a state second injury fund when the new injury and preexisting injuries combine to prevent the worker from continuing gainful employment. Several states have second injury funds that pay benefits above the disability rate, up to the pre-injury pay rate, when the injured employee's new and previous injuries combine to create an overall greater disability. Exhibit 8-3 is an example of recovery under a second injury fund.

EXHIBIT 8-3

Recovery Under Second Injury Fund

When Josh started work with Steel Inc., he had a 35 percent disability to his right foot because of a previous injury. While working as a welder for Steel Inc., he suffered a 40 percent disability to his right ankle. The combined disabilities rendered Josh unable to stand for more than ten minutes. The insurer for Steel Inc. paid him benefits and then filed for reimbursement from the state's second injury fund, stating that the ankle injury, when merged with the foot injury, caused a greater disability than the claimant would have had from the second injury alone. The claim against the second injury fund was honored.

An increasing number of states are eliminating second injury funds because the Americans with Disabilities Act (ADA) encourages employers to hire disabled workers. The ADA requires employers to make "reasonable accommodations" for workers with disabilities. The ADA does not compensate employers or their insurers for increased disabilities resulting from preexisting disabilities, but the ADA has helped eliminate the need for second injury funds, many of which were problematic and failed to meet their objectives.

Special Documentation Considerations in Workers' Compensation Claims

In addition to completing the documentation required for most claims, claim representatives must complete special types of documentation for workers' compensation claims. Because workers' compensation insurance is heavily regulated, insurers are required to complete many external reports that compile information collected by claim representatives.

As mentioned, an employer is required to file a First Report of Injury or Illness form with the compensation commission for its state. State compensation commissions are particularly interested in disability claims. They want to know who was injured, the length of time during which disability benefits were paid, and whether benefits were paid promptly. If the disability changes, most state compensation commissions require that a new report be filed. Recently, compensation commissions have become more interested in serious medical claims and rehabilitation efforts as well, and some require rehabilitation reports.

Insurers are also required to report detailed claim information on workers' compensation losses to advisory organizations to which they subscribe. The National Council on Compensation Insurance (NCCI) is one such advisory organization. Additionally, insurer financial departments might be required to report state-specific workers' compensation premium and loss information to an advisory organization.

Insurers that subscribe to NCCI obtain information on workers' compensation indemnity claims reported through Detailed Claim Information (DCI), which may be captured in automated reports from claim processing systems. DCI includes more specific information than the First Report of Injury or Illness form, such as personal information about claimants, nature of the injury, and types of treatment required. DCI is used to complete detailed claim analyses, which are used in rate filings, law evaluations, and cost containment efforts.

Determining Cause of Loss and Loss Amount in Workers' Compensation Claims

Another claim-handling activity that differs for workers' compensation claims is determining the cause of loss and loss amount. Under liability and property coverages, claim representatives determine the cause of loss; under workers' compensation coverage, claim representatives must determine whether an injury meets the requirements of compensability, as described earlier in the chapter. Rather than making loss payments, workers' compensation policies pay benefits to injured workers or their families, including medical, disability, rehabilitation, and funeral expenses, and survivors' benefits. Although the terminology used in workers' compensation claims differs from that used in property and liability claims, the concepts of determining cause of loss and loss amount are the same as determining compensability and benefits, respectively.

Claim representatives must remain aware that timeliness in paying workers' compensation benefits is crucial; some states penalize insurers for unjustifiable delays in paying benefits. The time required for claim representatives to determine a loss amount can vary considerably depending on the extent of injury. After a disability resulting from a compensable injury has been established, the claim representative must evaluate the extent of the injured worker's disability to determine the type of disability benefits payable.

This section describes medical benefits, disability types and associated benefits, rehabilitation benefits, and death benefits from a claim perspective. These benefits were introduced earlier in this text; however, further description will assist claim representatives in effectively determining the benefits payable for various compensable injuries.

Medical Benefits

Workers' compensation laws provide for payment of expenses for all reasonable and necessary medical care to injured workers, including fees for doctors, specialists, and nurses; surgical and hospital expenses; diagnostic testing; medications; therapy; travel expenses; prosthetic devices (such as glasses, hearing aids, dentures, and artificial limbs); and medical-related travel.

To determine the appropriate medical benefits, claim representatives must ensure that medical expenses are medically necessary and related to the occupational injury. Claim representatives often use the services of managed care organizations to help determine medical necessity. Paired with this resource, claim representatives who have a strong knowledge of medicine and medical procedures are well-equipped to determine medical expense benefit amounts under workers' compensation.

Disability Benefits

After determining the extent of the worker's injury, claim representatives must determine the likely length of any disability. Claim representatives use these determinations to assign one of the following four types of workers' compensation disability:

1. Temporary partial disability
2. Temporary total disability
3. Permanent partial disability
4. Permanent total disability

Claim personnel calculate disability benefits based on these disability types.

Temporary partial disability (TPD)

A disability caused by a work-related injury or disease that temporarily limits the extent to which a worker can perform job duties; the worker is eventually able to return to full duties and hours.

Waiting period

A statutory time period in which the injured worker must wait after an injury before benefits can begin.

The first type of workers' compensation disability is temporary partial disability. **Temporary partial disability (TPD)** is a disability caused by a work-related injury or disease that temporarily limits the extent to which a worker can perform job duties; the worker is eventually able to return to full duties and hours. After a specified **waiting period** (a statutory time period in which the injured worker must wait after an injury before benefits can begin), insurers pay compensation for TPD to workers who return to light duty or restricted work at a reduced pay rate or for fewer hours than the employee worked before the injury. For example, the doctor might allow a worker with a back strain to return to work with restricted lifting for half days until that worker has fully recovered. Employers have found that, by accommodating such work modifications, they can encourage job interest, boost morale, and help injured workers focus on the benefits of working.

The compensation rate for TPD is a percentage of the difference between the worker's gross pre-injury average weekly wage (AWW) and the worker's gross average weekly wage upon return to work. The percentage is mandated by state law and could be limited by a maximum or minimum rate allowable in that state. For example, the TPD compensation rate might be 66⅔ percent of the difference between a worker's AWW and post-injury wage or a maximum of $509 per week. TPD replaces the portion of income lost as a result of partial disability from a compensable injury.

The second type of workers' compensation disability is temporary total disability. **Temporary total disability (TTD)** is a disability caused by a work-related injury or disease that temporarily renders an injured worker unable to perform any job duties for a period of time; the worker eventually makes a full recovery and can resume all job duties. Like TPD, this disability also requires a waiting period before insurers begin making payments. TTD offers income replacement for a disabled worker during the time that the worker is unable to work at all as a result of a compensable injury.

As in TPD, the worker's gross pre-injury AWW is used to calculate the amount of weekly payment by applying a percentage (usually 66⅔ percent) to the AWW. Compensation is subject to maximum and minimum amounts in most jurisdictions. Generally, TTD benefits are paid until the worker is able to return to work or has reached maximum medical improvement. Some states impose limits on the amount of time that TTD benefits can be paid or on the maximum dollar amount that can be paid. In some states, if the TTD extends beyond a specified number of weeks (the retroactive period), the insurer must pay the injured worker for the wages lost during the waiting period.

The third type of workers' compensation disability is permanent partial disability. **Permanent partial disability (PPD)** is a disability caused by a work-related injury or disease that is permanent in nature but partial in degree. An insurer compensates an injured worker for future reduced earnings as a result of a compensable injury and/or for the disability to the injured part of the body. PPD cannot be measured until the worker has reached the maximum physical recovery.

The state where the injury occurred mandates the basis used to calculate PPD compensation. Compensation can be based on the decreased wages that the worker can earn after the work injury compared to the pre-injury wages. For example, a carpenter earning $19 per hour suffers a back injury and is unable to return to that type of work. Instead, he accepts a cashier job paying $8 per hour. His loss of earnings would be $11 per hour. His compensation rate might be a percentage of that $11 per hour, subject to a maximum.

Many states use a schedule to determine benefits for specific types of injury, such as loss of a limb. Usually a worker cannot receive disability benefits for both loss of earnings and a scheduled injury for the same claim. In states that apply a schedule for permanent disability benefits, the schedule lists body parts injured (most commonly toe, foot, leg, thumb, finger, hand, arm, and eye) and an appropriate disability period for each injured body part. For example, the schedule might specify 244 weeks of compensation for an amputated hand and 312 weeks of compensation for an amputated arm.

Some states also provide scheduled benefits for hearing loss or permanent disfigurement. The disfigurement benefit is greater when the disfigurement occurs on an exposed area of the body and the effect of the disfigurement on the worker's employability is considered. For example, a significant facial scar could reduce chances of employment for a salesperson.

Temporary total disability (TTD)
A disability caused by a work-related injury or disease that temporarily renders an injured worker unable to perform any job duties for a period of time; the worker eventually makes a full recovery and can resume all job duties.

Permanent partial disability (PPD)
A disability caused by a work-related injury or disease that is permanent in nature but partial in degree.

Compensation for losses not included in the schedule is based on lost earnings capacity. For example, if the worker's disability is 30 percent, then the worker's loss of earnings is 30 percent of the gross pre-injury AWW.

States that do not have scheduled injuries use several factors to determine the disability amount, such as the opinion of the treating physician, the appearance of the injured body part, and post-injury occupation and earnings. Physicians can apply rating guidelines, such as those prepared by the American Medical Association, to establish percentages of disability. Again, state laws must be consulted to determine the compensation amount for nonscheduled injuries.

Many states provide compensation for nonscheduled injuries based on loss of earning capacity. This compensation approach acknowledges the reduced post-injury earning capacity of the injured worker, compared to the worker's pre-injury earning capacity.

Permanent total disability (PTD)
A disability caused by a work-related injury or disease that renders a worker unable to return to gainful employment.

The fourth type of workers' compensation disability is permanent total disability. **Permanent total disability (PTD)** is a disability caused by a work-related injury or disease that renders a worker unable to return to gainful employment. Compensation for this type of disability is paid if the worker is unable to return to any type of gainful employment following a compensable injury. Some states refer to "suitable gainful employment," meaning that the worker must be able to return to employment in a position comparable to the pre-injury position. For example, an electrician earning $25 per hour becomes disabled and is able to obtain only a minimum-wage position after rehabilitation efforts. In a state where laws specify suitable gainful employment, this worker could request PTD compensation.

In some states, PTD is presumed by law for certain types of serious injuries. For example, many states presume PTD for loss of vision in both eyes, loss to both arms or both legs, or loss of mental capacity. Some of those states allow PTD compensation to stop if the worker returns to some type of employment.

PTD benefits generally continue as long as the disability continues, usually for life. A few states limit the number of weeks that PTD benefits are paid or the dollar amount of PTD benefits. Some states reduce the PTD benefit when social security benefits apply. All disability cases are reviewed periodically to ensure that the disability has continued.

Some states provide for an annual cost-of-living increase in the PTD benefit, usually by applying a percentage to the original PTD amount. In other states, the PTD amount is compounded (the percentage is applied to the most recent PTD benefit). The increased PTD benefit is subject to any maximum in effect at the time of the increase.

In summary, all of the disability benefits just described replace the injured worker's lost income. The type of disability determines the extent of benefits that the insurer provides. Insurers can sometimes reduce their disability costs by providing rehabilitation benefits, as described in the following section.

Rehabilitation Benefits

Insurers pay for rehabilitation services that assist disabled workers. **Rehabilitation services** integrate medical, vocational, and employer information to facilitate communication, return to work, and restoration of the individual to be able to function in society. Some states require rehabilitation for certain injuries. Medical rehabilitation includes supervising and coordinating worker care; providing physical rehabilitation, counseling, and emotional support; and helping the worker adjust to a lifestyle that accommodates the disability. Vocational rehabilitation could include modifying the pre-injury job to accommodate the disability, helping the injured worker find and apply for a new type of job, or training for a new career.

Vocational rehabilitation helps the injured worker prepare to return to work. Research has shown that returning to work encourages self-respect, improves earning power, gives purpose and structure to workers' lives, and offers a positive emotional outlook, which, in turn, improves workers' physical conditions.

Rehabilitation also helps the insurer by reducing the cost of paying ongoing TTD benefits. When insurers provide rehabilitation services, they typically pay less in TTD benefits for rehabilitated claimants.

Rehabilitation services
A workers' compensation benefit that integrates medical, vocational, and employer information to facilitate communication, return to work, and restoration of the individual to be able to function in society.

Death Benefits

Claim representatives determine a weekly (or some other agreed-upon schedule) death benefit amount for the surviving spouse and minor children of a worker who died from a compensable injury. Under some state laws, other people who were financially dependent on the deceased worker are also eligible for death benefits.

Insurers pay death benefits to partially replace the support that the deceased worker would have provided to dependents had the worker lived. Some states require a lump sum payment to the spouse and dependents in addition to the weekly benefit.

Insurers pay death benefits for a surviving spouse until the spouse remarries (with an extra lump sum benefit provided upon remarriage) or for a duration specified by state law. Some states limit spousal death benefits to a specific number of weeks, such as 500. Some states extend these benefits if the spouse suffers a disability. Insurers pay death benefits for dependent children until they reach a state-specified age, usually eighteen. In some states, these dependent benefits continue while the child is enrolled in an approved school or if the child suffers from a mental or physical disability.

As with disability benefits, the typical death benefit is 66⅔ percent of the deceased worker's AWW, subject to maximum and minimum amounts. The percentage could be adjusted if dependents no longer qualify for the death benefits and only the spouse receives it, or when a child reaches a state-specified age but enrolls in an approved school.

Workers' compensation laws also require payment of funeral expenses, subject to a maximum. Many states pay the expense to transport the body to a funeral home selected by the survivors, sometimes subject to a maximum. Claim representatives must consult state workers' compensation laws to properly determine all death benefits and payment terms.

Exhibit 8-4 provides a workers' compensation claim case study.

EXHIBIT 8-4

Workers' Compensation Claim

Darrell, age 46, worked as a roofer for MP Roofing Company. Darrell fell off a roof while shingling for MP. Darrell fractured his right femur and injured his back, requiring surgery to repair a herniated disc. After surgery, Darrell's physician recommended that he not return to any type of work that required him to climb a ladder or sit for long periods. Through rehabilitative efforts, Darrell learned to use a keyboard. After five months of recovery and rehabilitation, Darrell returned to MP Roofing in a clerical position. MP created a modified work area for Darrell including an ergonomic office chair, a wireless keyboard and mouse, and a telephone headset to give Darrell flexibility to move about while performing his duties.

Darrell's medical expenses were paid under the benefits of MP's workers' compensation policy with Stateside Compensation Carrier, Inc., including all expenses for the emergency room, hospitalization, surgery, physical therapy, and subsequent medical visits. Stateside paid Darrell's TTD for his back injury at a rate of $66^2/_3$ percent of his gross pre-injury AWW ($769.23), for a total of $512.82 per week during his recovery time:

$$\$769.23 \times 66^2/_3\% = \$512.82.$$

That amount was within the maximum allowed by the state. In addition, Stateside paid all of the costs for Darrell's rehabilitation.

Upon Darrell's return to work at MP, his annual pay was reduced from $40,000 per year to $36,000 per year, a $4,000 decrease. Because Darrell's post-injury annual salary was less than his pre-injury salary, he suffered a permanent wage loss. The final settlement that Stateside reached with Darrell provided him with a PPD benefit of $51.28 per week until his retirement:

$$\$4,000 \div 52 \text{ weeks} = \$76.92$$
$$\$76.92 \times 66^2/_3\% = \$51.28.$$

Concluding the Workers' Compensation Claim Through Adjudication

The final claim-handling activity that can differ for workers' compensation claims is concluding the claim. Some aspects of workers' compensation claims can be clearly determined, such as the amount of medical bills, whereas other aspects of workers' compensation claims are not as clear-cut. When a dispute arises about the compensability of an injury and the claimant disagrees with the claim representative, the dispute is settled by negotiation or adjudication. Negotiation was described in previous chapters; therefore, this section focuses on adjudication.

Occasionally, a dispute arises about the compensability of an injury. A claim representative or an employer who rejects a claim on the basis of compensability must notify the claimant and explain the reason for claim denial. If the claimant disagrees, the parties begin the adjudication process to reach a settlement. The **adjudication process** is the legal proceeding that an insurer, the employer, or a claimant must follow to dispute a workers' compensation settlement.

Adjudication process
The legal proceeding that an insurer, the employer, or a claimant must follow to dispute a workers' compensation settlement.

The insurer often begins the adjudication process by holding an informal conference. The injured worker and the worker's lawyer, the claim representative (representing the insurer and the insured), and a representative of the state compensation commission attend the conference. Other participants may include a special claim representative, called a hearing examiner, and a lawyer representing the insurer. The goals of the conference are to identify areas of agreement; isolate areas of disagreement; and achieve a calm, informal dispute resolution. Each side presents its position in an informal setting. The compensation commission representative may offer a recommendation or resolution at the conference or may respond within a specified number of days. If one party is dissatisfied with the resolution, that party can appeal at the next level, usually a formal compensation hearing.

A formal compensation hearing resembles a mini-trial before a single state compensation commissioner. Participants are the same as in an informal hearing, except that the insurer's legal representative should attend. Each party presents its case. Rules of evidence are less strict than in a civil trial, but the setting is not casual. The commissioner delivers the ruling sometime after the hearing. This ruling can also be appealed. Some state courts reserve the right to hear and decide workers' compensation cases without using a formal hearing.

Some states allow the injured worker or the employer to appeal the formal hearing and proceed to a hearing with the full state compensation commission present. Such a hearing is called a full commission appeal. One problem with this type of appeal is that the state workers' compensation commissioners might be reluctant to overrule the decision of one of their members.

The last possible step in the adjudication process is an appeal to a state court. If the claimant or the employer remains convinced that a poor decision was rendered, the claimant or employer can appeal to a court, usually a state appellate court. For an appellate review to be heard, the case must involve basic interpretation of the workers' compensation law or an issue of state constitutionality. The state supreme court uses discretion in reviewing workers' compensation cases. Most state appellate courts review only issues of law and not the facts that relate to the case. Very few states allow a jury trial.

After reaching a settlement through negotiation or adjudication, the claim representative prepares a written memorandum stating the details of the settlement. All parties must sign the memorandum, which is then filed with the state's compensation commission. If the settlement conforms to state law, the commission approves it and the claim representative makes the approved payments.

Insurers make partial benefit payments on some workers' compensation claims. For example, medical bills are paid throughout the course of the claim. Disability benefits are paid periodically.

When payments continue (such as with PPD or PTD), a workers' compensation claim is not closed when the settlement is reached and approved. The claim file remains open because benefits are still due and the file requires periodic monitoring. However, computerized payment generation eliminates the need for regular open-claim-file activity.

SUMMARY

State workers' compensation laws create a system whereby employers accept strict liability for work-related injuries and diseases. This system makes workers' compensation the injured worker's exclusive remedy for injury, except in limited circumstances.

Three statutory requirements must be met for an injury to be compensable under workers' compensation: (1) an employment relationship must exist, (2) the injury (or disease) must be covered, and (3) the injury must arise out of and in the course of employment. The employment relationship must include control, consent, and consideration, and certain employments are excluded.

Covered occupational injuries include accidental injuries, occupational disease, and mental injuries. Compensable accidental injuries must be unexpected and definite in time and place. Occupational disease can include hearing loss, allergic reaction to hazardous materials, accidental infectious disease, cumulative trauma, and progressive trauma. Workers' compensation coverage for mental injuries depends on the state's definition of "mental injury" and interpretations of mental injury coverage.

Most states require that an injury meet two tests to be covered by workers' compensation: (1) "arising out of" and (2) "in the course of" employment.

Voluntary private insurance, assigned risk plans, state funds, and qualified self-insurance plans are all sources through which employers can make workers' compensation benefits payments to injured workers.

Many insurers adopt the National Council on Compensation Insurance (NCCI) workers' compensation and employers' liability (WC&EL) insurance policy to provide benefits to injured workers, including medical benefits, disability benefits, rehabilitation benefits, funeral expense benefits, and survivors' benefits. State law determines the benefits payable. The employers' liability portion of the policy pays amounts that the employer is legally required to pay that fall outside workers' compensation laws.

When a worker is injured or contracts an occupational disease in the course of employment, the worker's employer files a workers' compensation claim with the insurer. The employee and the employer must file forms required by state laws. The claim is assigned to a claim representative, who must determine the compensability of the accident and the benefits to be paid.

In addition to the investigations that claim representatives conduct for most claims, they might conduct a post-accident activity investigation for workers' compensation claims. This investigation could invalidate a workers' compensation claim if evidence is collected that proves the claimant is not truly disabled as a result of the injury. In addition to recovering through subrogation, an insurer might recover workers' compensation benefit payments through second injury funds.

Claim representatives create special external reports on workers' compensation claims. These might include reports to state workers' compensation commissions, such as the First Report of Injury or Illness form required by most states and rehabilitation reports required by some states. Claim representatives also complete detailed claim information reports to advisory organizations such as the NCCI. Insurer financial departments might also be required to report state-specific workers' compensation premium and loss information to advisory organizations.

Workers' compensation laws provide payment of expenses for all reasonable and necessary medical care to injured workers. Claim representatives must calculate appropriate medical benefits. When the injury causes disability, they must determine whether the disability is a temporary partial disability (TPD), temporary total disability (TTD), permanent partial disability (PPD), or permanent total disability (PTD) and then calculate the appropriate disability benefits. Claim representatives may also determine rehabilitation benefits and death benefits, as they apply.

When claim representatives and injured employees dispute the compensability of a workers' compensation claim, they often resolve the dispute through adjudication.

As demonstrated throughout the text, the claim field offers variety and challenges to claim personnel. Claim representatives can develop expertise in certain claim areas, such as auto or property losses or workers' compensation claims. In all claim areas, successful claim handling helps keep an insurer financially stable and becomes its own reward for the claim representative.

Index

Page numbers in boldface refer to definitions of Key Words and Phrases.

A

APD (auto physical damage) coverage, **5.6**
Access security, **3.26**
Accident scene investigation, 4.13
Accidental injury, 8.6–8.7
Activity log, **3.24**
Actual cash value (ACV), **4.30,** 4.36
Actuary, **1.17**
Additional coverages and coverage extensions, 6.18–6.21
Additional living expense coverage, **6.15**
Adjudication process, **8.29**
Adjuster, public, **4.11**
Administrative law, **3.6**
Adverse selection, **1.12**
Aftermarket part, **5.14**
Agent
    direct writing, **1.14**
    exclusive, **1.14**
    independent, **1.13**
Aggregate limit, **7.12**
Alternative dispute resolution, 4.25
Annual Statement, **3.31**
Answer, **3.11**
Appraisal, **6.40**
Arbitration, **3.10**
Assigned risk plans, **8.10**–8.11
Assumption of risk, **7.8**
Audit, claim, **3.28**
Authority level, **3.27**
Auto physical damage claims
    dispute resolution and, 5.18
    investigating, 4.27–4.32
Auto physical damage (APD) coverage, **5.6**
Automobile first-party losses, coverage for, 5.3–5.14
Automobile physical damage coverages, 5.6–5.9

B

Automobile physical damage losses, 5.14–5.18
Average reserve method, **4.6**

Benefits
    death, 8.27–8.28
    disability, 8.24–8.26
    medical, 8.23
    rehabilitation, 8.27
Bodily injury, **2.4**
Bodily injury claims
    concluding, 4.43
    investigating, 4.37–4.43
        valuation of damages and, 4.40–4.43
    methods to evaluate, 4.42
Business income loss, **6.17**

C

Case law (or common law), **3.5**
Catastrophe, **6.41**
Catastrophe claim-handling
    communication with insureds during, 6.44
    issues regarding, 6.41–6.45
    need for stress management during, 6.45
    settlement costs and, 6.44
    standards for, 6.44
Cause of loss investigation, 4.27, 4.32–4.37
Causes of loss and related exclusions, 6.22–6.28
Civil law, **3.4**
    versus criminal law, 3.3–3.4
Civil procedure, rules of, **3.11**
Claim, **1.4**
Claim audit, **3.28**-3.29
    external, **3.29**
    internal, **3.28**

Claim considerations
    liability, 7.13–7.16
    workers' compensation, 8.17–8.30
Claim denial, 4.25
Claim file, **2.7**
Claim guidelines, **3.23**
Claim guidelines, policies, and procedures, 3.23–3.25
Claim handling, types of laws affecting, 3.3–3.6
Claim personnel
    claim representatives, 2.8–2.10
    customer service representatives, 2.11
    in-house counsel, 2.13
    managers, 2.6–2.7
    roles of, 2.5–2.14
    special investigation unit (SIU) personnel, 2.12–2.13
    supervisors, 2.7–2.8
    third-party administrators, 2.14
Claim representative, **1.17**
    essential skills and qualities of, 2.14–2.26
    interaction with other parties, 1.22–1.26
Claimant investigation, 4.13
Claim-handling practices
    federal laws that influence, 3.17–3.19
    state laws that influence, 3.15–3.17
Claim-handling process, 4.3–4.27
    acknowledging and assigning the claim, 4.4–4.5
    concluding the claim, 4.23–4.27
    contacting the insured or the insured's representative, 4.7–4.11
    determining the cause of loss and the loss amount, 4.23
    federal laws that influence, 3.17–3.19
    identifying the policy, 4.5–4.7
    investigating and documenting the claim, 4.11–4.23
    overview of, 2.3–2.5
Claims
    auto physical damage, investigating, 4.27–4.32
    automobile physical damage, dispute resolution and, 5.18

Formula reserve method, **4.7**
Fraud, investigating, 4.46

G

General damages, **4.39**
Good faith claim handling, **3.21**
Good faith claim-handling practices,
    3.21–3.22
Government insurance programs, 1.12
Gramm-Leach-Bliley Act, 3.18–3.19

H

Hazard, moral, **1.7**
Health Insurance Portability and
    Accountability Act of 1996
    (HIPAA), 3.18
Hearsay, **3.12**
Homeowners perils, 6.23–6.25

I

Indemnity, principle of, **1.8**
Independent agency and brokerage
    marketing system, 1.13–1.14
Independent agent, **1.13**
Indirect loss, **6.3**
Individual reserve method, **4.6**
Injury
    accidental, 8.6–8.7
    mental, 8.8
    occupational, **8.6**
Inland marine insurance claims, 6.46
Inside claim representative (or tele-
    phone claim representative), **2.8**
Insurable interest, **1.9**
Insurance, **1.3**
    benefits of, 1.4–1.6
    commercial, **1.10**
    costs of, 1.7
    employers' liability, 8.15
    liability, 7.9–7.13
    other states, 8.15
    personal, **1.10**
    professional liability
        for legal services providers, 7.20
        for medical services providers,
            7.20
    underlying principles of, 1.8–1.9

voluntary private, 8.10
    workers' compensation, 8.12
Insurance policy, parties to an,
    1.9–1.12
Insurance policy components,
    1.26–1.30
Insurance policy endorsements, 1.30
Insurance products and services, those
    who provide 1.13–1.17
Insured, **1.4**
Insured/witness investigation, 4.13
Insurer, **1.4**
Insurer response and reserving meth-
    ods, 6.43
Insurer's financial condition, evaluat-
    ing, 1.21–1.22
Insurers, private, 1.11
Insuring agreements, 1.27–1.28
Intentional tort, **7.8**
Intentional torts and strict liability,
    7.8–7.9
Internal claim audit, **3.28**
Investigation
    accident scene, 4.13
    cause of loss, 4.27, 4.32–4.37
    claimant, 4.13
    experts, use of in, 4.16–4.19
    insured/witness, 4.13
    medical, 4.14
    post-accident activity, 8.21
    prior claim, 4.14
    property damage, 4.14
    subrogation, 4.15–4.16

J

Jurisdiction, **3.6**

L

LKQ part, **5.14**
Large loss report, **4.20**
Law
    administrative, **3.6**
    case (or common law), **3.5**
    civil, **3.4**
    common (or case law), **3.5**
    contract, **3.5**
    criminal, **3.3**
    statutory, **3.5**
    valued policy, **6.39**
Law of large numbers, **1.8**

Laws
    licensing, 3.16
    privacy, 3.16
    unfair claim settlement practices,
        3.16
    unfair trade practices, 3.16
Laws affecting claim handling, 3.3–3.6
Lawsuits, 3.10–3.15
Lawyers, 1.17
Legal liability, 7.3–7.9
Legal requirements for handling claims,
    3.3–3.19
Liability
    legal, 7.3–7.9
    legal principles affecting, 7.6–7.8
    strict, **7.8**
    and intentional torts, 7.8–7.9
    vicarious, **7.6**
Liability claim considerations,
    7.13–7.16
Liability claims, special, 7.17–7.21
Liability coverages, 7.10
Liability dispute resolution, 7.16–7.17
Liability insurance, 7.9–7.13
Liability loss exposure, **7.10**
Licensing laws, 3.16
Limit
    aggregate, **7.12**
    each occurrence, **7.12**
    each person, **7.12**
Litigation, 4.26
Loss control, **1.4**
Loss control specialists, 1.16
Loss exposure, **1.3**
    liability, **7.10**
Loss of income claims, 4.36
Loss of use and business income cover-
    ages, 6.15–6.17
Loss
    business income, **6.17**
    diminished value, **5.18**
    direct, **6.3**
    indirect, **6.3**
Losses
    covered, 7.10–7.11
    diminished value, 5.18
    partial, 5.14, 5.16–5.17
    total, 5.17

M

Materiality, **3.12**
Mediation, **3.10**